InnGetaways
Virginia

A Photographic Guide to
Bed & Breakfasts and Inns

by Don Vandeventer

Published by
Down Home Publications
P.O. Box 1899
Candler, NC 28715

DISCLAIMER

Although the author has researched exhaustively to ensure the accuracy and completeness of the information contained in this book, we assume no responsibility for errors, inaccuracies, omissions, or any other inconsistency herein.

Published by:

Down Home Publications

P.O. Box 1899-B

Candler, NC 28715

Copyright © 1997 by Don Vandeventer.

Printed in the United States of America

10 9 8 7 6 5 4 3 2 1

Library of Congress Cataloging-in-Publication Data
Vandeventer, Don.
    InnGetaways Virginia: A Photographic Guide to Bed & Breakfasts and Inns
        Includes appendix and index
        ISBN 1-886443-03-3 (pbk.)
        1. Bed and breakfast accomodations—VirgippDirectories.
        2.Virginia—Guidebooks. I. Title II. Series
                        97-66416
                         CIP

Contents

Northern Region — Map 83

Central Region — Map 123

FOREWORD

Is there a B&B out there for me?

There is a B&B out there for everyone. The beauty of the industry is its incredible variety of sizes and shapes.

National Definitions and Distinctions

The following definitions attempt to codify what is presently being used in the field. They are only approximations and will vary by region or individual innkeeper.

Homestay, Host Home

This type of establishment is an owner-occupied private home where the business of paying guests is secondary to its use as a private residence. The hosts are primarily interested in meeting new people and making some additional monies while continuing their present employment or retirement. Frequently located in residential areas, zoning or other government restrictions may prevent the use of signs, public advertising, etc. Usually between 1-3 rooms, these homes are often a member of, and usually inspected by a reservation service organization (RSO) but are rarely required to be licensed or inspected by local applicable governmental agencies. Breakfast is the only meal served. In some instances, it may by an unhosted apartment where breakfast is self-serve.

B&B, Bed-And-Breakfast

Formerly a single family dwelling usually in the 4-5-room range, this owner-occupied establishment has an equally mixed use as home and lodging superseding home more often than not. It is located in a legally zoned area and meets all the tax, fire, building and health requirements for this size and use of property. This establishment advertises publicly and can legally post a sign. Like the homestay or host home, because of its size, these B&Bs usually cannot support a family unit, so the B&B is often one partner's job and the other has outside income. Often the property is purchased specifically to be a B&B, but many are converted family homes. Reservations may be made directly with the property.

Bed & Breakfast Inn

Generally small, owner-operated businesses providing the primary financial support of the owner. Usually the owner lives on premises. The building's primary usage is for business. Inns advertise, have business licenses, produce their own brochures, comply with government ordinances, pay all appropriate taxes and post signs. Breakfast is the only meal served and only to overnight guests. The inn may host events such as weddings, small business meetings, etc. Room numbers range from 4-20 with a small, but increasing number up to 30. Reservations may be made directly with the property. Note: The distinction between a "B&B" and a B&B inn" is not readily apparent, except with regard to building usage.

Country Inn

A business offering overnight lodging and meals where the owner is actively involved in daily operations, often living on site. These establishments are, in fact, B&B inns which serve at least one meal in addition to breakfast, and operate as "restaurants" as well as overnight lodging accommodations. Modified American Plan (MAP) country inns serve dinner to overnight guests only, and the cost of dinner and breakfast is generally included in the room rate. A country inn with a full-service restaurant serves these additional meals to the general public. To be a country inn, a property does not have to be located in a rural area. Room numbers tend to range from 6-30.

To understand *bed-and-breakfast/country inn* in the context of other properties that are confused with bed and breakfasts, the following definitions are included:

Bed & Breakfast And Self-Contained Cottage

A detached building affording more privacy and seclusion to guests, with owner providing minimal services. Breakfast is either delivered to the room, taken with others in a central dining room or placed prior to arrival (or upon daily cleaning) in the cottage kitchen facilities. Owner is usually available for questions, but generally guests choose this style of B&B when they want little help. Certain geographic regions see this type of lodging more than others. The light personal touch and memorable B&B decor further distinguish the genre from the vacation rental/condo.

Bed-And-Breakfast Hotel

These are 30+-room historic properties offering breakfast that can only be considered hotels. Only the historic structure, and perhaps some decorating components and breakfast provide the B&B feel.

Although all the above categories view themselves as providing these below-listed characteristics, in reality, the larger the property—and particularly if the owner is not actively involved in daily operations and guest interaction—the faster it moves into the "hotel" perception in the minds of the traveler.

• Generous hospitality and personal attention to guests

• Architecturally interesting or historic structure

• Owner involvement in business

• Clean and comfortable ambiance and surroundings

• Individually decorated rooms

What is a Reservation Service Organization (RSO)?

A reservation service organization is in business to match guests and B&Bs/Country Inns. RSOs represent a variety of properties—although most are private homes—and usually cover a specific geographic area. Guests call one telephone number, usually toll-free, to make reservations. The property pays the RSO directly for their services; guests do not pay a fee. Often, particularly in urban areas, this matching of guest and innkeeper gives you an opportunity to stay at a property not otherwise available.

What questions should I ask when I call a B&B?

Traveling the B&B way is a wonderful way to see the world and achieve a sense of place about where you are. You'll talk to owners who know and love where they live. They know the greatest local place to eat; the gallery or shop you must not miss; the best jogging trail, etc. It can be the greatest of serendipitous experiences. And because each is unique, complete with its own wonder, you want to know if this is the right place for you.

Some of these questions are only important as they relate to a specific geographic area. For example, there's rarely ever a need for air-conditioning in Mendocino, California. But don't hesitate to ask whatever you need to know:

1. The area. What is there to do and how far from the inn is it?

2. What are your policies on pets and children?

3. What is your cancellation policy?

4. Do you take credit cards?

5. Is the building air-conditioned?

6. Is there a telephone in the room? If not, is there someplace where a phone can be used in private?

7. Is smoking allowed?

8. Can you accommodate my (for example) low sodium diet?

9. Will you serve breakfast in my room?

10. If I have to leave really early to catch a plane, will you still provide some kind of breakfast?

11. What type of breakfast do you serve?

12. Do you have any special discounts, i.e. AARP, AAA?

13. Is there a parlor or common room where I'll have a chance to chat with other guests?

14. What are the sizes of your beds?

15. Do you have all private baths? (If not, how many rooms share a bath?)

16. Can you accommodate an early arrival? How about a late checkout?

17. Is the property handicap accessible? How about hearing or visual aids?

18. Where is the parking area for my car? Is there a charge?

19. What kind of fireplaces do you have, i.e. real wood, gas-burning?

20. Is there a two-night minimum?

You'll get the most out of your stay by asking questions *before* you arrive. Innkeepers want you to have a great stay. Carry this guidebook with you and use it often. Travel the B&B way; it's the only way to go!

PROFESSIONAL
Association of
INNKEEPERS
International®

How to Get the Most out of Your Stay

1. **Reservations:** Try to call the inn for information/reservations during off-peak hours. Keep in mind that most innkeepers are busy preparing breakfast and serving guests between the hours of 7AM and 10AM.

2. **Check-in:** Ask about check-in and checkout policies for each inn. Every operation is unique and each inn has its own policy. Some inns can be flexible and adjust to your needs and some cannot.

3. **Cancellations:** What is the cancellation policy of the inn? How does the inn handle credit card guarantees? If you have to cancel, what is the inn's refund policy? Again, each inn has its own policy.

4. **Payments:** What types of payment are acceptable at the inn? Most inns these days accept some type of credit card as well as personal checks. It takes only a moment to mention what kind of payment you would like to make and ask whether that is acceptable to that particular inn.

5. **Rules:** The rules are the rules! Each inn has its own set of rules regarding things like children, smoking, alcoholic beverages, etc. Find an inn whose rules are to your liking.

6. **Phone Numbers:** When leaving a number where you can be reached, DO NOT leave the inn's toll-free number. These 800 numbers are for reservations and information only. Each inn has a regular direct dial number that is usually on the brochure and other materials.

7. **Comment Cards:** Take time to write comments about the inn and leave it for (or mail it to) the innkeeper(s). Please take the time to tell us what we did right, as well as what we could be doing to make your next experience better.

Please carry this guidebook with you and use it often. Some of the best experiences of your life are sitting right here in your hands!

Diane Sheiry
North Carolina Bed Breakfast and Inns Association

The following abbreviations are used in this guide:

RATES

$ .... 50 and under
$$ 51-100
$$$ 101-150
$$$$ 151-250
$$$$$ .... 251 and over

AFFILIATIONS

AAA .... American Automobile Association
ABBA .... American Bed & Breakfast Association
BBAV .... Bed & Breakfast Association of Virginia
IIA .... Independent Innkeepers Association
NBBA .... National Bed & Breakfast Association
PAII .... Professional Association of Innkeepers International
RATHA .... Rockbridge Area Tourism and Hospitality Association
USB&B .... United States Bed & Breakfast Association

KEY TO SYMBOLS
PAYMENT

CHECKS =Checks

AMEX =American Express®

SSS =Cash

DISCOVER =Discover®

MC =MasterCard®

CARTE BLANCHE =Carte Blanche®

VISA =Visa®

Diner's Club =Diner's Club®

AMENITIES

A/C =Air Conditioned

=Jacuzzi in room

=Full Breakfast

=Phone in room

=Continental Breakfast

=TV Available

=Lunch and/or Dinner Available

VCR =VCR Available

=Fireplace Available

=Wheelchair access

=Hot Tubs

Eastern Shore Region

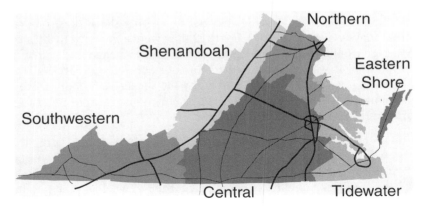

Bay Avenue's Sunset Bed & Breakfast
Cape Charles

One of the best beaches on the Eastern Shore is located in Cape Charles. As the beach is on the bay side of the Shore, it's a bit quieter than the ocean side, the waves more gentle, and the sunsets spectacular. Back in 1915, two sisters fell in love with the view of the beach, and they built their home directly across the street. For the next forty-three years, the Nottingham sisters lived just a stone's throw from the beach and a short walk from the center of Cape Charles.

Cape Charles was the Eastern Shore's first planned community. William L. Scott of Erie, Pennsylvania was the moving force behind the town. He was also primarily responsible for bringing the railroad to the Eastern Shore. Cape Charles was built as the terminus for the railroad. Ferries carried both passengers and freight across the 20-odd miles of the Chesapeake Bay. From 1886 to 1953 Cape Charles was the principal city of the Eastern Shore. During its heyday, more than two million people a year passed through the town.

Al Longo and Joyce Tribble first began visiting the Eastern Shore from Massachusetts in 1989. By 1992 they were convinced that Cape Charles would be their new home, and 108 Bay Avenue was a dream come true. It was perfectly suited for four comfortably sized guest rooms, a large porch on which to enjoy the sunsets and cool breezes coming off the Bay. They even had room to add Vermont Casting fireplace stoves to two of the rooms.

Rated three diamonds by AAA and holding a three-crown rating by the American Bed & Breakfast Association, Bay Avenue's Sunset Bed & Breakfast has become a favorite stopover for guests to Cape Charles. I think some folks come just for the views from the porch: the sunsets can truly be dramatic.

Al and Joyce have completely refurbished the Victorian style home by adding central air conditioning, Hunter fans to each guest room, as well as cable TVs, VCRs and queen-sized beds.

Breakfast each morning is served family style. Al and Joyce offer fresh fruit, homemade breads and a variety of entrées including oven baked egg dishes, sausage, bacon, grits, and French toast.

Since the Eastern Shore is only 70 miles long, it's a short drive to any of the area's attractions. Some of the more interesting include the Chesapeake Bay Bridge-Tunnel, Kiptopeke State Park, the Custis Farm Tour in Nassawadox and Chincoteague and Assateague Islands with their world-famous ponies.

While there is much to do in the area, let me recommend a very special stop: Charmar's County Store. Located at 213 Mason Avenue, it is one of the jewels of the entire Eastern Shore. This is the private collection of Charles & Margaret Carlson. The Carlson's, who own Charmar's Antiques next door, have outfitted the Country Store much as it might have been at the turn of the century. Entry to the store is made by stopping at the antique store next door. Just remember, everything at the antique store is for sale, but don't even ask to buy something at the Country Store; it's all a private collection.

Bay Avenue's Sunset Bed & Breakfast
108 Bay Avenue; Cape Charles, VA 23310
(888) 422-9283; (757) 331-2424; Fax: (757) 331-4877
Innkeepers: Al Longo & Joyce Tribble
Rooms: 4; All Private Baths; Rates: $$
Affiliations: AAA◆◆◆, BBAV, ABBA, NBBA, PAII, Mobil★★; Eastern Shore B&B Assoc.
Payment: $$$ CHECKS M C VISA AMEX DISCOVER
Amenities: ❄/C ▭ VCR ♨ ✆

Cape Charles House
Cape Charles

It's amazing the number of people, even map makers, who think that the Eastern Shore is a part of Maryland. Granted, on a map it looks like a logical extension of Maryland. However the area has always been a part of Virginia.

Since it lies some twenty miles across the Chesapeake Bay from the rest of Virginia, for years the only way to visit the area was to travel south from Maryland or to cross Chesapeake Bay by ferry. In 1964, the ferries were replaced by the 17-mile Chesapeake Bay Bridge-Tunnel which is considered to be the world's largest bridge-tunnel complex.

Located at the lower end of the Eastern Shore, Cape Charles was the shore's first planned community. It was created in 1883 to be the southern terminus of the New York, Philadelphia and Norfolk Railroad. More than 500 historic buildings constructed between 1885 and 1940 from the town's historic district.

For nearly half a century the town prospered. By the 1940's more than two million people were passing through the Cape Charles each year. But in 1950 the ferry closed and four years later, the railroad stopped carrying mail and passengers. Today, Cape Charles sits three miles off the beaten track taken by most tourists.

Cape Charles House innkeepers Bruce and Carol Evans first came to the Eastern Shore as guests at Cape Charles' only bed and breakfast at that time. They arrived on Saturday and by Sunday were looking for a location to open their own bed and breakfast. The Wilkins house was the first house at which they looked. After 18 months of searching elsewhere, they returned to the area, purchased the property and began the necessary remodeling to open it as Cape Charles House.

The house, located just a few blocks from one of the nicest beaches on the Eastern Shore, was built in 1912 by attorney Tucker Wilkins for his

wife and children. It is one of the largest and most luxurious homes in town. Its spacious wraparound porch welcomes guests and leads them into a stately foyer with Corinthian columns framing the grand staircase.

To this magnificent old house, the Evans' have added modern conveniences including individual zone climate control and in-room baths for each of the four spacious guest rooms. The interior decorations are highlighted by high ceilings, original moldings and maple-planked flooring. On the first floor Carol and Bruce have furnished the house with antique collections and Oriental rugs.

An accomplished cook (she has written recipes for Women's Circle magazine for a number of years now), Carol makes sure each morning meal is both delicious and unique. Breakfast brings an assortment of fresh fruit, homemade muffins or breads. The entrées vary from day to day and might include stuffed French toast, creamed eggs or omelets. Dinner is available upon request.

Guests are welcome to borrow beach chairs for a day on the beach, or use one of the inn's bicycles for a ride around town. Other activities in the area include fishing, boating excursions or a farm-wagon tour of the Custis Working Farm and Nursery. Antique shops in the area offer a variety of shopping opportunities.

Cape Charles House
645 Tazewell Avenue; Cape Charles, VA 23310
(757) 331-4920; Fax: (757) 331-4960
Innkeepers: Bruce & Carol Evans
Rooms: 4; **All Private Baths**; **Rates**: $$ - $$$
Affiliations: BBAV, Eastern Shore B&B Assoc., Northampton-Cape Charles Chamber
Payment: $$$ CHECKS MC VISA AMEX
Amenities: A/C 🖥 👥 ✉

Chesapeake Charm B&B
Cape Charles

The Eastern Shore community of Cape Charles is unique: it seems to be transplanted from somewhere up north. The historic district includes more than 500 structures built between 1885 and the 1940s. The main street is lined with crepe myrtle trees and the streets lie at perfect right angles to each other.

Cape Charles was the Shore's first planned community and was built in the 1880s as the terminus for the New York, Philadelphia & Norfolk railroad. During the early part of this century, more than two million people a year traveled through Cape Charles by train and ferry. Freight trains still travel through Cape Charles, but ferry service ended in 1953. With the 1964 opening of the bridge-tunnel across the Chesapeake Bay, Cape Charles has become a quaint village just three miles off the main highway.

When William H. Lambertson arrived in Cape Charles from Pocomoke City, Maryland, sometime before World War I, there were fewer than 50 houses in town. By the time he died in 1948, he is said to have built more than half the town. One of the most notable is the house he constructed at 202 Madison Avenue. It was built in 1921 for William Sanders as a gift for his niece Mary Louise Dix. Today is the site of Chesapeake Charm bed and breakfast.

Innkeepers Phyllis and Barry Tyndall were high school sweethearts in southeastern North Carolina. After marriage, their careers took them to Tampa, Florida for five years and then to Virginia Beach for another year. Barry had always wanted a small hotel but Phyllis wanted a bed and breakfast. They compromised. Guests to Chesapeake Charm know they made the right choice. As the only southerners owning a B&B in the area, they work hard to show their guests real Southern hospitality.

The American Four Square style home is located just two blocks from the beach and features natural heart pine flooring and moldings. The window

casings in the house are all original. In keeping with the early 1900s style of the house, Phyllis and Barry have decorated without using any reproductions. Most of the antiques are from the 1900s to 1940s and once belonged to four grandmothers plus several aunts, uncles, cousins, nieces and nephews. The organ is from the mid-1800s. In one room, Granny's Treasures, is a hand-carved antique full bed that was the property of Mary Louise Dix.

As Barry still works outside the home, most of the innkeeping duties fall to Phyllis who also works at home for a publishing house. Yet each morning she prepares a bountiful breakfast of cereals, homemade breads, cinnamon rolls, muffins, and fruit dishes. Beverages include fresh milk, orange juice, hot teas, coffee, apple juice and cranberry juice. Entrées vary each day and include delights such as: strawberry omelets with cheese grits; stuffed French toast; bacon or ham, egg and cheese casseroles.

Hot summer afternoons often bring ice cream, iced tea or lemonade. During the chilly spring or fall you can enjoy French bread, baked brie, pound cakes, cookies or sweets with hot cider and tea.

For a ride around town you can borrow the inn's bicycles. Towels, coolers and lounge chairs are available for your trip to the beach.

Cape Charles offers something for everyone, from cruises aboard the Cape Charles Delight to 9-hole golf or the area tennis courts. Kiptopeke State Park is just a few miles away, a sanctuary for birds of all types.

Chesapeake Charm B&B
202 Madison Avenue; Cape Charles, VA 23310
(800) 546-9215; (757) 331-2676
Innkeepers: Phyllis & Barry Tyndall
Rooms: 3; **All Private Baths**; **Rates**: $$
Affiliations: BBAV, Eastern Shore B&B Assoc., Northampton-Cape Charles Chamber
Payment: $$$ CHECKS M/C VISA
Amenities: A/C ▭ VCR 🔥 👪 ✉

Island Manor House (1848)
Chincoteague

Island Manor House is one of the oldest and most historic buildings on Chincoteague Island. It was built around 1848 by Nathaniel Smith, the first doctor to live on the island.

Now if that was as far as the story went, the history would be interesting enough but some of the details make it even more so. Dr. Smith built the house in partnership with the island postmaster, Joseph Kenny. For years they lived as bachelors until a young lady came from Baltimore to visit. She and Joseph fell in love and married. When her sister came to visit, she met Dr. Smith and they married. For a number of years they all lived in the same house until friction developed between the two sisters. They cared for each other very much, but just couldn't live under the same roof. So they literally split the house into two pieces and set one on the adjacent lot. Now each sister could run her own household.

Today the house has been rejoined and decorated in Federalist Style with fine antiques which give it great deal of charm. Because it was once two separate houses, it has lots of space, nearly 9,000 square feet. The lot is almost a half-block long and goes back 300 feet to include a large off-the-road parking area for guests.

Favorite areas of the Island Manor House include the library and the garden room which was built to rejoin the two houses. In addition to a fireplace, it offers passage to the courtyard and fountain. Many guests enjoy afternoon tea or breakfast in the courtyard.

Each afternoon innkeeper, Carol Kalmykow bakes several varieties of treats: lemon poppy seed cake, triple chocolate cake with hot fudge, apple crumb cheesecake, or blackberry cobbler. There are also imported cheeses, crackers, imported teas, iced teas and lemonade, cookies and or perhaps a Toll House Pie.

You won't walk away hungry from breakfast either. It's served each morning family style and might include fresh fruit and berries with their own Jack Daniels raisin yogurt sauce, homemade blueberry, lemon poppy seed, almond poppy seed, or apple cinnamon muffins. Hot dishes include "eggs extraordinaire," a baked version of eggs Benedict, or Belgian waffles with fresh strawberries or blueberries. Breakfast meats might include Canadian bacon or sausage and there are always teas, juices and coffees. As you will see, Carol and her husband Chuck love to pamper their guests.

Chincoteague is a very special place just off the coast of the Eastern Shore. Together with its sister island Assateague, it is known the world over for the wild ponies and the pony auction held each summer. However, Chincoteague offers a lot of which people are not aware.

It's an island that has survived flood, storm and fire and, as such, is a mixture of old and new. There are many nooks and crannies to explore. Two of the best ways to do this are by bicycle and by boat. The Island Manor House can provide the bicycles and Captain Barry's offers one of the better cruises around the area. In fact, you may pass on the bicycle ride but every visitor to the island should go out with Captain Barry at least once. Few know the local history better than he does.

Island Manor House (1848)
4160 Main Street; Chincoteague, VA 23336
(800) 852-1505; (757) 336-5436
Innkeepers: Carol & Charles Kalmykow
E-mail: imh@shore.intercom.net
Rooms: 8; **With Private Baths**: 6; **With Shared Baths**: 2; **Rates**: $$ - $$$
Affiliations: BBAV, Eastern Shore Chamber, Chincoteague Chamber
Payment:  Amenities:

Miss Molly's Inn
Chincoteague

Chincoteague and its sister island of Assateague are two of the most unique islands you will find off the Atlantic coast. While Chincoteague has become more tourist oriented in the past few years, it is still a very quiet place. You won't find mile after mile of gift shops, arcades, and amusement rides. What you *will* find is a quiet community that has been shaped over the years by flood, storm and fire leaving a collection of old and new architecture and streets full of interesting places to explore. Assateague on the other hand is mostly a wildlife preserve and the home of the famous Chincoteague wild ponies.

There are a number of bed and breakfasts on the island. In my opinion, Miss Molly's is the closest reflection of the Victorian era. The house was built in 1886, by J.T. Rowley, a clam merchant who was known to all as "the clam king of the world." Miss Molly, his daughter, was born in the house in 1887 and continued to live there until 1971, just six years before she died. During the 1930s, Miss Molly rented rooms to teachers, charging them $25 a month for room and board. In the 1940s, the plot of one of the island's most beloved stories, Misty of Chincoteague, was worked out while author Marguerite Henry rocked on the front porch.

Today, innkeepers Barbara and David Wiedenheft have lovingly restored the grand old house and offer comfortable accommodations and warm hospitality to island visitors. Barbara was with the British Embassy in Washington, DC when she met David, and they moved to the island to be closer to Barbara's twin sister in Salisbury, Maryland.

Recently they have purchased a second bed and breakfast, the Channel Bass Inn, just a block away. This structure was built in 1892,

and has been completely redecorated. Barbara has also opened a formal English Tea Room in the Channel Bass. The menu includes fresh brewed teas, scones, apple cakes, trifles, pecan pie, pound cake or sponge cake.

While both inns are in the heart of historic Chincoteague and within walking distance of restaurants and shopping, you will find them quiet and restful. In both Miss Molly's and the Channel Bass, David and Barbara have paid a great deal of attention to detail. Antiques have been carefully selected and rooms decorated to reflect the appropriate period.

Chincoteague is famous for the wild ponies that live on Assateague Island and the pony auctions held each July on Chincoteague. However, there's enough to do on Chincoteague and Assateague that a visit anytime is well worth while. A wildlife tour of Assateague Island provides an excellent opportunity to see not only the ponies but hundreds of other forms of wildlife

One of the best ways to really appreciate Chincoteague is to take one of the bay cruises. Our favorite was Captain Barry's. A New York transplant, he has taken time to learn many stories about the island and is a wealth of information. I can guarantee that you will not be disappointed.

Miss Molly's Inn
4141 Main Street; Chincoteague, VA 23336
(800) 221-5620; (757) 336-6686; Fax: (757) 336-1342
Innkeepers: David & Barbara Wiedenheft
Rooms: 7; **With Private Baths**: 5; **With Shared Baths**: 2; **Rates**: $$ - $$$
Affiliations: Mobil, BBAV, Chincoteague Chamber
Payment:
Amenities:

The Watson House
Chincoteague

The islands of Chincoteague and Assateague are famous around the world for the wild ponies that live on Assateague and for the pony auction that takes place every summer. During the auction, the islands are packed with visitors, and reservations must be made well in advance. But people are discovering that the islands offer hundreds of reasons to visit during the rest of the year and it's the only part of the Eastern Shore where you will really encounter tourism.

I should probably explain the differences between the two islands. Chincoteague is the smaller of the two islands, but the one that is populated. Chincoteague is also the name of the bay that separates the islands from the mainland and the name of the ponies that actually live wild on Assateague. The larger island, Assateague, is more than 30 miles long. Only the southern tip lies of it within Virginia. The northern part of the island is part of Maryland. Assateague is also the name of the National Seashore Park located on the island.

The Watson House and its companion bed and breakfast, the Inn at Poplar Corner, are owned by Tom and Jacque Derrickson and Jacque's parents, David and JoAnne Snead.

Watson House, a member of the Bed and Breakfast Association of Virginia, was built in the late 1800s by David Robert Watson. It's located just a few blocks from shops and a number of good restaurants, one of our favorites being the Landmark Crab House & Waterfront Lounge. In addition to good food, I think it has one of the best views of the sunset on the island.

Directly across the street from the Watson House is a brand new (built 1995-96) Victorian-style house that offers an atmosphere of the mid-1800s and all of the amenities that 1996 construction can provide.

I'm often amazed at the number of people who think bed and breakfasts are strictly a woman's thing. It is often far from the truth, and here is a case in point. The whole project began with David and Tom's idea of buying and restoring the Watson House as a bed and breakfast. After several successful years, they purchased the house across the street, knowing that it was too far gone to repair, and built a modern replica of a Victorian home.

The two properties are basically treated as one bed and breakfast. You can call either for reservations, and you might be served afternoon tea at the Watson House and have your breakfast in the formal dining room of the Inn at Poplar Corner.

Afternoon tea at either home yields cookies or truffles plus pie, cake or cheesecake along with fresh brewed ice tea, lemonade, or hot tea. Breakfast is generally served buffet style and offers a variety of entrées and breakfast meats along with cereals, juices and coffee or teas.

Both houses have been carefully decorated with period antiques and reproductions set off by drapes and wallpapers that reflect the Victorian era. Rooms at the newer Inn at Poplar Corner are a bit larger than the Watson House, yet both are very comfortable and reasonably priced.

The Watson House
4240 Main Street; P.O. Box 905; Chincoteague, VA 23336
(800) 336-6787; (757) 336-1564; Fax: (757) 336-5776
Innkeepers: David & JoAnne Snead/Tom & Jacque Derrickson
Rooms: 6; **Cottages**: 2; **All Private Baths**; **Rates**: $$ - $$$
Affiliations: BBAV, Eastern Shore B&B Assoc.
Payment: $$$ CHECKS M/C VISA
Amenities:

Garden and The Sea Inn
Chincoteague Area (New Church)

Architecture is one of the major draws of the Eastern Shore, not only the variety of architecture but the history of the buildings themselves. A good example is the Garden and The Sea Inn & Restaurant.

Originally built as Bloxom's Tavern in 1802, it served as an ordinary on the old stagecoach line to Salisbury, Maryland. As a stagecoach stop, it served not only the traveling public but was also a major focal point for the entire community. It functioned as post office, polling station and even the local general store.

The coming of the railroad to the Eastern Shore changed life in the small community. The stagecoach was no longer needed. With its passing, Bloxom's Tavern became the summer home for the owner's family. The Nelson's purchased the property in 1896 and added a new three-story facade with a Victorian look. For the next 90 years the property served as the Nelson family home.

It wasn't until 1989 that the first changes took place to return the property to its original purpose. With the goal of operating a country inn in mind, the owners first opened the restaurant. In 1991, they opened as an inn and the first overnight guests were accepted.

Innkeepers Tom and Sara Baker spent nearly a year looking at more than 40 properties before discovering that they and the Garden & The Sea were a perfect match. Tom's background had been in the restaurant business since he was 17. With Sara's background in accounting, human resources and personnel, they knew their combination of talents would work well as innkeepers. They took over the Inn in 1994.

Currently the inn has six large bright rooms featuring bay windows with stained glass and private baths. Some rooms have Jacuzzis. All beds are queen-sized and vary from a Victorian wrought-iron bed to

a wicker sleigh bed. The Chardonnay Room, on the first floor, is wheelchair accessible. Television is available on request for all the rooms.

While the rooms at the inn are great, I must confess that I fell in love the dining room. Dinner is served five nights a week during the summer months and Thursday through Sunday during the off-season. The inn closes after Thanksgiving and reopens April 1.

Tom offers either four-course *prix fixe* dinners or an *à la carte* menu. Both change daily and the entrées can vary from Veal Virginia with sautéed veal slices served on Virginia Ham or a wonderful rack of lamb to many, many fresh local fish and some interesting seafood combinations. Whatever the evening fare, dinner is not to be missed.

Refreshments are available in the Garden House all afternoon and include brownies, fresh fruit, chips and cookies. Sherry is also available as well as wine and beer. While breakfast is served continental style, there is an abundance of choices to satisfy anyone's taste.

Tom and Sara have three resident Maltese dogs that help with the day to day operation of Garden and the Sea Inn. They are available for the guests' enjoyment or you may bring your own pet (with prior arrangements) in certain rooms. There are more than four acres plus many miles of side roads to roam.

Garden and the Sea Inn
4188 Nelson Road; P.O. Box 275; New Church, VA 23415
(800) 824-0672; (757) 824-0672; Fax: (757) 824-5605
Innkeepers: Tom & Sara Baker
E-mail: baker@shore.intercom.net
Rooms: 6; All Private Baths; Rates: $$ - $$$$
Affiliations: PAII, Mobil★★, BBAV, Eastern Shore Chamber, Chincoteague Chamber
Payment: Amenities:

Bay View Waterfront Bed & Breakfast
Davis Wharf Area (Belle Haven)

Bay View Waterfront consists of 140 acres of woods, farm land and creek shore property that has been in innkeeper Mary Will's family since the early 1820s. The house is more than one hundred feet long with five different roof levels. Its style is unique to the Eastern Shore and is called 'big house, little house, colonnade, kitchen.' This architectural style came about in the 1700s and 1800s as homeowners prospered and began to add to basic one-room and two-room homes. New sections were added and the old and new were connected with an enclosed passageway or "colonnade." The older parts of the house are only one room deep to take advantage of the summer breezes coming off Occohannock Creek and the Chesapeake Bay. An official history of the Eastern Shore says the house was built in 1801. However, bricks have been found dating back to 1797.

Mary Will grew up in the house and returned to it as an adult with her husband, Wayne, in 1961. Together they raised five children before turning the home into a bed and breakfast in 1992. While part of the land is farmed, there are plenty of acres to wander through woods, along the creek and by the shore. Ice Lady, a Labrador Retriever, is frequently willing to act as a guide around the property. Warm afternoons often find guests relaxing by the pool or just sitting on the dock.

The Brownings call the furnishings "family comfortable" but you'll find many antiques and family heirlooms throughout the house. There's truly a feeling of Colonial America in each of the three guest rooms, and they each provide excellent views of the shore.

Breakfast at Bay View can truly be called a country breakfast, with sausage made locally, farm fresh eggs, grits or biscuits or both. On some mornings Mary Will serves French toast with caramel under-

neath along with bacon and there are always fresh fruit, juices and plenty of coffee or tea. Guests have a choice of privacy or eating family style. We were lucky enough to enjoy our breakfast with the innkeepers.

Because Mary Will grew up in the area, she can provide directions and maps to most of the points of interest along the Eastern Shore. She can also tell you about some of the 'off the beaten track' places typically missed by the tourist.

In addition to the peace and quiet of the area, guests can enjoy biking, hiking and bird watching. Take a trip to Davis Wharf to watch the fishing boats come in or rent your own at Wachapreague. You can also make arrangements to go out on a charter at Wachapreague or drive up to Hacks Neck and get fresh crabs.

If your interest is architecture, there are four Colonial churches in the area. St. George's Episcopal Church in Pungoteague was built about 1738. You can enjoy live dinner theater at the Trawler Restaurant and the North Street Players in Onancock features local talent.

Bay View Waterfront Bed & Breakfast
35350 Copes Drive; Belle Haven, VA 23306
(800) 442-6966; (757) 442-6963
Innkeepers: Wayne & Mary Will Browning
Rooms: 3; Suites: 1; With Private Baths: 2; With Shared Baths: 2; Rates: $$ - $$$
Affiliations: BBAV, Eastern Shore Tourism

Payment: CHECKS

Amenities:

The Gladstone House
Exmore

Exmore is a perfect destination for anyone who wants to really explore all that the Eastern Shore has to offer. Because of Exmore's location near the center of the Eastern Shore, it is located between Assateague State Park to the north and Kiptopeke State Park to the south.

While Exmore isn't as historic a community as some of the others on the Shore, in addition to its location, it does have several things that make it memorable. The most important is Gladstone House. Built by Dr. Gladstone and his wife in 1938, The Gladstone House is an elegant 7,000-square-foot brick Georgian home. The brick walls on the first floor are nearly 18 inches thick, and on the second floor the walls are about 12 inches. Dr. Joe, as he was known locally, even added a special elevator that guests with special needs may use. Construction cost today for a house like this would be prohibitive.

Innkeepers Al and Pat Egan came from New Jersey to create a retreat at Gladstone House. I believe you will find they have truly mastered the art of Southern hospitality. From the warm greeting when we arrived to the last good-bye hugs, I can say that I enjoyed everything about Gladstone House. Every antique and decoration seems to fit Gladstone House perfectly. The rooms are large and comfortable, and offer special features such as cable TV, VCRs, and a complimentary video library. The living room is especially inviting with its player piano, organ and gas-log fireplace.

Your day at Gladstone House will begin with hot coffee or tea delivered to your bedroom door. A trip down the curved staircase brings you to a breakfast served in the formal dining room. Their motto of "you will never leave the breakfast table hungry," is

backed up by plates of fresh fruit, sticky buns, and a variety of entrées. Baked eggs, crêpes, eggs Benedict, sunrise pancakes or French toast is accompanied by a selection of breakfast meats.

Eat too much? Don't worry, the Gladstone House has bikes for guests and they have detailed maps for everything from five-mile warm-up rides to trips that will take you 64 miles around the Eastern Shore. Ready for lunch? You might want to stop at Exmore Diner, one of the last original diners on the Shore. While the fare is simple, we found our lunch to be quite good and very reasonably priced. Of course, Pat and Al can suggest a number of other sites in the area for lunch or dinner.

One of the new points of interest in the area is the Railroad Museum in Exmore. Exmore was a major stop on for the New York, Pennsylvania and Norfolk Railroad. Many of the people in the area were employed by the railroad and their help should make the Railroad Museum a first class exhibit. I would also recommend taking a trip to Tangier Island. The island is two and one-half miles long, one mile wide and only seven feet above sea level. You can take a boat ride on the Captain Eulice from Onancock, a 300-year-old town located right on the Chesapeake Bay.

The Gladstone House
12108 Lincoln Avenue; P.O. Box 296; Exmore, VA 23350
(800) 262-4837; (757) 442-4614; Fax: (757) 442-4678
Innkeepers: Pat & Al Egan
E-mail: egan@gladstonehouse.com
Rooms: 3; **All Private Baths**; **Rates**: $$
Affiliations: NBBA, AAA◆◆◆, BBAV, Eastern Shore B&B Assoc.
Payment: Amenities:

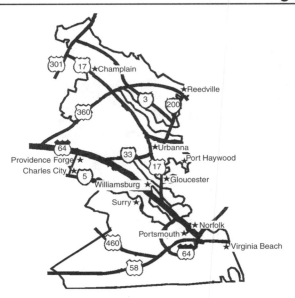

Tidewater Region

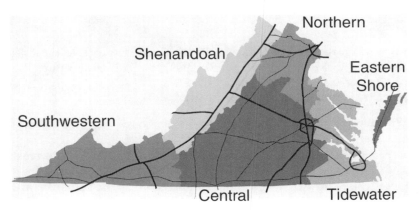

Inn at Tabb's Creek Landing
Mathews Area (Port Haywood)

You will find that most innkeepers are very interesting people with very diverse backgrounds. Cabell and Catherine Venable are no exception. Over the years they have owned and operated a gourmet restaurant as well as a wine shop. Two of their more notable enterprises were white-water rafting and dog sled companies in Jackson Hole, Wyoming.

Catherine is a producing artist of fine art and poster art. She takes part in many area festivals such as the Mathews Market Day Festival, the Gloucester Daffodil Festival, the Fredericksburg Dog Festival and Arts in' the Park in Richmond. You'll find her works throughout the bed and breakfast. Cabell is a consultant and writer in the computer field.

Their interest in bed and breakfasts arose when Catherine took a cross-country trip with her son. While on the road, they stayed at a number of B&Bs across the country. When she came back, she felt that the property at Tabb's Creek would be a perfect location for a bed and breakfast.

Located on the banks of Tabb's Creek, there is access to the East River and to Mobjack Bay, both opening to Chesapeake Bay. The original house was built in the 1820s for a Captain Billups and it remained in his family until the 1950s.

With ancient magnolias taller than the main house, as well as maples and elms, shade is abundant at Tabb's Creek Landing. The many screened porches around the house become favorite places to read. They also make great places to enjoy the fragrance drifting in from more than 100 rose bushes in the cutting garden which connects the guest cottage and swimming pool to the main house.

The area is alive with geese, gray herons, blue herons and doves. You can often see otters, deer, foxes and rabbits as well as bald eagles, osprey and sometimes dolphins. The creek is full of blue fin crabs.

With years of experience in the restaurant business, Cabell's breakfasts are memorable. He does a modified Southern breakfast with fried apples, grits (his own secret recipe), scrambled eggs, country sausage or bacon, English muffins, fresh fruit (such as bananas and cream) and juices. Other breakfasts include crêpes or pancakes with breakfast meats. Many of the vegetables, including tomatoes, cantaloupes and blueberries, come from their own large vegetable garden.

The area around Mathews and Port Haywood is ideal for bicycling and long walks on shady country lanes with virtually no traffic. Canoeing and paddle boating on Tabb's Creek are also popular activities. Many folks come just to watch the sunset from the dock. Some guests never leave the thirty acres of grounds. They spend their days reading, strolling by the creek or swimming in the pool. When you're ready to explore more of the area, Williamsburg is only 55 minutes away and another 30 minutes will take you to Norfolk.

Closer to Tabb's Creek you will find Virginia's Northern Neck with its colonial and antebellum homes and churches. Presidents George Washington, James Monroe and James Madison were born in the area, as was General Robert E. Lee.

Inn at Tabb's Creek Landing
Rt. 14, Mathews County; P.O. Box 219; Port Haywood, VA 23138
(804) 725-5136
Innkeepers: Cabell & Catherine Venable
Rooms: 2; Suites: 2; All Private Baths; Rates: $$$
Affiliations: ABBA, BBAV, Mathews County Chamber

Payment:

Amenities: 🅰️/c 🖥️ 📼 🔥 🍴 ⊘

Page House Inn
Norfolk

Norfolk's Ghent Historic District is a neighborhood filled with history and culture. Originally farmland, by the late 1800s and early 1900s it had become the fashionable place for the wealthy to live and build stately homes. The area began to decline as new suburbs were developed. It wasn't until the early 1970s that restoration began. Today it has become a center of fine restaurants, boutiques and both historic and cultural sites.

In the Ghent Historic district you will find the Chrysler Museum of Art, one of America's premier art collections, including works by Andy Warhol as well as Hopper, Cassatt and many others. Other major sites in the Ghent Historic District include the Harrison Opera House and Stockley Gardens, a three-block-long park.

Here in the urban area of the Ghent Historic District you will find the Page House Inn. This 1899 Georgian Revival mansion has been completely restored and turned into one of Virginia's premier bed and breakfasts.

Award-winning preservation along with nineteenth and turn-of-the-century antiques and artwork has created a bed and breakfast that is elegant yet comfortable. The Inn has four rooms, three of which are located on the third floor, and two suites. The fourth room and both suites are located on the second floor. Each room and suite has its very own personality. There are suites and rooms with gas fireplaces and skylights. There are rooms with twin four-poster beds (which can be pushed together and made up as a king) and others with queen-sized beds. In the bathrooms, you may find a claw-foot tub with a brass ring for stand-up showers, oversized built-in showers, and even whirlpool baths. In the suites you can have breakfast by candlelight.

All rooms, of course, include a gourmet continental-plus breakfast served either in the dining room or in your room. Breakfast consists

of a selection of premium fresh juices, fresh-baked sourdough bread or other crusty European-style bread, fresh-baked cream scones or other pastry, butter, assorted jams and imported cheese. There is a selection of low-fat cereals, poached or baked fruits or a fruit compote, a basket of fresh fruit, yogurts, fancy and herbal teas as well as coffee, espresso and cappuccino. Stephanie & Ezio are also happy to accommodate special dietary needs.

Afternoons bring fresh-baked cookies and cappuccino or hot tea in winter, and iced tea or lemonade in the summer. Guests have access to a refrigerator stocked with complimentary soft drinks and juices and there is also a basket filled with snacks at all times.

Located just a short walk from the financial district yet close to major points of interest, Page House Inn is an enjoyable place to stay for those who wish to be truly pampered while seeing the sites of the Virginia Waterfront. This area includes Norfolk, Chesapeake, Hampton, Newport News, Portsmouth, Suffolk and Virginia Beach.

Stephanie knows the city well and can recommend a number of good places to dine such as the Baker's Crust, or one of my favorites, Doumar's. This is an old fashioned drive-in restaurant that is home of the first ice cream cone machine, used to introduce ice cream cones at the 1904 St. Louis World's Fair.

Page House Inn; 323 Fairfax Avenue; Norfolk, VA 23507
(800) 599-7659; (757) 625-5033; Fax: (757) 623-9451
Innkeepers: Stephanie & Ezio DiBelardino
E-mail: innkeeper@pagehouseinn.com
Rooms: 4; **Suites**: 2; **All Private Baths**; **Rates**: $$ - $$$
Affiliations: AAA◆◆◆◆, PAII, Mobil★★★, BBAV, Norfolk Hotel & Motel Assoc.
Payment: $$$ CHECKS MC VISA
Amenities: A/C ⟨icons⟩

Olde Towne Inn
Norfolk Area (Portsmouth)

Portsmouth is an amazing city and I fell in love with the waterfront the moment I arrived. There is so much to see and do that I will plan a longer stay on my next visit. For history lovers, Portsmouth offers over 300 years of history to explore in the Olde Towne Historic District. There's a self-guided walking tour, a harbor tour on the stern-wheeler Carrie B and a tall sailing ship, American Rover. There are also trolley tours to places like the Naval Shipyard Museum, the Lightship Museum and the historic Hill House.

At almost any time of day, art lovers can walk along the waterfront and find artists painting, or visit one of the galleries such as the Olde Towne Gallery or Art Atrium. Movie lovers will want to visit the Commodore Theater. It's a restored 1945 art deco style movie theater where you can enjoy dinner while watching first-run movies the way they were meant to be seen.

Since Norfolk is just across the river and easily accessible by ferry, the National Maritime Center (NAUTICUS), the Chrysler Art Museum, and the Harrison Opera House are all within easy reach. Every weekend during the spring, summer and fall, you will find a variety of festivals and free public concerts at Towne Point Park in Norfolk or Portside in Portsmouth.

Regardless of your interests, you'll find plenty to do within a few blocks of the Olde Towne Inn. Within just a 45-minute drive, vacationers can visit historic Williamsburg, Jamestown and Yorktown, visit Busch Gardens or swim in the warm waters of Virginia Beach.

The Olde Towne Inn is a grand Italianate style house that was built for a wealthy local merchant in the mid-1880s. Innkeepers Dede and John Braley have carefully restored this beautiful home and decorated it with an eclectic assortment of antiques and traditional

furnishings. Its blend of historic ambiance with twentieth-century conveniences is wonderfully suited to the historic area.

Each bedroom in the house has its own theme. The Garden Room overlooks the city-like garden and a deluxe room that would appeal to guests celebrating a special occasion. Three rooms have access to the second story veranda with unique doors called "jib windows" that were common in the latter part of the nineteenth century but rare today. These windows raise and the bottom section opens to create a doorway for guests to enjoy the veranda.

Breakfast brings Dede's special recipes that include pineapple pancakes, stuffed French toast with boysenberry sauce, overstuffed omelets or breakfast casseroles. There are always muffins, banana breads, coffee cake, or apple cakes along with juices, teas and fresh coffee. Seasonally, afternoons bring refreshments of iced tea, lemonade or cocoa. There are cookies, scones and other snacks to hold you until dinner at one of the area's fine restaurants.

With the world's busiest harbor only a few blocks away, you are guaranteed that Portsmouth will keep you busy with all that it offers. Then again, you may want to just curl up with a good book on the veranda and watch the world pass by below.

Olde Towne Inn
420 Middle Street; Portsmouth, VA 23704
(800) 353-0278; (757) 397-5462
Innkeepers: Dede & John Braley
Rooms: 3; Suites: 1; All Private Baths; Rates: $$ - $$$
Affiliations: BBAV
Payment:
Amenities:

Linden House Bed & Breakfast
Northern Neck Area (Champlain)

The year was 1735. Buckingham Browne, formerly of Norfolk, England, had just completed the construction of a magnificent two and a half-story brick home. His plantation was located on the 1,265-acre land grant that he had been awarded in 1719.

This area of Virginia is called the "Land of Independence" because it is where the ideas of freedom were first voiced. It is the land of George Washington, James Monroe and James Madison, all three born in an area just across the Rappahannock River in an area known as the Northern Neck.

Also prominent in the area was the Lee family of Stratford Hall. Four generations of Lees were born here including Richard Henry and his brother Francis Lightfoot, the only brothers to sign the Declaration of Independence. In 1807 another Lee was born, Robert E., who was destined to become the commanding officer of the Army of the Confederacy.

With my love of history, there could be no better area for us to begin our 14,500-mile odyssey researching Virginia for this book. Our first bed and breakfast in the state was Linden House, where innkeepers Ken and Sandra Pounsberry have created a hideaway on 200 acres. Its blend of hospitality, history, and comfortable surroundings makes Linden House perfect for romantic interludes.

In addition to his having been a police officer for 20 years, Ken and his wife, Sandy, had also been caterers and restaurateurs. The idea of a bed and breakfast had been a dream for several years before they found Linden House. They had lived on a farm so they needed enough land to bring their animals with them. It was on a trip to see their daughter in Williamsburg that they first saw the plantation. It had been sitting empty

for more than 30 years and they knew it would take considerable talent to bring this two-and-a-half-century old home back to life.

More than three tons of plaster and 185 gallons of paint went into the project. It also took weeks of restoration, numerous trips to area estate sales for furnishings and many family heirlooms to complete Linden House. The result is one of the finest bed and breakfasts in a historical setting that exists in the area.

The most recent addition has been the two-story Coach House. The brick work of the Coach House blends so amazingly well with the old brick of Linden House, you would think they were built at the same time from the same brick. Downstairs is the Carriage Suite with country furnishings, antiques, a fireplace and its own porch. Upstairs the couple have built two very comfortable modern rooms, appropriately named the Coachman and the Footman. Other rooms located in the main manor house include the Robert E. Lee Room, the Jefferson Davis Room, and the Linden Suite.

As caterers and former restaurateurs, they have learned the secret of making breakfast a special treat. A "full plantation breakfast" is served each morning and features a half dozen varieties of waffles with bacon or sausage, pancakes, biscuits and eggs. Other mornings bring omelets with vegetables and ham or eggs Benedict.

Linden House Bed & Breakfast
P.O. Box 23; Champlain, VA 22438
(800) 622-1202; (804) 443-1170; Fax: (804) 443-0107
Innkeepers: Ken & Sandra Pounsberry
Rooms: 4; Suites: 2; All Private Baths; Rates: $$ - $$$
Affiliations: AAA, ABBA, BBAV, Chamber of Commerce of Essex

Payment:

Amenities:

The Morris House
Northern Neck Area (Reedville)

It would be impossible to forget the imposing façade of the house Albert Morris built for his wife, Annie, in 1895. Albert was a fishing tycoon and one of the original residents of Reedville. Materials for the mansion built on "Millionaires Row" came from all over the country by boat and landed at the dock he had built for the purpose. Bricks were specially made with steel particles to ensure they would withstand both time and weather. The grand wrap-around veranda enhances the appearance of this three-story mansion that also includes a full English basement. The house covers more than 4,000 square feet and sits on more than an acre of land on Cockrells Creek.

Reedville was established following the Civil War by Captain Elijah Reed who came to fish for menhaden. The Atlantic menhaden is only about 15 inches long but rich in oil. At the time, they were caught in large numbers and used as bait as well as for animal feed and fertilizer. The industry brought such wealth to the community that at one time Reedville had the highest per capita income of any town in the United States.

Innkeepers Erin and Heath Dill spent nearly a year looking for the right place for their bed and breakfast. They knew they wanted to be able to work together, to be around people, and they needed a place that would showcase their interest in antiques. The Morris House has served all three interests and the antiques seem to belong there.

Over the years, Erin and Heath had collected a number of family heirlooms like the pharmacy cabinet in the dining room that belonged to Erin's great-great uncle, Richard Furman, who was a doctor in South Carolina for more than 60 years. There's a secretary in the living room that belonged to Erin's grandmother. In the dining room there is a painting of John Blount Miller, Erin's great-great-great-great grandfather who fought in the War of 1812. The painting was done by

Scarborough, who had also been commissioned to paint Miller's seven daughters. During the months of painting, Scarborough became such a member of the family that he married the seventh daughter!

Morris House has also benefited from Erin and Heath's collections such as the antique beaded-purse collection that fills an entire case in the hall. The beadwork ranges in age from the 1800s to the 1920s. There are many rocking horses and much horse memorabilia around the house from Heath's years of work in the horse industry. Two of my favorite collections are the miniature furniture (salesmen's samples) hanging on the wall of the balcony suite and Heath's collection of toy soldiers. Some of them are rare British-made hollow-cast circa 1895.

The Northern Neck is formed by two great rivers, the Potomac to the north and the Rappahannock to the south. Three presidents, George Washington, James Monroe and James Madison, were born in the area. One of the finest restorations in the nation, Stratford Hall, the birthplace of General Robert E. Lee, is just a short drive from Reedville. Historic Christ Church, built by Robert "King" Carter in 1735, is located in Irvington and the Mary Ball Washington Museum in Lancaster. Other points of interest in the area include the Reedville Fishermen's Museum, just a few blocks from Morris House and the ship Chesapeake Breeze which will take you from Reedville to Tangier Island.

The Morris House
Lower Main Street; P.O. Box 163; Reedville, VA 22539
(804) 453-7016; Fax: (804) 453-9032
Innkeepers: Heath & Erin Dill
Rooms: 2; **Suites**: 2 **Cottages**: 1; **All Private Baths**; **Rates**: $$ - $$$
Affiliations: PAII, BBAV
Payment:  $$$ CHECKS MC VISA
Amenities: A/C VCR

Angie's Guest Cottage
Virginia Beach

You'll find real hospitality here, with people who are always happy to see you, but this isn't your typical bed and breakfast. It's more informal than most, more laid back. Part of that is because it's only a block-and-a-half from one of the most popular beaches on the eastern seaboard. Another reason is that while Angie's is a bed and breakfast open to couples, families, and singles, it's also a youth hostel and a member of Hostelling International—American Youth Hostels.

As a bed and breakfast, it's like staying at your grandmother's beach house, with its "old-timey" bedspreads, comfortable furnishings and its easy-going atmosphere with a bit of a European twist. It offers three upstairs rooms, each with its own refrigerator and three downstairs rooms that share a full-size refrigerator in the hall. There is a kitchen with a range, dishes and a microwave and an outside barbecue pit with picnic tables available for guest use.

The youth hostel is part of an international system of low-cost, supervised dormitories for young travelers. Hostels provide sleeping areas, bathrooms, kitchens, and common areas for meeting other travelers. You may find guests staying there from almost anywhere in the world. It's not unusual for guests to work off part of their expenses. When we arrived, a number of world travelers were giving Angie's a spring coat of paint. They add richness to the experience of staying at Angie's.

Barbara Yates first became interested in hostels at age 21 when she and a friend backpacked across Europe for three months. Still the world traveler, her most recent trip included trekking in parts South America.

The house was built early in the 1900s and hosted families enjoying summer vacations while their "surfmen" were stationed at the Coast Guard Station. The "original" Angie purchased the property when the station closed and began operating a rooming house for 12 years in the late

1960s and early 70s. In 1978, the property sold to Barbara's parents. They started operating the bed and breakfast three years later and the hostel four years after they opened the B&B. While the "original" Angie is gone, Angie's Guest Cottage has always had a good reputation for cleanliness.

Angie's is located in the heart of Virginia Beach so finding a good place to eat or something to do isn't a problem. Allowing enough time to do everything you want, however, might be. One of your first stops should be Old Coast Guard Museum of Virginia located only a block away, right on the way to the beach.

There are two miles of boardwalk along the beach and more than 45 miles of bike paths in the area. There is shopping, dining, and the Ocean Breeze amusement park. A trolley ride will take you to the Virginia Marine Science Museum with more than 400,000 gallons of aquariums and a new IMAX theater. Another place to visit is the Back Bay National Wildlife Refuge, located just a short drive from Angie's Guest Cottage. This 7,700-acre refuge of beach woodland and marsh provides habitat for migratory waterfowl.

There is always something going on beachside from concerts to live stage performances, music dance, comedy clubs, and live opera performances. No matter what time of day or night, you'll find Angie's is only minutes away from something to do.

Angie's Guest Cottage
302 24th Street; Virginia Beach, VA 23451
(757) 428-4690
Innkeepers: Barbara Yates and Parents
Rooms: 6; Cottages: 2; With Private Bath: 1; With Shared Baths: 5; Rates: $ - $$
Affiliations: BBAV, VA Beach Hotel & Motel Assoc., American Youth Hostels
Payment:
Amenities: 🖳 🙂

Barclay Cottage
Virginia Beach

Believed to be the second-oldest beach house in Virginia Beach, Barclay Cottage has enjoyed a rich history during its 100 years. It began as a summer cottage in 1895. From 1905 to 1917, it was the home of the Williamson family.

For a while it was a boarding house and then for 50 years a school. Its history as a school is the most interesting of all. Christopher Columbus Barclay, father of Lillian Sinclair Barclay, purchased the house in 1917. Lillian, who never married, ran a guest house with her parents for many years. In 1922, Lillian began tutoring three or four students. As the numbers grew, the guest rooms gave way to classrooms as she converted the upstairs bedrooms one by one. For the next 50 years she taught kindergarten through third grade. At the age of 80 she closed the doors to her small school. She continued to live in her home until she passed away at the age of 97.

Peter & Claire Catanese came from New Jersey and purchased the property in December of 1990. At that time all that remained was a shell. The furnishings had been sold and the inside of the house had been torn out. It was almost miraculous but the contractors had the work done on the house in just four months and it opened as a bed and breakfast in May of 1991.

There are a number of historic collections in the house, many to honor the home's former owners. Over the years a number of former students have brought items, like the teapot and rocker, that had been there when Miss Barclay taught school in the house.

Barclay Cottage is large enough to be comfortable yet small enough to be cozy. The wraparound porches on the first and second floors make a great place to sit and plan a day of exploring Virginia Beach, or better, a place to relax in the cool of the evening.

After a breakfast of fresh fruit, homemade muffins or cinnamon buns, and scrambled eggs with bacon or sausage, Peter will suggest a number of interesting things to do in the area. Be sure to ask about Virginia's Marine Science Museum located just a short drive from the Barclay Cottage.

While I enjoyed the beach and the two-mile boardwalk with its variety of restaurants and shops, the Marine Science Museum has to be one of the best stops in Virginia Beach. A $35 million expansion program has increased both acreage and exhibits. A 300,000 gallon deep-sea aquarium is part of the new expansion along with a six-story IMAX theater.

The Old Coast Guard Museum of Virginia is located on the boardwalk and tells the history of the U.S. Life-Saving/Coast Guard stations along our coast. The historic station was operational by 1903 and decommissioned in 1969.

Other major places to visit might the Old Cape Henry Lighthouse, the oldest government built lighthouse in America (commissioned by George Washington in 1791) or the Association for Research & Enlightenment the headquarters for the work of Edgar Cayce, a medical clairvoyant.

Edgar Cayce came to Virginia Beach in 1929 as a result of a vision which told him to come to a safe part of the country. For a time he lived just down the street from the Barclay Cottage and even gave lectures on the veranda during the time Miss Barclay taught school here.

Barclay Cottage
400 16th Street; Virginia Beach, VA 23451
(757) 422-1956
Innkeepers: Peter & Claire Catanese
Rooms: 5; With Private Baths: 3; With Shared Baths: 2 Rates: $$
Affiliations: BBAV
Payment:
Amenities:

Church Point Manor
Virginia Beach

On a three-acre tract of land in one of Virginia Beach's most prestigious neighborhoods, we found Church Point Manor. It's one of the most lavish bed and breakfasts you will ever visit. Every detail of this 10,000-square-foot manor has been painstakingly designed to pamper you. There are plush Oriental carpets showing off polished floors, rooms elegantly furnished with antiques, and each guest room is meticulously accessorized.

The original land grant where Church Point is located was made to Adam Thoroughgood by Charles I in 1635. The area was named Church Point because it was the sight of the first Old Donation Church built in 1639. However, by the mid-nineteenth century the property was a farm owned by James Garrison and was used to breed and raise race horses. It was during his ownership that the 1860s farmhouse was built. Abandoned in the early twentieth century, the farmhouse was virtually forgotten. When development began in the Church Point area, it was rescued from demolition. In 1992, an architectural survey of the city recommended the house be placed on the National Register of Historical Places as it is one of the rare surviving nineteenth-century farmhouses in the area.

After months of restoration, Church Point Manor was opened as a bed and breakfast with Angela Craig and her husband Peter Gagnon as innkeepers. Both are well suited for the task as Angela tutored under Carl Glassman, a nationally known consultant to the bed and breakfast industry. Peter's background had been in the restaurant business.

While Church Point Manor is nearly six miles from the boardwalk along the ocean front, it is only a half-mile from the Chesapeake Bay. The area is also rich with fine restaurants, small shops and

antique dealers. You may find, however, that there is enough to do at the bed and breakfast that you never leave during your stay. In addition to six rooms and a suite, work has recently been completed on a carriage house which adds an additional three rooms. The tap room is also now open to guests and area residents.

The property also includes a pool, a deck for sun bathing and your own private tennis court. The Historic Thoroughgood House is accessible through a path next to the manor house. There are bicycles for touring the historic areas or you might want to take the canoe from Church Point Manor's private dock and paddle the Lynnhaven River. After a full breakfast prepared by Peter, you'll find more than 30 acres of hiking trails nearby.

When you are ready to explore Virginia Beach, you'll find that it is easy to go from Church Point to any part of the Bay area. The Chesapeake Bay Bridge-Tunnel is only a few miles away and will take you to the Eastern Shore. Of course there is also the two-mile boardwalk along one of the east coast's finest beaches. City parks, state parks and national wildlife areas can be found throughout the area. The Seashore State Park contains almost 3,000 acres with 27 miles of nature trails. Rainy days are an excellent time to visit the many museums in the area. Our personal favorites include the Virginia Marine Science Museum and the Old Coast Guard Museum of Virginia.

Church Point Manor
4001 Church Point Road; Virginia Beach, VA 23455
(757) 460-2657; Fax: (757) 460-2845
Innkeepers: Angela Craig & Peter Gagnon
Rooms: 9; Suites: 1; All Private Baths; Rates: $$$ - $$$$
Affiliations: PAII, BBAV, Virginia Beach Chamber
Payment: $$$ MC VISA AMEX Diner's Club
Amenities:

Applewood Colonial Bed & Breakfast
Williamsburg

The restoration of Colonial Williamsburg began with a dream of Dr. W.A.R. Goodwin. His vision not only captured the attention of locals but also the interest of John D. Rockefeller. With Rockefeller's involvement in the early 1920s came the necessary funding to begin the project. Elton Holland was hired as construction manager and artisans came from around the world to begin the task of restoring Williamsburg.

Needing a home for his family, Holland built a private residence just a few blocks from the historic area. Much of the detail work on the house was done by the artisans who worked on Colonial Williamsburg and with materials similar to those used in the historic district. Within Applewood Colonial you will find Flemish bond brickwork, brass door locks, handmade hinges and the same style of crown dentil molding that can be seen in the Governor's Palace.

The house served as a tourist home or guest house for more than 25 years until the 1980s when it was used for college housing. Innkeeper Marty Jones already owned another bed and breakfast in the area when she learned that this property was for sale in 1988. Together with her family, they have returned it to its former glory. Over the last nine years it has become one of Williamsburg's favorite bed and breakfasts.

Marty, who grew up in Tell City, Indiana (named for William Tell), has decorated the bed and breakfast with an apple theme. There is an amazing collection of items all with the apple motif, including pictures and antique china. The collection grows on a regular basis as former guests send pieces not only from their own collections, but who also frequently buy special pieces that they think would fit perfectly within the decorating scheme. Dr. Jones, Marty's husband, hand-crafted the walnut mantel in the front parlor and serves as a consultant when guests' medical needs arise.

Breakfast is served in a dining room that features a beautiful built-in corner cupboard. Its hand-crafted wood sets off the display of antique china and apple teapots. The centerpiece of the table is a hand-crafted miniature gazebo set in a seasonally decorated courtyard.

There are three guest rooms and one suite at Applewood, all well appointed and with private baths. The rooms, which are named Gilliflower, Margil, and the Golden Pippin each have their own distinct style. They are decorated with quality antiques, oriental rugs, and queen-sized beds. My personal favorite is the spacious Colonel Vaughn Suite with its private breakfast room, private entrance and large sitting area. From the queen-sized canopy bed to the wall of bookcases featuring a large selection of books to the wood-burning fireplace, the suite was perfect to return to after a day of exploring Colonial Williamsburg.

And there is so much to see and do in the area besides Colonial Williamsburg. There are also Yorktown, the Jamestown settlement, Busch Gardens and the James River Plantations. With so much to do, you need to plan several days in the area, and a perfect way to get a bird's-eye view is to take the Historic Air Tour over the Virginia peninsula. When it comes to dining out, be sure to try a colonial tavern with its eighteenth-century ambiance. Williamsburg also offers a number of other choices from American to Vietnamese cuisine.

Applewood Colonial Bed & Breakfast
605 Richmond Road; Williamsburg, VA 23185
(800) 899-2753; (757) 229-0205; Fax: (757) 229-9405
Innkeepers: Marty Jones/Jan Brown
E-mail: applewood@widomaker.com
Rooms: 3; Suites: 1; All Private Baths; Rates: $$ - $$$
Affiliations: ABBA, NBBA, PAII, BBAV, Williamsburg Chamber
Payment: AMEX Amenities:

Cedars Bed & Breakfast
Williamsburg

Located directly across from the College of William and Mary and only a ten-minute walk from Colonial Williamsburg, the Cedars is Williamsburg's largest bed and breakfast and also one of its oldest. Built in the 1930s for a doctor with eight children, the house was constructed of 200-year-old brick taken from a warehouse that once stood in Williamsburg. The family only lived in the house for about a year before relocating. The sisters who purchased the property ran it as a guest house for 35 years, then sold it to a second set of sisters who also ran it as a guest house for a number of years.

Jim Malecha and his wife Bróna together with Jim's sister, Carol, wanted a business they could operate as a family. Over the years they had traveled a great deal and had stayed in many bed and breakfasts. It was Carol's background as an American history major that brought them to Williamsburg, and they saw that the Cedars offered them the perfect opportunity.

Guests at the Cedars have a variety of accommodations from which to choose. There are six rooms, two suites and a two-story brick guest cottage hidden away behind the inn. Great care has been taken in the decoration of the Cedars. While there are many antiques and elegant furnishings, there is still a feeling of comfort to the inn. You get the impression that it's okay to sit back, prop your feet up and relax. The innkeepers' goal was to offer traditional colonial elegance and hospitality with the modern comfort that today's travelers want and need. In this writer's opinion, they have done an excellent job. Candlelight and fresh flowers accent the full breakfast that's served buffet style on the handhewn huntboard on the tavern porch. Breakfast includes items such as smoked salmon flan, oatmeal pudding, fresh fruit, home-

made muffins or breads, as well as a selection of juices, coffees and teas.

The Cedars' location is perfect for visiting area attractions. While staying at the Cedars, I took the Historic Air Tour of the area. It really helped orient me to the location of the Jamestown settlement, Yorktown, where the revolutionary war ended, the James River Plantations and, of course, to Williamsburg and the historic area.

Of course the best way to tour historic Williamsburg is by carriage. The ride acts as a time machine taking you back to the early days of this colonial capital. Lunch at the Kings Arms Tavern helps to complete the feeling. After lunch, take a leisurely walk among the shops, artisans and craftsmen.

Midweek seems to be the best time to visit Busch Gardens. The crowds are smaller, and you'll have more time to enjoy the old country flavor that the theme park works to create. While there is much to do in Williamsburg, Jamestown, and the area, remember it is only a short drive to Newport News, Norfolk and across Hampton Bay to Virginia Beach. You could spend several months in the area and not see everything. There are many museums near Williamsburg such as the Mariners' Museum, Virginia Air and Space Center and the Virginia Living Museum.

The Cedars Bed & Breakfast
616 Jamestown Road; Williamsburg, VA 23185
(800) 296-3591; (757) 229-3591; Fax: (757) 229-0756
Innkeepers: Carol, James & Bróna Malecha
Rooms: 6; Suites: 2; Cottages: 1; All Private Baths; Rates: $$ - $$$
Affiliations: PAII, BBAV, Williamsburg Chamber

Payment:

Amenities:

Colonial Capital Bed & Breakfast
Williamsburg

Built in 1926, this three story Colonial Revival style home is located only three blocks from the historic area of Williamsburg, just across from the College of William and Mary. Its columned portico leads to a spacious entry foyer where you are greeted by innkeepers whose motto is quite simply "we're here to spoil you." From the welcoming refreshments to the nightly turn down service, innkeepers Phil and Barbara Craig have a way of making you feel comfortable.

Phil and Barbara's first experience at bed and breakfasts came in 1986 when they went to England for their 25th wedding anniversary. One stay and they were hooked. In fact, they both agreed that owning a bed and breakfast would be a part of their future. It turned out that the future came sooner than they had expected. In August 1988, they bought property in their home state of Virginia and opened Colonial Capital Bed and Breakfast in December.

They have managed to completely renovate the Colonial Revival home and yet retain its elegance and graciousness while providing private baths for each of the four guest rooms and the two-room suite. There is a rich blend of warmth, style and comfort. The decor is enhanced by antique furnishings and Oriental rugs. The four guest rooms and one suite all include cozy canopied four-poster beds, private baths, and remote control ceiling fans. In case you might have forgotten anything, luxury bath amenities including soaps, body lotion and bath beads are provided.

Every guest I spoke with had favorite things they remembered about the house. The classic plantation-style parlor and the screened side porch, patio and deck came out on top. During cool weather you will find guests curled up with a good book in front of the parlor

fireplace. The porches are great for summer relaxation with a glass of iced tea or lemonade.

Breakfast is generally served at 8:30 a.m. The menu is so varied that you could stay 14 days and never have the same thing twice. There's Virginia ham, bacon or sausage, French toast, a variety of casseroles, omelets, or waffles. Anyone who eats all their grits gets a freshly baked chocolate chip cookie. Specially-blended coffee and, of course, herbal teas and fresh juices accompany the meal.

When you're ready to explore Williamsburg, you might try one of the bicycles that are available for guest use. Once you've finished your tour of the 173-acre outdoor living history museum, there are also Jamestown and Yorktown nearby. Jamestown is where America began, and Yorktown, where Lord Cornwallis surrendered for the British. Many of the James River Plantations are open to the public and offer a look at sixteenth- and seventeenth-century life in the new world.

One of the best ways I found to explore the area was to take the Historic Air Tour. It helped to orient me to the area. Later, back on the ground, I found I had a much better understanding of not only the area, but even of the chain of events that helped to forge this nation of ours.

Colonial Capital Bed & Breakfast
 501 Richmond Road; Williamsburg, VA 23185
(800) 776-0570; (757) 229-0233; Fax: (757) 253-7667
Innkeepers: Barbara & Phil Craig
E-mail: ccbb@widomaker.com
Rooms: 4; Suites: 1; All Private Baths; Rates: $$ - $$$
Affiliations: PAII, Mobil, BBAV, Williamsburg Chamber
Payment: SSS CHECKS MC VISA AMEX DISCOVER Amenities: A/C ✈ ▢ VCR ♨ ✆

Colonial Gardens Bed & Breakfast
Williamsburg

Located just five minutes from the historic area of Williamsburg, Colonial Gardens occupies a quiet, secluded woodland setting. Built in 1965 for the Dean of the School of Law at William and Mary, it was constructed of bricks from the old city hall which was built in the late 1800s.

The 3,950-square-foot home with its understated elegance combined with a natural setting on two acres has made Colonial Gardens a favorite stop for travelers to the area. I was captivated by the beautifully landscaped grounds the moment we pulled into the driveway. The grounds are covered with century-old oaks and poplars and the gardens are alive with color most of the year. The garden theme is carried throughout the home with seasonal flowers in every room and suite. Accordingly, three of the rooms are named the Primrose Room, the Rhododendron Suite and the Azalea Suite.

Innkeepers Scottie and Wilmot Phillips came to Williamsburg from Atlanta in 1995. They bought the property on Memorial weekend and, after extensive cosmetic renovation, opened October 1, 1995. Scottie is retired after 20 years in the medical profession but Wilmot continues to do architectural renderings. Most of the paintings and drawings throughout the house were done by him. They are based on travels in England, Italy, France and Wales. His paintings have been marketed commercially in Atlanta, Hilton Head, Highlands, North Carolina, and New York City.

Colonial Gardens has been carefully decorated and furnished with antiques collected over the last 30 years. Many are family heirlooms that have been passed down through generations. One such piece is the museum-quality punch bowl produced in New York in the 1880s that belonged to Scottie's grandmother. The English gateleg table in

the entrance hall belonged to Scottie's great-great grandmother. Ask Wilmot to see the converted flintlock carried by his great-great-great grandfather in the Battle of Atlanta when he was only 14 years old.

Scottie and Wilmot have tried to anticipate every need. They devote themselves to details such as afternoon refreshments of iced tea or lemonade served in the sunroom and plush, monogrammed robes. They do a nightly turn-down and put either individually-wrapped gourmet candies or almond cookies on the pillows. Breakfast brings stuffed baked blueberry French toast with blueberry syrup from Maine or egg casseroles in individual ramekins. There's also sausage, links or patties, Canadian bacon, fresh fruit, and beverages.

With Colonial Williamsburg just a short drive away and only minutes to the parkway to the Jamestown settlement, there is always something to do while staying at Colonial Gardens. However, you may just want to relax on the porch with one of the outdoor cats.

The huntboard in the foyer provides a large selection of menus. The innkeepers are familiar with local restaurants and can help with selections and reservations. We ate at a number of places in the area that I would recommend, but a stop at the Kings Arms Tavern in the historic section is a must on anyone's trip. It may be the closest you ever get to taking a ride in a time machine.

Colonial Gardens Bed & Breakfast
1109 Jamestown Road; Williamsburg, VA 23185
(800) 886-9715; (757) 220-8087; Fax: (757) 253-1495
Innkeepers: Scottie & Wilmot Phillips
E-mail: colgrdns@widomaker.com
Rooms: 2; **Suites**: 2; **All Private Baths**; **Rates**: $$$
Affiliations: BBAV, Williamsburg Chamber
Payment:  **Amenities**:

Liberty Rose Bed & Breakfast Williamsburg

Often referred to as "Williamsburg's most romantic bed and breakfast," Liberty Rose brought innkeepers Brad and Sandi Hirz together.

Back when he and Sandy were just friends, Brad told Sandy that he had been reading about something called a bed and breakfast. He felt with her background in interior design and her work as a wedding consultant, that she would make a great innkeeper. In 1986, Sandy decided to come to Virginia and find a bed and breakfast. Her first stop was Williamsburg where she found a property that had been sitting empty for two years. After just 15 minutes, she knew it was the right place and bought it that night. When she moved to Williamsburg three months later, people were lined up wanting the property.

Brad came to Virginia from his farm in the state of Washington to help her with the house and what had been a friendship grew into romance. When time came for Brad to go back to the farm, he said they would get together the next year. A few days later he called and said he would be there on Thursday. They were married on Friday and the empty house became their honeymoon project.

Built in the early 1920s, the bed and breakfast is an eclectic mix of English, Victorian, and French antiques, fabrics and wallpapers. Much of the brick used in building the two-story, white clapboard house came from Jamestown where the original owner had gathered bricks to build the house. The most unusual thing about the house is that because it turns enough corners, it has three sides of windows in every room: a back view, a side view and a front view. Sited on one of the few hills in town, the one-acre lot contains many oak, beech, and poplar trees that are over 100 years old.

From the entryway to the grand piano in the elegant guest parlor and the guest rooms, the house is filled with treasures from bygone years. Sandi has crafted all the bed coverings, drapery treatments and wall coverings.

Brad's special touches show at breakfast when he prepares a delightful array of meats such bacon and sausage, or breakfast boboli, (a breakfast pizza with a big crust, honey mustard, bacon, ham, three types of cheeses and fresh broiled tomatoes). Some mornings bring granny smith hotcakes, also called apple fritter hot cakes, with roasted pecans. The guest refrigerator is always well stocked, and Brad's homemade chocolate chip cookies are famous with guests who return year after year.

The entire area around Williamsburg is really amazing. The beginnings and the end of Colonial America are both here. The Jamestown settlement was the first English colony. Many of our founding fathers lived in and around Williamsburg or at plantations along the James River. Williamsburg was also the site of the First Continental Congress in 1774. Colonial America and the Revolutionary War ended in 1781 at Yorktown with the surrender of the British.

When you make your reservation to stay at Liberty Rose, be sure to allow enough time to visit not only the historical sites in the area, but also to take in modern attractions like Busch Gardens Old Country. You might even want to take a plane ride with Historic Air Tours over the peninsula for a bird's eye view of where America began.

Liberty Rose Bed & Breakfast
1022 Jamestown Road; Williamsburg, VA 23185
(800) 545-1825; (757) 253-1260
Innkeepers: Brad & Sandra Hirz
Rooms: 2; **Suites**: 2; **All Private Baths**; **Rates**: $$$ - $$$$
Affiliations: AAA♦♦♦, NBBA, USB&B, Mobil, BBAV, Williamsburg Chamber
Historic Preservation Society
Payment: 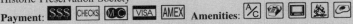 **Amenities**:

Magnolia Manor
Williamsburg

The best alarm clock I've ever had was the aroma of cinnamon rolls fresh from the oven at Magnolia Manor. The buns, known locally as Bonjour Buns, along with gourmet coffee and a choice of teas, are available each morning about an hour before breakfast is served in the dining room.

Magnolia Manor was opened in October 1994 by Bill and Robyn Eshleman on their return to the United States after 15 years in the Middle East. Bill, originally from Pennsylvania, went to Abu Dhabi in the United Arab Emirates to fly for an aviation company shortly after the couple married in 1978. While his job was to fly helicopters, his reputation was for his gourmet cooking talents. Now this culinary expertise is put to practical use with Bonjour Buns and Patriot Pretzels. These are delivered to customers all over the Williamsburg area but yours come first.

Robyn, a New Zealander, moved with her family to Honolulu in 1960. Over the years she has photographed a wide range of subjects while on world travels. They have ranged from offshore oil rigs to a sought-after set of prints of traditional life in the Emirates.

Together they operate the Magnolia Manor, a three-story Georgian revival built in 1941. The furnishings are a mix of contemporary, Oriental and eighteenth-century. The Korean medicine and Kashmiri brass inlaid chests, the large rosewood dining table and grandfather clock were all brought back from overseas. A recent gift from Bill's mother is a beautiful curved mahogany sideboard ideal for serving tea and coffee before breakfast. The eighteenth century rice-carved canopy beds which grace every suite or room at Magnolia Manor, originally all came from North Carolina. However, two of the canopy beds have made the sea voyage to the Middle East and back again. They graced the master suite and guest room of the Eshleman's Abu Dhabi penthouse which overlooked the Gulf.

All rooms have either a separate living room or a sitting area, a direct outside line telephone and TV with cable and VCR on request. Bathrooms have whirlpool tubs or huge glass and marble showers (with four heads). The bathrooms, the beds and the relaxed atmosphere make Magnolia Manor a haven for getaways, anniversaries and honeymoons.

Magnolia Manor breakfast specialties include shirred eggs, apple-cured bacon, hash brown potatoes and ham. For a leisurely Sunday breakfast you might try cranberry and pecan pancakes topped with rich maple syrup and whipped cream. Juices include the traditional orange as well as apple and cranberry served at the large Chinese rosewood table. In cold weather, fireplaces in both living and dining rooms are ablaze with wood fires.

The Williamsburg, Jamestown, Yorktown triangle has something for everyone in the family. Magnolia Manor is within walking distance of Merchant's Square and Colonial Williamsburg. You may choose from antique shops to the largest outdoor living history museum in America. You can take a cruise on the James River or fly over the peninsula with Historic Air Tours. When the weather is hot, take a dip at Water Country, Busch Gardens' water park, and then spend your evening taking the rides and seeing the sites of Busch Gardens Old Country. By the end of the day, you will appreciate the turn down service and Godiva chocolate waiting on your pillow.

Magnolia Manor
700 Richmond Road; Williamsburg, VA 23185
(800) 462-6667; (757) 220-9600; Fax: (757) 253-0088
Innkeepers: Bill & Robyn Eshleman
Rooms: 2; **Suites**: 2; **All Private Baths**; **Rates**: $$$ - $$$$
Affiliations: BBAV, Williamsburg Chamber
Payment: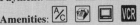
Amenities:

Primrose Cottage Bed & Breakfast
Williamsburg

Innkeeper Inge Curtis has made Primrose Cottage a wonderful escape from the routines of daily life. The beautiful surroundings help guests relax immediately, and Inge's warm, friendly manner invites them to become friends.

On display is a Bavarian dollhouse that Inge built by hand. Look beyond the hand-carved balcony through the windows and you'll see miniature lights, wallpapered rooms, tile floors, a tiny tub, tables and chairs. Other signs of the innkeeper's talent include the harpsichord she built (and keeps tuned) in the living room. She has also built a dulcimer and a clavichord, but it was the harpsichord on which her daughters learned to play.

Inge is German born, but she has been in the United States for more than 30 years. She has lived in Florida, Connecticut and New York City. She was living in Mason Neck, Virginia, on the Potomac River, when her daughters left for college. Her move to Williamsburg gave her peace of mind and allowed her to own the bed and breakfast she had dreamed of for years.

Primrose Cottage was built in the early 1950s by two maiden sisters as a tourist or guest house. The last three owners have operated it as a bed and breakfast, so its history of hospitality goes back nearly 50 years. The various innkeepers have made improvements to the house over the years. When Inge arrived in 1993, it required only cosmetic changes and a lot of work in the garden to bring Primrose Cottage to its present charm.

Inge was trained as a gardener in Germany and she will always love flowers. In the spring, the front walk is lined with primroses. Inge has also planted over 2,000 tulips. As the seasons change, so do the gardens with new flowers in bloom.

Breakfast is served family style each morning at 8:30 a.m. and Inge tries never to repeat a meal during a guest's stay. One of her most popular dishes is the oven baked apple pancakes or "Dutch babies," served with real whipped cream, juice, coffee, tea, hot chocolate, or other requested bever-

age. Other favorites include sausage or bacon with bread pudding soufflé, waffles with raspberries, French toast or quiche. The fresh fruit always served varies according to the season.

Primrose Cottage is located less than a ten-minute walk from Merchants Square at the edge of Colonial Williamsburg. More than 40 stores offer everything from arts and crafts to clothing and gifts. The Historic Area just beyond the shops is a trip back to eighteenth-century Colonial America. Eighty-eight preserved and restored original structures function as America's largest outdoor living history museum.

When you're ready to step back into the twentieth-century, Busch Gardens theme park will delight you, young and old. From the newest attraction, "Escape From Pompeii" to the German Oompah Band, the theme park is a fanciful recreation of Old World Europe.

Other major points of interest in the area include Jamestown, where the first permanent English settlement in America was established. There's also Yorktown, where the British surrendered, ending the Revolutionary War, and the James River Plantations along Route 5. A flight with Historic Air Tours or a river cruise on the Hampton II will provide an overview of the area.

Whatever your interest while in the Williamsburg area, Primrose Cottage is in the center of it all.

Primrose Cottage Bed & Breakfast
706 Richmond Road; Williamsburg, VA 23185
(888) 800-1705; (757) 229-6421; Fax: (757) 259-0717
Innkeeper: Inge Curtis
Rooms: 4; **With Private Baths**: 3; **With Shared Bath**:1; **Rates**: $$-$$$
Affiliations: BBAV, Williamsburg Chamber
Payment: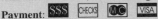
Amenities:

War Hill Inn
Williamsburg

Just three miles from Colonial Williamsburg is a pleasant farm with Angus cattle grazing in lush pastures. At night you'll hear the sounds of owls, frogs and crickets. Mornings are signaled by the crowing of the cock. The busy world of Williamsburg seems a million miles away. Yet the drive is pleasant and takes only minutes to return you the heart of early American history.

Shirley and Bill Lee built the house in 1968 with the guidance of an architect from Colonial Williamsburg. It began as a replica of the James Anderson house in Colonial Williamsburg, but over the years, new wings have been added to the house.

This house wasn't built by a contractor, but created by the owners themselves. It is a composite of many different things: old building materials from Lancaster, Pennsylvania; bricks from the Norfolk harbor area; stairs from an old Lutheran church; and beams in the living area from an old barn. It took a lot of vision, years of hard work and loving care to build a home with all the conveniences of the twentieth century. Yet it still retains the charm of the eighteenth-century architecture after which it was modeled.

You will find three guest rooms and a suite in the main house. The Washington Cottage is located just across the drive. Each of the rooms, like the common areas, has been carefully decorated with an eclectic mix of period antiques. Still, this is a bed and breakfast where children are welcome. All the accommodations include private baths, air-conditioning, and cable TV. Queen-sized, double and twin beds are all available depending on the room you choose.

With more than 6,200 square feet in the house plus the cottage, there is plenty of room for guests to feel comfortable and yet enjoy their privacy. If you need a bit more space, the house sits in the middle of a 32-acre farm that you are welcome to wander.

While it has not been possible to ascertain from where the name War Hill came, the earliest reference is from records dating back to the early 1700s. It's believed that the original tract of land covered thousands of acres. The existing 32 acres of land were given to a slave after the Civil War. Over the years the Lees have found artifacts on the property such as a rifle barrel, a bayonet, horn instruments and even a whale bone.

Bill was a veterinarian in Williamsburg for 30 years. Now that he is retired, his interests are centered in horticulture and he spends much time tending the orchard. He grows kiwi, peaches, blueberries, plums, grapes, blackberries, strawberries and, of course, apples. The fruit isn't for sale, but mainly for their own consumption and use at the bed and breakfast. Guests are encouraged to help themselves if the fruit is ripe when they visit. Breakfast at War Hill is thankfully very country. With fresh laid eggs, country ham, bacon or sausage, rosemary potatoes and applesauce made on the farm, it's just like a trip to grandma's.

Like any farm, there are outdoor pets: the yellow Labrador is Dakota; the Dachshund is Sophie; a black and white Border Collie/Elk Hound mix is named Scottie; and the barn cat is Maria. And, of course, Bill has named every one of the Black Angus cattle.

War Hill Inn
4560 Long Hill Road; Williamsburg, VA 23188
(800) 743-0248; (757) 565-0248
Innkeepers: Shirley, Bill & Will Lee
Rooms: 3; Suites: 1; Cottages: 1; All Private Baths; Rates: $$ - $$$
Affiliations: AAA◆◆◆, Mobil, BBAV, Williamsburg Chamber
Payment:
Amenities: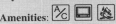

North Bend Plantation Bed & Breakfast
Williamsburg Area (Charles City)

Very seldom have I had the opportunity of staying at a historic bed and breakfast owned by the descendants of the original owner. However, innkeeper George Copland's family has lived in the area for the last 200 years. The great house at North Bend Plantation, a Federal period Greek Revival style home, was built in 1819 by John Minge for his wife Sarah Harrison. Sarah was the sister of William Henry Harrison, ninth President of the United States. Today, William and Sarah's great-grand nephew George and his wife Ridgely are innkeepers at North Bend.

This isn't George's only claim to the area. His mother was Mary Harrison Ruffin Copland of Evelynton Plantation and his maternal grandmother was Jane Cary Harrison of Berkeley Plantation. He is also the great-great grandson of Edmund Ruffin, who is known as the father of agriculture in America. Ruffin is also credited with firing the first shot in the Civil War for the South.

North Bend was built in 1819 and remained in the family until 1843 when it was sold to the Wilcox family. The Wilcoxes doubled the size of the house in 1853 and sold the property just after the Civil War. For a time in 1864 there were 30,000 union troops in this area under the commands of General Philip Sheridan and General Ulysses S. Grant. Sheridan used the house as his headquarters. The plantation desk used by General Sheridan is located in the guest room named after him.

In 1916 the property once again returned to George's family when his grandfather purchased the plantation. George still actively farms the 1,200 acres growing corn, wheat and soybeans.

Operated as a bed and breakfast since 1984, North Bend Plantation is rich in history. Great care has been taken to preserve that history. Throughout the house you will find antiques and family heirlooms dat-

ing back several generations. There are historic maps and rare books including the *Harpers Pictorial History of the Civil War* from 1869.

On the grounds guests will find a swimming pool, croquet, horseshoes and volleyball. For the golf enthusiast, a public golf course is only 20 minutes away. Several excellent restaurants are also located in the area, but one of our personal favorites is Indian Fields Tavern, just down the road from North Bend Plantation.

While Williamsburg is within a half-hour drive, there are several plantations in the area that are well worth your time. Remember that many of these were owned or are still owned by families related to your innkeeper. One of the best ways to see the plantations is aboard the Annabel Lee. This 3½ hour cruise on the James River begins in Richmond and travels down the river to Westover, Berkeley and Evelynton Plantations.

The area along the James River, including the historic triangle of Williamsburg, Jamestown, and Yorktown, holds more of our history than any other place in America. The first English settlement was at Jamestown, Williamsburg was the site of the first Continental Congress, and Yorktown was where the Revolutionary War ended with the surrender of Cornwallis. The river plantations are where many of our founding fathers lived, worked, and planned the future of our county. What better way to see the area than to stay in one of its finer plantations.

North Bend Plantation Bed & Breakfast
12200 Weyanoke Road; Charles City, VA 23030
(800) 841-1479; (804) 829-5176; Fax: (804) 829-6828
Innkeepers: George & Ridgely Copland
Rooms: 4; **Suites**: 1; **All Private Baths**; **Rates**: $$$
Affiliations: ABBA, USB&B, BBAV, Historic James River Plantation Group

Payment:

Amenities:

Piney Grove at Southall's Plantation
Williamsburg Area (Charles City)

Just twenty miles west of Williamsburg is the James River Plantation country. The 300-acre Southall Plantation, on which the original log portion of Piney Grove was built in 1800, was a typical Tidewater plantation with hundreds of acres. Today the seven acres that surround the original house are listed on the National Register of Historic Places. Beyond lie cultivated fields and Tidewater woodlands.

When Furnea (Fur-now) Southall established his prosperous plantation, the ride from Williamsburg might have taken two days by carriage. Visitors were a rare treat. Hospitality became a way of life among plantation owners. Today the drive from Williamsburg takes only thirty minutes and visitors are many, but hospitality is still a way of life with the Gordineer family. Whether it's a cool refreshing mint julep served on the porch swing, a hot toddy enjoyed before a roaring fire or a candlelit plantation breakfast in the 1800 Log Room, Piney Grove offers true Southern hospitality.

The Chickahominy Indians were early residents of the site and guests still find arrowheads and other signs of their habitation on the property. The original log portion of Piney Grove is the only surviving building from Southall's Plantation. In 1820, the structure was converted into a general merchandise emporium. In 1855 it was purchased by Edmund Archer Saunders, a successful Richmond wholesale grocer. Saunders later sold the store to his clerk, Thomas Fletcher Harwood. In 1905, Harwood built a new store across the street and enlarged Piney Grove as a residence for himself, his wife and his son, Dr. Ashton Harwood. The Harwood family cemetery remains on the property. In 1984, after it had been abandoned for over two decades, the Gordineers purchased Piney Grove and undertook a five-year restoration.

Guest rooms are located in the two-story Ladysmith House, originally built in 1857 in nearby Caroline County. The house was carefully dismantled and meticulously reconstructed and restored by Joseph and Joan Gordineer

and their son, Brian. Each spacious room is furnished with antiques, many of which are family heirlooms. Special amenities include private baths, coffeemakers and hair dryers. Nightly turn-down service is another one of the special touches provided by the Gordineers. During cool weather, they will lay a fire for you while you are dining at nearby Indian Fields Tavern and enjoying your complimentary desserts (arranged by the innkeepers at Piney Grove).

Other buildings on the grounds include Ashland (c. 1835), Duck Church (c. 1900) and the Dower Quaker (c. 1860). You will also find gardens and barnyard animals including two ponies, a goat, ducks, geese and six sheep. You also might want to enjoy your complimentary bottle of Virginia wine or cider on the gazebo or along the half-mile-long nature trail that winds around the swimming hole (pool) and down the ravine to Piney Springs, the headwaters of Rippon's Run. Take time to learn about Piney Grove. You'll find that Brian is well-versed in the history of the James River Plantation country.

Many of the plantations along the James River date back to the early 1600s. Berkeley Plantation for example was built in 1619 and Shirley Plantation in 1613. Berkeley was the birthplace of Benjamin Harrison, a signer of the Declaration of Independence. Benjamin's third son, William Henry Harrison, was the ninth president and was also born at Berkeley. Both of these plantations and several others along the James River are open to the public.

Piney Grove at Southall's Plantation
P.O. Box 1359; Williamsburg, VA 23187
(804) 829-2480
Innkeepers: The Gordineer Family
Rooms: 4; All Private Baths; Rates: $$$ - $$$$
Affiliations: PAII, BBAV

Payment:

Amenities:

Airville Plantation
Williamsburg Area (Gloucester)

Though the Revolutionary War was still 20 years away, the French and Indian War was raging across the colonies. During the conflict, colonial merchants continued to trade with the enemy and smuggle goods while refusing to provide English officials with men and supplies. It was also during this time that huge plantations were established by rich merchants and planters. John Dixon built Airville Plantation on 680 acres of prime land near Virginia's Northern Neck. His manor house was constructed in 1756 on the highest point in the area, nearly 75 feet above sea level. The waters of Mobjack Bay were visible and, farther on, Chesapeake Bay. During both the Revolutionary and Civil Wars, guards were posted on the porticos 24 hours a day to watch for enemy ships.

Old documents show that Thomas Jefferson was a visitor to Airville and offered suggestions for landscaping and crops. Airville was also the boyhood home of John Dixon, Jr., the famed leader of "Dixon's Light Horse Cavalry" during the Revolutionary War.

The plantation was sold a number of times from one generation to the next to avoid inheritance taxes. In 1828, 550 acres were sold to Thomas Smith, a wealthy merchant who was responsible for increasing the manor house to its present size of 6,500 square feet. Some of the more notable additions were the hanging curved stairway that extends to the third floor and the formal parlor with its black marble mantle shipped from Italy. Most of the dependencies that stand today are also from the time of Smith's ownership. The overseer's cottage now serves as a two-story suite for guests. The round ice house has become the pool house, complete with dressing rooms.

In the mid-1840s the land, house and furnishings were bet and lost in a poker game. From 1848 until 1928 it was in the Thomas Seawell Harwood family. Today, 250 acres plus a secluded half-acre on Mobjack Bay re-

main. Innkeepers Larry and Kathie Cohen along with their two teenage daughters (Jennifer and Courtenay), a pair of cats (Tessa and Molly), an English Setter (Oliver) and a Golden Retriever (Jake), have made Airville into a prime getaway for their guests.

With Colonial Williamsburg less than 30 minutes away, Airville offers the luxury of plantation living near major attractions. Gloucester is one of the oldest counties in Virginia, known for lush farmland and daffodil fields. Captain John Smith once said of the area, "Heaven and earth never framed a better place for man's habitation."

Consider visiting the Rosewell Ruins, all that remains of perhaps the largest and finest of the Colonial mansions. While fire consumed the interior in the early 1900s, it is still worth a visit. You might also want to visit the Gloucester Point Archaeological District at Tyndall's Point Park. Both Union and Confederate forces had fortifications on this site during the Civil War.

A true treasure in the area is Seawell's Ordinary, just a few miles from Airville Plantation. Built as a residence in 1712, Joseph Seawell opened the doors to serve travelers in 1757, just a year after Airville Plantation was constructed. Early Thomas Jefferson maps refer to Seawell's Publick House. George Washington was a frequent visitor while staying with his aunt and uncle at Warner Hall Plantation just three miles away.

Airville Plantation
6423 T.C. Walker Road; Gloucester, VA 23061
(804) 694-0287; Fax: (804) 694-0287
Innkeepers: Lawrence & Kathleen Cohen
Rooms: 2; Cottages: 1; With Private Baths: 1; With Shared Baths: 2
Rates: $$$ - $$$$
Affiliations: BBAV
Payment: $$$ CHECKS Amenities:

Jasmine Plantation Bed & Breakfast Inn
Williamsburg Area (Providence Forge)

History and hospitality abound at Jasmine Plantation. It was settled in 1680 by George Morris who was a member of the Virginia House of Burgesses. Morris also was a surveyor and a captain in the civilian guard. The existing house was built in the 1750s by his descendants and sits in front of the original home site. In 1779 the house was used as a headquarters for the Revolutionary Army.

Joyce and Howard Vogt purchased the property in 1987. Though previously occupied, the house required gutting and rebuilding of the interior.

Avid collectors, Howard and Joyce saw a bed and breakfast as a way they could share their collections and, at the same time, share in the lives of others. The 5,400-square-foot house on 47 acres has worked well as a bed and breakfast, and guests love their collections. Its location makes it a great place to stay whether your touring interest is Williamsburg (25 miles away), the James River Plantations (7 miles) or Richmond (25 miles). There's a new golf course across the road, and the Colonial Downs race track is nearby, (scheduled for completion September 1997). For dinner in the area, you can't beat David's White House Restaurant. This is the tied-for-first-place winner of my "Best Filet Mignon in Virginia" award.

When you arrive at Jasmine, you're taken to the "country store," given refreshments and checked into one of the six guest rooms. The "country store" is my favorite room at Jasmine, with its collection of antiques from the early 1930s and 40s. When Joyce was growing up, there was a general store to which her father used to go. (She had to wait outside because they served beer in the store.) The old store is gone now, but the cash register and old counter now sit in the "country store" room. There are also many metal signs from the 1930s, 40s

and 50s in this room as well as in the dining room. An old stove and checkered tablecloths add to the atmosphere of an old general store.

There are six fireplaces in the house, one each in the parlor and the den, and the other four in guest rooms. The dining room has a wood-burning cook stove used for heat during winter. Each of the guest rooms has its own personality. The George Morris Room, the most spacious, is also the most romantic with its own sitting area and fireplace. The Plantation Room is decorated with antique farm tools and other memorabilia from the early years of farming in the James River Valley. Other rooms include the John Morris Room with its 1750 features, the Brenneman Room, Jasmine Room and the Rose Room with a whirlpool tub.

The innkeepers told me quite simply that "they don't do quiches." The traditional farm breakfast varies from day to day. There are buttermilk, pecan, or blueberry pancakes, an egg dish on the side, and breakfast meats such as bacon, country ham or sausage. Other mornings bring Belgian or regular waffles, or possibly a cheese, egg & sausage casserole. There is always homemade bread, biscuits or sweet rolls, and of course fresh fruit. Special attention is paid to dietary restrictions. Basically, if the guest wants it, Joyce will do her best to provide it.

Jasmine Plantation Bed & Breakfast Inn
4500 North Courthouse Road; Providence Forge, VA 23140
(800) 639-5368; (804) 966-9836; Fax: (804) 966-5679
Innkeepers: Joyce & Howard Vogt
Rooms: 6; **Suites**: 1; **With Private Baths**: 5; **With Shared Baths**: 1; **Rates**: $$ - $$$
Affiliations: PAII, BBAV, New Kent Chamber, West Point Area Chamber
Payment:
Amenities:

Seward House Inn Bed & Breakfast
Williamsburg Area (Surry)

Located just a short ferry ride from the Jamestown settlement across the James River, the Seward House Inn is one of our favorite places in Virginia. It's the innkeepers who make a bed and breakfast. At the Seward House there is a feeling of coming home to visit favorite aunts you haven't seen for a while. Innkeepers Jackie Bayer from Norfolk and British-born Cynthia Erskine are as warm and friendly as any innkeepers I have ever met.

The community of Surry is just one square mile in size. The few businesses and homes are scattered among working farms. Tourists to the area often see it as just a stop in the road on your way either to the ferry at Scotland or to Smithfield, home of Smithfield Hams. Yet the area is one of simple country beauty. It's easy to forget how close you are to the metropolitan areas of Portsmouth and Williamsburg.

In the early 1900s, Surry was a major stopover for commerce heading for Portsmouth or for river barges on the James River. Dr. William Seward set up practice here and, in 1902, built a large country house for his wife, Lizzie. His practice, until the mid-1930s, was run out of the small attached cottage next door.

Dr. Seward's great niece, Jackie, along with her friend, Cynthia, purchased the property near the end of 1988 and opened it as a bed and breakfast in early 1991. Its country charm, ten-foot ceilings and gingerbread trim complemented by family heirlooms from both Cynthia and Jackie's families have created a very comfortable bed and breakfast. Today the doctor's office serves as the cottage suite.

Cynthia and Jackie like to remind you that while the house is gracious, it is not pretentious. They want you to feel at home. You're free to walk around barefoot or curl up with a good book and fall asleep on the couch. You might even do as we did, fix some popcorn and watch a good movie in the

parlor. For those who prefer, there's always a jigsaw puzzle needing some attention.

The three guest rooms and suite are furnished with more than three generations of family mementos. Hand-carved beds, family pictures, old toys, and bits of needlework adorn each room. A two-person hammock swings from a huge pecan tree, and the croquet set is ready and waiting. There are even two mountain bikes for guests' use.

While there aren't many places in Surry to dine, a quick trip on the ferry will take you to Williamsburg, with its many fine restaurants. Cynthia and Jackie can help with suggestions and even tickets for the ferry. With advance notice, they'll prepare an excellent dinner for guests at a very reasonable rate. Breakfast, too, is a treat at the Seward House with Edwards sausage, ham or bacon (this is from a local company and I highly recommend it), sourdough waffles, homemade yeast pancakes, fruit, yogurt, sweet rolls, juices, coffee and/or tea. When the need arises, they can accommodate special diets and tastes.

While you're in the area, stop at Bacon's Castle. It doesn't look like a castle, and it certainly was never visited by its namesake, but it is believed to be the oldest brick structure in North America. Just down the road is Chippokes Farm and Forestry Museum, a tribute to those ancestors who lived in the area in the 1850s.

Seward House Bed & Breakfast
193 Colonial Trail East; P.O. Box 352; Surry, VA 23883
(757) 294-3810
Innkeepers: Jacqueline Bayer & Cynthia Erskine
Rooms: 3; **Suites:** 1; **With Private Baths:** 2, **With Shared Baths:** 2; **Rates:** $$
Affiliations: BBAV, U.S. Chamber
Payment: $$$ | CHECKS | AMEX | DISCOVER
Amenities: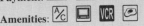

Hewick Plantation
Williamsburg Area (Urbanna)

Ownership of this 300-plus-year-old plantation reads like a Who's Who of Colonial America. Part of what makes its history so interesting is that the innkeepers are tenth generation descendants of its builder. Christopher Robinson arrived in Virginia from Yorkshire, England in 1666. He built his home in 1678, by an offshoot of the Rappahannock River that is still known as Robinson's Creek. Christopher served two terms in the House of Burgesses and was one of the original trustees of the College of William and Mary. In 1692 he was designated by the British Crown to be the Secretary of the Foreign Plantations.

The plantation was first called The Grange. It was Christopher Robinson II who renamed it Hewick for the ancestral home in England. Old records show that the plantation was almost a village, having had its own blacksmith, carpenter, cobbler and butcher shops. Digs conducted by the archaeology department at William and Mary have uncovered more than two dozen dependencies on the property.

The Honorable John Robinson (1704-1766) was born in the house and served as Treasurer of Virginia. For seven sessions he was the speaker of the House of Burgesses in Williamsburg, the lower house of legislature in colonial Virginia. George Washington, George Madison, Patrick Henry, Richard Henry Lee, and Francis Lightfoot Lee all served in the House during this period.

The two-story manor house served as a gathering place for the important families of Colonial Virginia. Carter Braxton, a signer of the Declaration of Independence, married Judith Robinson, the granddaughter of Christopher Robinson I. Another of Christopher's sons, John, was acting Governor of Virginia in 1749.

Ed and Helen Battleson bought the 66-acre plantation from a distant cousin in 1989 with the goal of restoring the family's historical home.

The idea of operating it as a bed and breakfast came later. The Battleson's live in a more recent addition to the original structure. The parlor, dining room, and guest rooms are in the original part of the house. You will find the that the Battleson's have taken great care to restore these rooms as they would have been in the late seventeenth century. Although perhaps a bit Spartan by today's standards, they are decorated with period pieces and each has its own private bath. But the charm of Hewick Plantation is the opportunity to stay in one of the most historic homes in America. It is a chance to walk under enormous pecan trees to the family cemetery with its nearly 300-year-old tombstones.

The house sits a full third of a mile from the highway and is surrounded by much acreage. The only sounds you will hear are the family pets which include a rooster or two, geese, several dogs, and a couple of cats as well as quarter horses.

Hewick Plantation is located just a short drive from the attractions of Williamsburg and just across the Rappahannock River from the Northern Neck. Day trips to the birthplace of George Washington and Robert E. Lee as well as stops at Jamestown Settlement and Yorktown are easy to accomplish. I found that I appreciated Colonial Williamsburg even more for having stayed at a plantation manor that dates to the same period as historic Williamsburg.

Hewick Plantation
VSH 602/615; P.O. Box 82; Urbanna, VA 23175
(800) 484-7514 (PIN Code 1678); (804) 758-4214; Fax: (804) 758-4080
Innkeepers: Helen & Ed Battleson
E-mail: hewick@prodigy.com
Rooms: 2; All Private Baths; Rates: $$ - $$$
Affiliations: BBAV, Urbanna Merchants Assoc., Middlesex County Chamber
Payment:  Amenities:

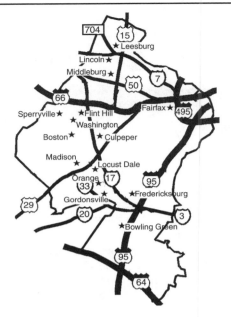

Northern Region

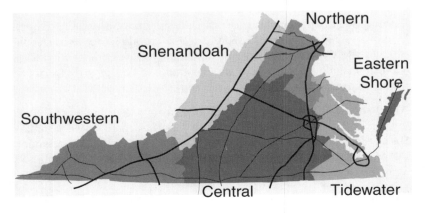

Fountain Hall
Culpeper

You may remember from American history class a flag inscribed "Liberty or Death—Don't Tread On Me." It was the battle flag of the Culpeper Minute Men during the American Revolutionary War. This is an area that has always seemed to be in the thick of things. For example, 37 Civil War engagements took place within the county. During the winter of 1863-64, General Ulysses S. Grant, with 100,000 men, camped at the edge of the town, and the largest cavalry engagement in U.S. history took place at nearby Brandy Station.

The area's first recorded history is being a part of a 5.2 million-acre inheritance of Lord Fairfax in the early 1700s. In July of 1740, Fairfax hired 17-year-old George Washington to define the boundaries of a land grant to then Governor Spotswood. While it wasn't Washington's first surveying job, it was the first of this size. For the next three years, Washington lived and worked in the area. The first settlement was called Fairfax. However, the courthouse has always been known as Culpeper, in honor of Fairfax's grandfather, Lord Thomas Culpeper.

History in Culpeper can be seen in a walking tour of South East Street. Within a few blocks you can see the architectural history of a new nation. Greek, Gothic, Colonial and Italianate Revival homes as well as Victorian, and even the American Foursquare of the early 1900s can be found on the tour.

Along this walk through architectural history, one of the most imposing structures is located at 609 South East Street. In 1859, Fountain Hall began as a simple country Victorian. In 1923, extensive remodeling created a two-story Colonial that almost dwarfs the other houses along the walk.

Armed with a bachelor's degree in hotel administration, Steve Walker and his wife, Kathi, moved to Culpeper and took possession of Foun-

tain Hall in 1985. They too have made changes to the property, not structural changes but changes nonetheless. They have converted Fountain Hall into a first class bed and breakfast.

With 18 total rooms and over 5,000 square feet of space to work with, Fountain Hall provides room for guests to feel comfortable and yet still remain intimate. The acre-and-a-half grounds are covered with large boxwoods and the formal flower gardens. A carefully maintained lawn adds to the feeling of a country house. In addition to all this, downtown Culpeper is a just a short walk away.

Period antiques, collectibles and photographs accent the inlaid columns and high ceilings. Each of the six guest rooms is larger than you might expect in a house constructed in the mid-1800s. A two-room suite, Pulliams Retreat, with its own parlor and private porch, is a house favorite.

Steve and Kathi are knowledgeable about the history of the area and can suggest a variety of things to do. This is the center of the Virginia wine country and steeplechase. Point-to-point races are held in the area on a regular basis.

When dining out in the area, you will find a number of good restaurants. Chef/owner John Yarnall has brought European Country Cuisine to Culpeper recently at his It's About Thyme restaurant. Steve and Kathi can help with other suggestions as well.

Fountain Hall
609 South East Street; Culpeper, VA 22701
(800) 298-4748; (540) 825-8200; Fax: (540) 825-7716
Innkeepers: Steve & Kathi Walker
Rooms: 4 Suites: 2; All Private Baths; Rates: $$ - $$$
Affiliations: AAA♦♦♦, Mobil★★★, BBAV, Culpeper Chamber, Foothills Travel Assoc.
Payment: $$$ CHECKS MC VISA AMEX DISCOVER Diner's Club CARTE BLANCHE
Amenities: ♿ A/C 🖋 💻 VCR ⛷ 👥 ↻

La Vista Plantation
Fredericksburg

There is so much to do in the Fredericksburg area that we just barely touched the surface. Our lodgings were at the La Vista Plantation, just a few miles south of Fredericksburg. While the Civil War raged all around them, La Vista was spared. There is still the sense of history that you can feel throughout the area.

La Vista was originally a 1,000-acre plantation owned by the Boulware family. The manor house was built in 1838. At the time of its construction it was called "The Grove." It wasn't until sometime just before the Civil War that the name was changed to La Vista.

Edward and Michele Schiesser purchased the manor house and ten acres in 1983 when their children were small. Over the years they have completely restored the house. They came to the area from the Washington, DC suburbs. However, Edward's job as chief of exhibits and design for the Hirshhorn Museum and Sculpture Garden at the Smithsonian Institute requires him to commute back to the city every day.

While La Vista may be called a homestay because it has less than four guest rooms, its accommodations were a real treat. The main-floor guest room features a magnificent king-sized mahogany rice carved four-poster bed, working fireplace and Empire style antiques. The second accommodation is an English basement apartment with its own sitting room and fully equipped kitchen. This 1,200-square-foot apartment is perfect for the couple who want or need more room or for two couples traveling together. It can be rented as a single guest room, a two-bedroom unit with shared bath or as a suite.

Throughout the house you will find a number of limestone sculptures that are very humorous. They were all made by Edward and reflect the more comical side of man's life on planet earth. My favorite pieces are in the dining room where Michele serves a full country-style breakfast.

The property offers woods in which to walk, a one-third-mile jogging path and a pond where you can fish for large mouth bass. Still, the time will come when you want to explore some of the area around La Vista.

Some of the fiercest fighting of the Civil War took place at Chancellorsville, Fredericksburg, Spotsylvania Court House and at the Battle of the Wilderness. All are just a few miles away.

The 40-block National Historic District in Fredericksburg features more than 350 original eighteenth- and nineteenth-century buildings. The best way to view the area is by taking a trolley or carriage ride through the city. Living history exhibits are presented at the Fredericksburg/Spotsylvania National Military Park. Walking tours guided by park historians are also available in certain locations in season. However, long before the Civil War, Washington and Jefferson both spent time in the area.

Kenmore is considered to be one of the most beautiful Colonial mansions in America. It was built by Fielding Lewis for his wife Betty, the only sister of George Washington. Any stop in Fredericksburg should include a trip to this historic mansion.

In the downtown area, a walking tour will take you to the Mary Washington House, purchased by George for his mother, and to the Rising Sun Tavern. The tavern, built in 1760 by Charles Washington, was once the only "ordinary" in town. I guarantee that if you love American history, you won't run out of things to do and see in the area while you stay at La Vista.

La Vista Plantation
4420 Guinea Station Road; Fredericksburg, VA 22408
(800) 529-2823; (540) 898-8444; Fax: (540) 898-9414
Innkeepers: Michele & Edward Schiesser
Rooms: 1; Suites: 1; All Private Baths; Rates: $$
Affiliations: NBBA, BBAV
Payment: $$$ CHECKS MC VISA
Amenities:

Mansion View Bed & Breakfast
Fredericksburg Area (Bowling Green)

The mansion referred to in the name is the "Old Mansion" directly across the highway. This mansion is the third-oldest surviving structure in the state of Virginia, and the oldest building continuously inhabited since its construction. It was built in 1669 for Major Thomas Hoomes on a 7000-acre land grant given by the British Crown. Wanting the best that money could buy, Colonel Hoomes had all the bricks for the house shipped from England. That's not a major task today, but imagine the work required at the end of the seventeenth century to transport enough brick to the New World on those small ships.

Hoomes came from Bolling Green, England and named his plantation the same. However, over the years the spelling has changed to Bowling Green. As the community grew, Hoomes donated much of his land to the community. While the mansion is not open for visitation, there is so much to do it the area that the location of the bed and breakfast has proven to be perfect.

Mansion View is located on property that was once a part of the Hoomes estate, but the structure was constructed much later, between 1925 and 1927. A prosperous local merchant, Hinton B. Smithers, wanted to build a home for his wife, Laura, that "would stand through the ages." Since he owned two portable saw mills, he was able to be very particular about the wood that was used. Together with his wife, they hand-picked every piece of lumber used in the house. After each piece was selected and cut, it was then stored in a barn to dry before construction began.

During the two years of construction on their home, the Smithers lived in the little cottage located behind the main house. Here they could keep a watchful eye on the construction. The Smithers had no

children but they loved to entertain and it shows throughout the house. For example, in addition to the master bedroom, there are six bedrooms where house guests would come and stay for long periods of time. The formal dining room and a large drawing room were incorporated into the design for social functions.

The size, location and construction of the house attracted Dennis and Jane Donachy who purchased the property in October 1995. Their goal for years had been to operate a bed and breakfast. By November of the same year, they were ready to greet their first guests.

Dennis and Jane's goal is for guests to feel at home. Often it's homemade ice cream that does the trick. For others it is a generous breakfast and there is always such a variety that you will never get the same thing two days in a row. Mornings may bring casseroles, waffles, pancakes or French toast. Some mornings there are farm fresh eggs, sausage, fried apples, or homemade biscuits, with fried potatoes and gravy.

Washington, DC is only 75 miles to the north and the state capital of Richmond is less than 40 miles to the south. A favorite with many people is Paramount's Kings Dominion theme park. It's just a 20-minute drive away. There are also a number of Civil War battlefield parks, vineyards and historic sites to visit.

Mansion View Bed & Breakfast
16041 Richmond Turnpike; P.O. Box 787; Bowling Green, VA 22427
(800) 251-9335; (804) 633-4377; Fax: (804) 251-9335
Innkeepers: Dennis & Jane Donachy
Rooms: 5; With Private Baths: 3; With Shared Baths: 2; Rates: $$
Affiliations: BBAV, Caroline County Chamber
Payment: SSS CHECKS MC VISA AMEX DISCOVER
Amenities: A/C 💻 📧

The Norris House Inn
Leesburg

Californians Don and Pam McMurray stayed at or visited more than 200 locations before selecting the Norris House as their bed and breakfast. I think they made the right choice, and so will you. The three-story brick Federal style residence has been painstakingly renovated with attention to every detail.

It's within walking distance of Leesburg's historic district and the Loudoun Museum. There are great restaurants in the area including one across the street and it's an easy walk to the Lightfoot Café where we had an excellent lunch. Our dinner choice, the Tuscarora Mill, was just a short five-block walk and well worth it.

Outside, the award-winning gardens and grounds, along with the long, side veranda, are a delight. Inside, the common rooms are elegantly decorated. Three of the six guest rooms include working fireplaces, and all the rooms have the same charm as the rest of the property. You'll find one room decorated with a country hunt motif, another in an English garden decor and still others decorated with pinks, blues and whites. The colors and fabrics work together to create a restful atmosphere. Homemade gourmet candies and turn-down service help to fulfill the fantasies of most guests' getaways.

Part of the building, the library and the room above it, was constructed between 1757 and 1760. The original owner was John Huff, a surveyor. He had three years to build his 16 by 28 foot structure. If he didn't finish it, the land would go back to the original owner who would, in turn, split it into smaller lots and return them to the market. Huff completed his task and the property remained in his family until the early 1800s. The first major change to the property took place in 1833 when the house was doubled in size by its new owner, a Mr. Memory. In the mid-1800s, the Norris brothers, the architects for almost every major building in town, acquired the property and added

the north wing. The Norris brothers were known for their detailed woodwork, and the Norris House shows off their handiwork. The main-floor library features beautiful built-in cherry woodwork.

While the Norris house is located on historic property within a major community, the McMurray's have made the most of their ample side yard by creating beautiful gardens. The yard and Federal colors, period antiques, and reproductions give the Norris House the feeling of a country manor house instead of one in an urban area.

Across the yard is the Stone House Tea Room, owned by Don and Pam, but leased to Sandy Ruefer. On weekends at the Tea Room, you can enjoy a formal tea with all types of tasty treats.

Leesburg is rich in history and close to everything in northern Virginia. This is part of the famous hunt country and during the season you can still hear the sounds of the hunt in places such as Middleburg. The community of Round Hill, surveyed in 1725, served as an observation point during the Civil War. Waterford, founded by Quakers in 1733, is one of the few National Landmark villages in the nation. The village is well worth visiting and retains most of its charm from the 1800s. The Oatlands Plantation, just a few miles from Leesburg, is one of the finest plantations to survive the Civil War. It was built in the early 1800s by George Carter, great-grandson of Virginia's famed "King" Carter.

The Norris House Inn
108 Loudoun Street SW; Leesburg, VA 20175
(800) 644-1806; (703) 777-1806; Fax: (703) 771-8051
Innkeepers: Pam & Don McMurray
E-mail: jrtpolb@prodigy.com
Rooms: 6; With Shared Baths: 6; Rates: $$ - $$$
Affiliations: BBAV, Loudoun County Chamber, Loudoun County B&B Guild
Payment: Amenities:

Springdale Country Inn
Leesburg Area (Lincoln)

It's believed that the Quaker, Samuel Janney built Springdale in 1832 as a front for the underground railroad. Its location was perfect, only 14 miles from the Potomac River. Once the slaves made it to the Potomac, they were free. Officially it was called the Springdale Boarding School, and it was for high school age girls. Most probably, the girls and slaves learned to read and write side by side.

The underground railroad was started in the 1780s by the Quakers and the activity acquired legendary fame after the 1830s. It was once estimated that more than 60,000 slaves gained their freedom in this way, but that is probably an exaggeration. Many of the fugitive slaves came from the upper South because of its proximity to the North. They traveled by night to avoid detection and sought isolated "stations" where they could effectively be concealed. The school was one of the last stops on the underground railroad.

A trip up a narrow twisting stairway reveals a cubby hole behind the wainscoting. Slaves could hide here when professional slave catchers were in the area. When the Civil War came, the school continued its role as a stopover for blacks heading north. At the same time, it was used as a hospital and served both Northern and Southern soldiers.

Located just 45 miles west of Washington, DC, Springdale is in the heart of the Virginia wine country and only a few miles from a number of historic sites. When innkeepers Nancy and Roger Fones first saw the property, they knew its location would be great for a bed and breakfast. With four floors, 28 rooms and six acres of land with which to work, Springdale can accommodate not only getaway travelers, but also weddings and small meetings.

Nancy and Roger did extensive research on the property. Their exacting restoration shows throughout the house and property. Wide plank pine

floors, rich colors and historic wallpaper all add to the elegant yet comfortable decor. The six acres include sloping lawns, babbling brooks with wooden bridges, and plenty of benches along the walking trails through the woods.

There are nine guest rooms, six with private baths and three with shared baths. Each room is furnished in a different period. You may choose from Federal, Regency, Victorian or Quaker decor. Four of the rooms have working fireplaces, and all are decorated with representative antiques. One of the special pieces in the inn is the cherry server in the parlor. The server was made more than 170 years ago by Nancy's great-great grandfather when he was 17.

Since Springdale is a country inn, dinner is available on weekends with advance reservation. The head chef has taken century-old recipes and adapted them to current taste. Most of the vegetables and herbs come from the inn's gardens.

Springdale is only a short drive from Harpers Ferry, West Virginia where John Brown and 21 followers seized the government arsenal on October 16 and 17, 1859. Belle Grove Plantation and the Virginia hunt country are in nearby Middleburg. To the east is Leesburg, where you will find Morven Park with its Greek Revival mansion and the famous Oatlands Plantation. Both are open to the public and well worth the tour if you're interested in Civil War history.

Springdale Country Inn; Lincoln, VA 20160
(800) 388-1832; (540) 338-1832; Fax: (540) 338-1839
Innkeepers: Nancy & Roger Fones
Rooms: 9; **Suites**: 2; **With Private Baths**: 6; **With Shared Baths**: 5; **Rates**: $$$
Affiliations: PAII, BBAV, Loudoun County Chamber

Payment:

Amenities:

Middleburg Country Inn
Middleburg

Middleburg Country Inn was one of the very first country inns at which we ever stayed. This entire series would never have come about if it hadn't been for how pleased I was with our first stay, our room, and the excellent food. While it had been several years since our first visit, I was pleased to find that the Middleburg Country Inn has improved. I expect it will continue to do so.

Of course, the running of any successful inn is the result of good innkeepers. Because John Pettibone's background is that of an executive, he runs the inn with dedication and efficiency. His wife, Susan, learned the art of innkeeping from her mother who had a bed and breakfast in North Carolina at Nag's Head which is still in operation.

Middleburg Country Inn has a long history in the community. The first part of the building was constructed by Richard Cochran in 1820. In 1856, Saint Johns Episcopal Church purchased the property and the adjoining lot for the parsonage. William Benton added the east side of the parsonage in 1858. For the next 200 years it belonged to the church. The Pettibones purchased it in 1987 as a home for Susan's mother, but it turned out to be too large so they decided to make it into an inn.

While the structure was remarkably sound, it took quite a bit of expensive repair and modernization to be converted into a bed and breakfast. After all, the house had been built before nails were invented. On the older side, you can still see where the wood was joined by drilling a hole and inserting a pine knot. When the wood was moistened, it would swell. The joints still hold today.

The entire lower level had a dirt floor and was used as a root cellar. The basement also contained the house's original kitchen. It had a huge stone fireplace complete with hangers for pots. The Pettibones literally had to raise the roof to add air conditioning before the remodeling was

complete and now there are four floors. The changes had a side benefit as they gained two large suites.

Each of the six guest rooms and the two suites has been named and carefully decorated to reflect historic Virginian mansions. The rooms feature Colonial furnishings with either canopy or four-poster beds, working fireplaces, and each offers color cable TV with VCR and in-room phones.

The homes of James Madison and James Monroe are in the area and a frequent visitor was General Lafayette. John and Susan felt that he, too, should be honored so they named the dining room after him. Susan calls John her closet chef because she discovered, after the inn was opened, that he really loved to cook. After graduating from La Academe De Cuisine—a professional cuisine course in Gaithersburg, Virginia—John did most of the cooking. While they now have a full time chef, Anna Caravageau, who insists on things being done as they were in her native village in France, John still gets to cook occasionally.

The area around Middleburg is known as Virginia's hunt country. It is some of the most beautiful land in the state. It's rich in history and located close to most of the major points of interest not only in northern Virginia, but Washington, DC, Dulles International Airport, Harpers Ferry, West Virginia and even Gettysburg, Pennsylvania are within an easy drive.

Middleburg Country Inn
209 East Washington Street; Middleburg, VA 22117
(800) 262-6082; (540) 687-6082; Fax: (540) 687-5603
Innkeepers: John & Susan Pettibone
Rooms: 6; Suites: 2 All Private Baths; Rates: $$$-$$$$$
Affiliations: ABBA, PAII, Mobil, Loudoun County B&B Guild, Loudoun County Chamber

Payment:

Amenities:

Holladay House
Orange

The house on Main Street has been the residence for the Holladay family for nearly a century. Innkeeper Pete Holladay's grandfather first purchased the property in 1899. Dr. Lewis Holladay was the local doctor and he bought the house to serve as both family residence and doctor's office.

Located just a block or so from the center of Orange, the building was built in the 1830s as a store. It only lasted for a few years as a store before it became a private home. For Dr. Holladay, its location was perfect. In a short time, however, his family as well as his practice needed more space. Holladay's answer was to enlarge the house. Between the years of 1910 and 1917, he more than doubled its size. While making these changes, a speaking tube was added to run from just inside the front door up to the doctor's bedroom. This way, if someone came during the night, they could wake him and not the entire family. You'll find other reminders of Dr. Holladay throughout the house such as the massive bookcase that hides his desk and the display case with his shingle, medical bag and surgical instruments.

Because this has been the family home for the last three generations, the house is full of family antiques and heirlooms. There are four-poster beds, marble-topped dressers and quilts stitched by hand. One guest room includes the walnut bed with acorn carvings that belonged to Dr. Holladay and his wife. It all works together to bring a feeling of family to the Holladay House...and you're a part of that family.

Pete and his wife, Phebe, lived for years on the campuses of private schools while he was working in school business management. After 24 years, and a four-year period as manager of a thoroughbred

horse farm just outside Orange, Pete and Phebe turned their talents to converting the family home into a bed & breakfast. This was an idea that originated with Pete's father years before, and I am sure he would approve of the way Pete and Phebe have accomplished it.

Built of brick laid in Flemish bond and set on an English basement, the house is characteristic of the Federal period. Since additions have been made over the years, the size of the rooms varies greatly. However, each of the guest rooms is well decorated and very large with private baths. Each room has its own breakfast nook to accommodate their custom of breakfast served in your room.

Since Phebe is also a part-time art instructor, breakfast is often a part of Pete's daily responsibilities—and he does a very impressive breakfast at that. Whether you choose to have breakfast served in your room or in the formal dining room, you can look forward to a full three-course meal. Breakfast at Holladay House is a treat, especially Pete's apple muffins. They once won first place in a contest sponsored by the Bed and Breakfast Association of Virginia.

Be sure to set aside time to see Orange after breakfast. Montpelier, the lifelong home of James Madison, Father of the Constitution, is only four miles away. Also close by are both the Exchange Hotel & Civil War Museum and the Wilderness Civil War Battlefield.

Holladay House; 155 West Main Street; Orange, VA 22960
(800) 358-4422; (540) 672-4893; Fax: (540) 672-3028
Innkeepers: Phebe & Pete Holladay
E-mail: holladay@symweb.com
Rooms: 4; **Suites**: 2; **All Private Baths**; **Rates**: $$$$
Affiliations: PAII, Mobil, BBAV, Orange County Chamber, Orange County Historical Society
Payment:
Amenities:

Sleepy Hollow Farm Bed & Breakfast
Orange Area (Gordonsville)

Just a short drive from the Exchange Hotel & Civil War Museum in Gordonsville is a bed and breakfast where hospitality isn't just a word; it's a way of life practiced at a historic farm. The only way to Sleepy Hollow Farm is down Virginia Scenic Byway Route 213. Along the drive you go past forgotten encampments of Colonial and Civil War soldiers. These troops may have even stopped at Sleepy Hollow Farm for some of its delicious spring water.

While it's not known exactly when the first dwelling was constructed at the farm, part of the early 1700s foundation would have been here when Colonial troops used the historic road. The first known building was a two-story, three-room clapboard house built in the 1850s, a decade before the Civil War. The old slave cabin, totally renovated, now serves as a guest cottage. The rest of the house has been expanded and bricked over.

Beverley Allison first saw the farm as a new bride in 1950. Raised in Montreal, Canada, she met her husband while attending the University of Delaware. He brought her to Sleepy Hollow and it was here that they raised five children.

When the children were grown, Beverley moved away for 14 years. For part of that time she worked as a journalist for ABC in Washington, DC. She also worked as a missionary in Latin America with the South American Missionary Society, a part of the Episcopal church. It wasn't until 1984 that she was able to return to Sleepy Hollow to create the bed and breakfast.

Accommodations vary at Sleepy Hollow Farm. You'll find rooms with fireplaces or Franklin stoves and whirlpools. Furnishings include a queen-sized canopied four-poster bed and a fine antique mahogany bed. Some rooms offer views of the meadow while others look out on the pond

where a half-dozen ducks can be seen swimming. Each room we visited looked inviting and was comfortably furnished with antiques and period reproductions.

A full country style breakfast of farm fresh eggs, local bacon or sausage, fried potatoes or grits, biscuits, hot cakes, fresh fruit and juices greet you each morning. Breakfast is served in the main house's dining room or, when the weather permits, on the north terrace.

Since the bed and breakfast is located on 11 acres, there is plenty of room for guests to get out and 'smell the roses.' There's a pond where guests can swim or fish for bass, perch and catfish. There are pastures and woods for hiking or you can enjoy a picnic under the gazebo. For the equestrian, horseback riding is available in the area. There is even a golf course nearby. However, leave some time to explore all that Orange county has to offer.

Be sure to plan a visit to Montpelier, home of James Madison, Father of the U.S. Constitution. A museum dedicated to the life of Madison is in Orange. The Barboursville Vineyards are located at the ruins of James Barbour's plantation where "Shakespeare at the Ruins" is presented each summer.

For dinner, I suggest the Toliver House Restaurant in Gordonsville. While Toliver House is most famous for their fried chicken, I can also recommend their steaks.

Sleepy Hollow Farm Bed & Breakfast
16280 Blue Ridge Turnpike; Gordonsville, VA 22942
(800) 215-4804; (540) 832-5555; Fax: (540) 832-2515
Innkeepers: Beverley H. Allison and Dorsey Allison Comer
Rooms: 6; Suites: 3; Cottages: 1; All Private Baths; Rates: $$ - $$$
Affiliations: NBBA, BBAV, Orange County Chamber

Payment: MC VISA

Amenities:

Tivoli
Orange Area (Gordonsville)

High on a hill outside Gordonsville is Tivoli, a three-story 24-room Victorian mansion. In the distance are the Blue Ridge Mountains, while around you is a 235-acre working cattle farm. Since nearly a third of the land is wooded, there is room to take a walk, mountain bike, or bring your cross-county skis and follow the trails. There is wildlife everywhere. There are wild turkeys, Canadian geese, and hummingbirds as well as deer, an occasional fox and raccoons.

Tivoli was built in 1903 by James Allison of Richmond. The mansion was built to be just a summer home. The family would pack up each May, bring grandparents, children, servants and nannies, and come to Tivoli until September. Then the entourage would return to Richmond for winter. Because the house was closed up during the winter months, the only heating came from fireplaces in each of the bedrooms.

The fireplaces remain, and innkeepers Phil and Susie Audibert (pronounced O.D. Bear) make sure that during cooler months, a fire is laid and waiting for you to strike the match. Of course, now there is other heat in the house. For years the house was the Audibert family home. In fact, Phil grew up here and inherited the property from his mother in 1987.

Phil and Susie began a major renovation project inside and out. Each of the 14 Corinthian columns needed repair or cleaning and all required scraping and painting. Roofs, porches, and hundreds of other details plus remodeling and improving each guest room and bath took nearly three years. Oh, there's still a place or two where the grand old lady shows her age, but it only adds to the character of the house. However, Phil and Susie have taken great care in each of the guest rooms and made certain that they were

carefully restored and decorated. They added baths so that each guest room has its own.

Phil and Susie don't actually live in the mansion, but in a 1850s farmhouse about a half-mile away. However, one of them or a resident innkeeper stays at the house when they have guests. Yet the house is so large I think you could hold a family reunion here and never make it to see all the family. Tivoli is available for groups and meetings. Often, families have reunions and weddings here.

Breakfast is served either in the dining room or on the veranda. Either way, be sure to bring an appetite. Phil and Susie pride themselves on a "you can't leave the table hungry" breakfast. While you can look forward to a real farm breakfast, they will gladly accommodate special diets.

The area around Tivoli is rich in history and culture. Fine dining can be found at a number of good restaurants but we found that we liked the Toliver House Restaurant in Gordonsville. It has been around for years and is a favorite with locals. For something to do, a stop at Montpelier should be high on the list. This is the home of James Madison, Father of the U.S. Constitution, and has only recently been opened to the public. A museum dedicated to the life of Madison is located in Orange. One of the best wineries is located at the Barboursville Vineyards. Here too are the ruins of James Barbour's plantation where "Shakespeare at the Ruins" is presented each summer.

Tivoli
9171 Tivoli Drive; Gordonsville, VA 22942
(800) 840-2225; (540) 832-2225; Fax: (540) 832-3691
Innkeepers: Phil & Susie Audibert
E-mail: tivolibnb@aol.com
Rooms: 4; **All Private Baths; Rates:** $$$
Affiliations: PAII, BBAV, Orange County Chamber
Payment:  **Amenities:**

Inn at Meander Plantation
Orange Area (Locust Dale)

After breakfast, I kidded the innkeepers that they should change the name of the inn to 'meander inn, roll me out.' I can not remember a better (or bigger) breakfast in the more than 300 bed and breakfasts at which I have stayed. Then again, it may have just been the setting. There was really a feeling of staying at an old plantation. The only thing missing was a morning horse ride and the innkeepers could even have arranged that for me.

The known history of Meander Plantation dates back to 1727. Colonel Joshua Fry, a member of the House of Burgesses and a professor at William and Mary, received the patent to build the first plantation in Madison County. Fry has a very interesting history. He and his partner surveyed Virginia and drew its first official map. His partner was Peter Jefferson, father of Thomas. Fry also commanded the Virginia militia during the French and Indian War. When Fry was killed at the battle of Cumberland, his second-in-command, George Washington, took command of the troops.

When Col. Fry died, the plantation passed to his son, Henry, who enlarged the manor house and added to the acreage. As with many early plantations, hospitality was a way of life. Thomas Jefferson and General Lafayette were frequent guests at the plantation.

While the Civil War raged around the property and one of the largest cavalry battles ever fought in America took place a few miles away at Cedar Mountain, the plantation remained untouched. Its only known involvement was that Robert E. Lee once rested here under the shade trees while his horse 'Traveler' was shod.

Innkeepers Bob and Suzie Blanchard with their partner and fellow innkeeper, Suzanne Thomas, share a common goal; making the Inn

at Meander Plantation one of Virginia's finest. They began by taking a year to restore the manor house. Within its walls you will find the elegance of a bygone age. Polished floors, fine antiques and comfortable queen- and king-sized beds all help add to the romance of this Colonial plantation.

Whether it's a walk through the formal boxwood gardens, a hike in the woods, or a game of croquet, there is plenty to do and room to do it in without feeling you're in someone's way. Throughout the manor house there are nooks and crannies to read a book. You can play the baby grand piano or just sit on the veranda. While there is much to do on the grounds, there is also much to do in the area. It's located only nine miles south of Culpeper and eight miles north of Orange. To the southwest is Charlottesville. Washington, DC is only 70 miles to the east.

My only regrets were that time did not permit us to sample the five-course, candlelight dinner available at the inn or the picnic basket lunches that can be prepared for your journeys throughout the area. But if dinner is anything like breakfast, then I missed a treat. Now I do have to admit they indulged me the morning I was there with a full plantation-style breakfast with all the trimmings including excellent sausage and bacon. By request, they will prepare a meal that is lower in fat and more healthful.

Inn at Meander Plantation
HCR 5, Box 460A; Locust Dale, VA 22948
(800) 385-4936; (540) 672-4912; Fax: (540) 672-4912
Innkeepers: Suzanne Thomas, Suzie & Bob Blanchard
E-mail: inn@meander-plantation.com
Rooms: 3; Suites: 4; Cabins: 1; All Private Baths; Rates: $$$ - $$$$
Affiliations: NBBA, PAII, BBAV, Madison County Chamber, Charlottesville Chamber
Payment: **Amenities:**

Shenandoah Springs Country Inn B&B
Orange Area (Madison)

You'll think you're lost as you drive down the dirt and gravel lane looking for Shenandoah Springs. It will seem as though there is nothing but forest, crops and pasture. However, if you saw the sign for Camp Shenandoah, you're on the right road.

The camp is owned by the same folks who own the bed and breakfast; in fact, the camp came first. And the road really isn't that bad, buses travel it all the time going to the camp.

The farm was first established in 1740 by Walker Yowell and his wife, Jane Snyder. They were the first land owners in the area to acquire 1,000 acres. It was a working farm that raised tobacco with the help of 12 to 14 slaves. They're buried on the farm.

Anne and Doug Farmer saw an ad for the farm in the Washington Post and came down in February of 1981 to look at it. The house hadn't been lived in for more than a year. They added to the house and restored the barn and other buildings on the property. On the far side of the property they built log cabins and teepees for young campers who come for summer camp. You don't need to worry about the campers. With a thousand acres to wander, it's a long way from your bedroom window to their camp.

If you're looking for a getaway, this is it. The camp just adds to all there is to do. There's a seven-acre lake (with diving board), sail boating, fishing for catfish, perch and bass, a basketball and a volleyball court, sand beach volleyball, ping-pong and archery. If that's not enough, there are horses on which you can go horseback riding for a reasonable rate and mountains to hike.

The main house has four rooms with two shared baths. The seven working fireplaces in the house are all original. Just down the road

is the cottage containing two suites. Upstairs is "Morning Side" with three bedrooms, bath, sitting room and deck. Downstairs is "Sunset" with its own kitchen, bath, bedroom, sitting room and deck.

If you're looking for something a bit more private, try Uncle J's handhewn log cabin. This is a two-story cabin with a pot-bellied stove and a beautiful view of the lake. Now, there's no lights and it's two bedrooms and a *path* instead of two bedrooms and a *bath*. For running water, "You take the bucket and run from the fountain." Sure, it's primitive compared to the rest of the bed and breakfast, but people enjoy the cabin.

Because the property is at an elevation of about 1,000 feet, you can see the Shenandoah National Park just a few miles away (as the crow flies). It's only seven miles to Madison, 30 miles to Charlottesville and a little under two hours to Richmond or Washington, DC.

There are a number of good places to eat and things to do in the Madison area. The innkeepers can help with recommendations. However, you might want to try the Bavarian Chef near Shelby for dinner. A small zoological park, On The Wild Side, is located just south of Madison. Here, you'll find a variety of exotic cats, monkeys and more.

Shenandoah Springs Country Inn B&B
P.O. Box 770; Madison, VA 22727
(540) 923-4300
Innkeepers: Anne & Doug Farmer
Rooms: 4; **Cabins**: 2; **With Private Baths: 4 With Shared Baths**: 2; **Rates**: $$ - $$$
Affiliations: BBAV, Madison County Chamber

Payment:

Amenities:

Thistle Hill Bed & Breakfast Inn
Rappahannock Area (Boston)

There really isn't much to the community of Boston. It doesn't even appear on some maps, but it's close to most points of interest in northern Virginia. To the northwest is Sperryville and to the southeast, historic Culpeper. A short drive will take you to Skyline Drive and the Shenandoah National Park. A drive over the Blue Ridge Mountains will take you to Luray and the world famous Luray Caverns. Monticello, Montpelier and Ashlawn-Highland are all within an hour's drive.

Boston's location makes it a destination and the place to stay is Thistle Hill. Here, on ten acres of land, Charles & Marianne Wilson opened bed and breakfast in May of 1989. You will find the food excellent and the accommodations very comfortable.

Opening a bed and breakfast had been Charles Wilson's dream for years. When he met Marianna, one of the first questions he asked was "Do you like bed and breakfasts?" Thistle Hill was the result of that courtship.

The inn is named for the wild thistle that blooms abundantly from late June to early July. As the bird feeders and plants draw hummingbirds, cardinals and gold finches, the thistle draws hundreds of butterflies. Together with the gardens and the ornamental fish pond, complete with fountain and goldfish, the area around the house is almost park-like. A gazebo in the center of the yard adds to the picturesque style of the property.

The Colonial-style home was built just 30 years ago. A great room with cathedral ceiling and fireplace was just recently added, and acts as the dining room. It is open to both guests and the public by reservation. You will often find the work of area artists displayed

around the room because Charles and Marianne are avid supporters of local art.

Naturally, the menu changes regularly at Thistle Hill. A sampling might include Cornish game hen, roast pork, rack of lamb or New Zealand domestic venison. Our dinner was very good; probably the best we had in the area. Just be sure to reserve in advance.

Two of the guest rooms are located in the main house, while the other three are located in two cottages just a short walk down the drive. While the home is not historical, you will find wonderful antiques in every room, many of which are available for purchase if you fall in love with that special piece that was in your room.

For the nature lover, there are miles of hiking and biking trails in the area. Thistle Hill has all-terrain bicycles you may use. Several wineries in the area offer tours and there are a number of historic battlefields within an easy drive. However, you may want to just relax, play croquet or spend some time in the hot tub.

Culpeper is only about 11 miles from Thistle Hill. If you have a love of fine architecture, it is well worth the trip. Within the few blocks of South East Street's walking tour you will see Greek Revival, Italianate, Queen Anne, American Foursquare, Gothic Revival and Colonial Revival structures.

Thistle Hill Bed & Breakfast Inn
5541 Sperryville Pike; Boston, VA 22713
(540) 987-9142; Fax: (540) 987-9122
Innkeepers: Charles & Marianne Wilson
Rooms: 2; **Cottages**: 3; **All Private Baths**; **Rates**: $$ - $$$$
Affiliations: BBAV, Rappahannock B&B Guild, Culpeper Chamber, Foothills Travel Assoc.

Payment:

Amenities:

Fairlea Farm Bed & Breakfast
Washington

In my opinion, Fairlea Farm Bed and Breakfast has the best of two worlds. It sits at the edge of town and is surrounded by a 40-acre farm with sheep and cattle roaming the pastures. The 270-degree views are spectacular. It's an easy walk to all there is to see and do.

A fieldstone manor house with oriental rugs, quality antiques, and queen-sized beds, Fairlea takes its name from the fact that it sits on the site of the old county fairgrounds in the 1920s. *Fair*, of course, is for fairgrounds and *lea* is from the Old English word for pastures.

The house was built in 1961 by Judge Sneed and his wife. They raised five children on the property. Susan and Walt Longyear started the bed and breakfast in 1992, when their oldest daughter went off to college. Before the bed and breakfast, Susan was the managing editor of a magazine. Walt still does direct-mail fund-raising for organizations as he has for the last 21 years.

With three rooms and one suite, Fairlea is large enough to take care of your needs and small enough to be intimate. The Magnolia Room on the main floor is named for its view of several beautiful magnolias. A mirror collection (59, if I counted right) decorates one wall. Upstairs you will find the Rose Room and the Meadow Room. The first has a canopied bed and windows overlooking the garden. The second comes with a brass bed and some really great views of the fields. My favorite room is the ground level suite with its stone fireplace and kitchenette.

Fresh fruit and flowers in each room and nightly turn-down service help to add to the feeling of being pampered. A homemade country breakfast is served at your convenience and varies depending on your needs.

Washington was the first of 28 towns in the United States to be named after George Washington. Its population is only about 250, not much different from what it was early in the eighteenth century. The streets are laid out exactly as they were when surveyed by George Washington in 1749. It's one of the most charming communities in northern Virginia. Susan and Walt agree with me.

Washington is located just 65 miles west of that other Washington. There are quaint shops, live theater and one of the best restaurants in the state, if not the country. To the west, the Blue Ridge Mountains rise to an elevation of 4,000 feet. To the east is the famous hunt country of Virginia highlands.

Admittedly, Washington's recent growth as a tourist destination came as a result of the popularity of the Inn at Little Washington. While it is the only establishment in the country to ever be awarded both a five-star and a five-diamond award, it isn't for everyone. Some of us prefer the pastoral beauty of a quaint and comfortable bed and breakfast.

Naturally, while you're in the area, you will want to try the restaurant at the Inn at Little Washington, but there are a number of other good restaurants in the area. Just a few miles away, in Flint Hill, Four & Twenty Blackbirds is a new restaurant that I am told is very good and more affordable.

Fairlea Farm Bed & Breakfast
636 Mount Salem Avenue; P.O. Box 124; Washington, VA 22747
(540) 675-3679; Fax: (540) 675-1064
Innkeepers: Susan & Walt Longyear
Rooms: 3; **Suites**: 1; **All Private Baths**; **Rates**: $$ - $$$
Affiliations: NBBA, USB&B, BBAV, Fauquier County Chamber, Foothills Travel Assoc., Warren County Chamber, Rappahannock B&B Guild
Payment: $$$ CHECKS **Amenities**: ▢ ▢ ▢ VCR ▢ ▢

Foster-Harris House
Washington

Innkeeper Phyllis Marriott's turn-of-the-century home in Washington first became a popular place for guests to stay in the 1930s. Of course, in the early part of the twentieth century such places were called guest homes or tourist homes. Guest homes were the forerunners of today's bed and breakfasts. The Foster-Harris House operated in this capacity throughout the 1940s.

Pat Foster and Camille Harris purchased the house in 1981. It required nearly three years before it was ready to open as a bed and breakfast in 1984. Phyllis, a former caterer from the other Washington (the capital), arrived in 1992 and made her own changes to the bed and breakfasts. Most important, all four guest rooms now have private baths and queen-sized beds. Since she's a very good cook, guests look forward to homemade cookies, as well as a great breakfast.

The area was originally surveyed by George Washington when he was only 17 years old. It was the first of 28 towns in America named after the president. It also has the distinction of having been the only town named before he became president. The community has changed little over the years; the streets are still laid out the way he surveyed them and the population hasn't increased a lot over the last hundred years.

Washington was really a very sleepy little community until a couple of enterprising young men opened a restaurant in a garage near the middle of town. Now, the town is only six or seven blocks long and perhaps three blocks wide. But from this small beginning, the restaurant went on to become the first five-star, five-diamond facility in America. With the Inn at Little Washington's rise to fame, the community has become a favorite place for weekend getaways.

There are two very good art galleries, some craft shops and the Theatre At Washington that is well known for its professional performances. In addition to the Inn at Little Washington, there are several other good restaurants within an easy drive of the Foster-Harris House. Two of the more favorite places are the Four & Twenty Blackbirds and Flint Hill Public House. Within a short drive of the Foster-Harris House you'll find Virginia's hunt country to the northeast, the Shenandoah National Park and Skyline Drive to the west, and Front Royal just 17 miles to the north.

The Foster-Harris House has an easy and comfortable feeling that I enjoyed; country crafts, perennial gardens and plenty of things to do nearby. The suite, the Mountain View, with its wood-burning stove and whirlpool bath is a favorite with guests. Other rooms include the Americana, the Meadow View and the Garden View. Regardless of which room you have, you can look forward to a good breakfast. Examples of Phyllis's breakfast entrées are baked French toast with smoked chicken and apple sausage and poached eggs with caper sauce and smoked salmon.

Of course Phyllis couldn't run the bed and breakfasts alone. She has an assistant named LuLu, a Labrador mix who is loved by everyone.

Foster-Harris House
189 Main Street; P.O. Box 333; Washington, VA 22747
(800) 666-0153; (540) 675-3757
Innkeeper: Phyllis Marriott
Rooms: 3; **Suites**: 1; **All Private Baths**; **Rates**: $$$
Affiliations: PAII, BBAV, Rappahannock B&B Guild, Foothills Travel Assoc.
Payment:
Amenities:

Middleton Inn
Washington

MaryAnn Kuhn's résumé is really quite impressive. It begans with her position as a legal reporter covering the U.S. Supreme Court. It ends at CBS where, as a producer, she produced segments of *Nightwatch* and *America Tonight* with Charles Kuralt and Lesley Stahl. Mary Ann is still doing productions, except now the set is a beautiful bed and breakfast in Washington, Virginia. She works to make sure everything is just right for guests. For example, everything that comes from the kitchen is served on a silver platter.

Middleton Inn is a grand Federal home built in 1850 by Middleton Miller, who designed and manufactured Confederate uniforms during the Civil War. Great care went into both the house design and construction. To ensure quality materials, all the brick was fired on the property. The main house, with its grand center hall, has eight working fireplaces, including one in each bedroom. The interior walls are a full eight inches thick.

The six-acre property of the Middleton Inn is located on a knoll that faces the Blue Ridge Mountains. There are three of the original dependencies on the property: the old smoke house, the summer kitchen, and the slaves' quarters (which has been converted into a guest cottage). There's an interesting story about the last building. It seems that a slave named Mamie, when freed, went to Washington, DC to make her fortune. She returned with a brick of gold and her old master said she could stay in the slaves' quarters for the rest of her life. When she died, she left the brick of gold to her old master's children.

Mary Ann bought the house in October 1994 and lived in it for four months before starting renovations. Restoration took longer than

expected. Two nights before opening the inn in September 1995, she still had carpenters working on the porch. Brick masons were working until midnight with flood lights and a generator trying to get everything finished. In the middle of it all, she received a call from a lady saying she was Director of Public Relations with the Ritz-Carlton Hotel and would like a room for herself and an Ambassador. Mary Ann thought it was a friend playing a joke, but it turned out to be true. When the Ambassador arrived, the silver was polished, sheets were pressed and draperies hung.

The Middleton Inn is only a few blocks from the center of Washington, yet cattle and horses graze in the adjoining pastures. Mary Ann has restored an original barn on the property that is home to two horses and a pony. As in any rural setting, there are several dogs and cats running around outside, except hers are kept playing in an area away from the guests by an invisible fence.

Expect to be pampered at Middleton Inn. The rooms are much lower in price than the Inn at Little Washington. Aside from that, I think you will find the same quality in everything the Middleton has to offer. Its location makes it an easy walk to the quaint shops of Washington. There are a number of good restaurants within a short drive. You might want to try Four & Twenty Blackbirds, a few miles away in Flint Hill. Everyone who has tried it has given it a good report.

Middleton Inn
176 Main Street; P.O. Box 254; Washington, VA 22747
(800) 816-8157; (540) 675-2020; Fax: (540) 675-1050
Innkeeper: Mary Ann Kuhn
E-mail: middlein@shentel.net
Rooms: 4; Cottages: 1; All Private Baths; Rates: $$$$ - $$$$$
Affiliations: Mobil★★★, PAII, BBAV, Washington Business Council
Payment: Amenities:

Sunset Hills Farm Bed & Breakfast
Washington

There is no way that I can do Sunset Hills Farm justice with text or black and white photographs. The place is simply beautiful from the pond at the bottom of the drive to the Belgian horses grazing in the pasture. The orchards and flower gardens by the gazebo deck seem to accent it all. I have placed my name on the already long list of people who are ready to move into the northern Virginia paradise that Betty and Leon Hutcheson have created.

When the Hutcheson's purchased the 25 acres on the side of Jenkins Mountain, it was nothing but trees and 'man-eating briars.' A road had to be constructed before they could even begin doing anything else. The property was purchased in 1978. It was 1981 before construction began on the house.

After seeing a house they liked in Marion, Virginia, they approached Kamal Amin, a former student of Frank Lloyd Wright, to design the house. Kamal, from Cairo, Egypt, designed the house to be built in two stages. The first stage required nearly a year to complete and the second demanded another year and a half. It was 1986 before the final work was done. When the last nail was in place, they had created a showplace; one that was balanced with its setting, yet provided room to raise a family. When their children had gone, friends and family suggested they turn the property into a bed and breakfast. I'm glad they did.

Betty and Leon cleared the land for the orchard and nursery themselves, long before there was a bed and breakfast. The apples and peaches from the orchard are used in Leon's business that markets "A Basket of Virginia." Leon and his staff combine their own brandied peaches, peach butter, or delicious apple butter with some of

the finest of Virginia's gourmet food products to create beautiful gift baskets for any occasion.

The first two rooms, each with queen-sized beds and fieldstone walls, have private marble baths and color TV. While smaller than the extra-large Gazebo Room, these two rooms are comfortable in size and furnishings. The Gazebo Room comes with a king-sized bed, its own sitting area and an enormous bath with Jacuzzi tub. This room has direct access to a large deck and screened gazebo.

The expansive windows in the great room offer magnificent views of the Blue Ridge Mountains. Here or in the gazebo, Betty serves a full breakfast with many of Virginia's finest items such as Smithfield ham or bacon, brandied peaches, apple butter for the fresh baked biscuits, along with eggs, waffles or pancakes. On other mornings she might serve an egg casserole. It's not unusual to see coffee cake or fresh peach cobbler on the table tempting you.

Sunset Hills Farm is located only a few miles outside Little Washington. It takes only minutes to drive to the quaint shops and restaurants in the area. A drive over the mountains to the west will take you to Luray, home of the world famous Luray Caverns. To the north are Front Royal, the beginning of the Shenandoah National Park and Skyline Drive. To the northeast is the Virginia Hunt Country. Washington, DC is just an hour away.

Sunset Hills Farm Bed & Breakfast
105 Christmas Tree Lane; Washington, VA 22747
(800) 980-2580; (540) 987-8804; Fax: (540) 987-9742
Innkeepers: Betty & Leon Hutcheson
Rooms: 2; Suites: 1; All Private Baths; Rates: $$$$
Affiliations: BBAV
Payment: $$$ CHECKS MC VISA DISCOVER
Amenities: A/C 📺 👪 📧

Caledonia Farm—1812
Washington Area (Flint Hill)

Caledonia Farm is without a doubt the most unusual bed and breakfast at which I have ever stayed; firstly because of its setting, and secondly because of its innkeeper. Owner Phil Irwin, who has visited more than 330 bed and breakfasts across the country, will tell you that he runs his bed and breakfast differently than any other. I can attest to the truth of that statement.

Caledonia is the ancient name for Scotland. It was used for the farm to honor those who settled this area back in the early nineteenth century. While the name of the stone mason who built the marvelous stone house with its two-foot-thick walls and 32-foot solid wood beams has been lost, what he constructed will be with us for years to come. We do know that the house was built for Captain John Dearing, a veteran of the Revolutionary War, in 1812. It is believed that the work was done by Hessian soldiers, German mercenaries in the British army, who settled in the area at the end of the war.

On a 52-acre working farm, Phil has turned Caledonia into a first class bed and breakfast. It's only an hour from America's capital, a short drive from Front Royal and in the heart of Virginia's hunt country.

Phil makes a great tour guide as he takes you around the 180+ year-old house. On your tour you will discover six fireplaces, all operational, paneled window wells, wide pine-planked floors and narrow stairs leading to the upstairs guest rooms. If not rented as a suite, the two rooms share a bath and Phil provides quality bathrobes for the short distance between your door and the bath. The rooms are comfortably sized and decorated with pine furniture. The thick foam mattresses gave us a restful night's sleep. Views of the Skyline Drive may be enjoyed from all the guest rooms.

The Summer Kitchen dependency has been converted into a suite and is accessed by a 30-foot long covered portico. What was once the kitchen with its huge stone fireplace is now the living room. The upstairs slave quarters provides both bedroom and bath. Like the manor house, this building is also constructed of fieldstone and like the rooms in the main house is air conditioned and perfect for honeymooners.

Phil serves a "custom made-to-order breakfast" at an hour of choice. House specialties include items like eggs Benedict, smoked salmon and custom-made omelets. The meal begins with sparkling cider and generally ends with a delicious apple strudel.

Five generations of Phil's family worked for the railroad, but Phil chose a life of radio broadcasting. His job with Voice of America made him famous for the morning "Breakfast Show" beamed to listeners around the world.

Phil is one of the most self-assured individuals I have ever met. It's a trait that most of us would like to have. He knows who he is, and what he wants for his guests. I enjoyed his direct approach to life. It makes for an unusual bed and breakfast, one that works well and is very comfortable.

Caledonia Farm—1812
47 Dearing Road; Flint Hill, VA 22627
(800) 262-1812; (540) 675-3693; Fax: (540) 675-3693
Innkeeper: Phil Irwin
Rooms: 1; **Suites**: 1; **Cottages**: 1; **With Private Baths**: 2; **With Shared Baths**: 1
Rates: $$ - $$$
Affiliations: NBBA, BBAV, Rappahannock B&B Guild, Front Royal/Warren County Chamber, Foothills Travel Assoc.
Payment:  **Amenities:**

Apple Hill Farm Bed & Breakfast
Washington Area (Sperryville)

Just a short drive west of Washington, Virginia, on the way to the Blue Ridge Mountains, you'll find the small community of Sperryville. Only two things in Sperryville make it famous, the Sperryville Emporium and Apple Hill Farm Bed and Breakfast. Its location makes it a great place for either a hideaway weekend or for those looking to enjoy the outdoor attractions of the Shenandoah National Park and the Skyline Drive.

Here in this beautiful valley the Adkins family built a large dairy farm back in 1849. All that remains today is the 20 acres and a 3,100-square-foot farm house that Wayne and Dot Waller have turned into a very comfortable bed and breakfast.

Wayne and Dot came to this region from the Mojave Desert area of California, so the climate was quite a change for them. When they discovered their future home, it had been empty for nearly 15 years. It took a considerable amount of work to prepare the two-story house for bed and breakfast guests.

Wayne and Dot have done a great job in restoration and decorating. With its location just a short drive from town, there's a feeling of "going off to stay at grandma's." The country antiques and decorations help contribute to this feeling. Cozy fireplaces throughout the house add to the overall ambiance. Dot has done a great job in picking fabrics that help to accent the country motif.

Even though each guest room has a comfortable sitting area, my favorite place to relax is on one of the porches. Here we listened to the sound of wild birds and watched Bear Dog as he tried to catch the woodpeckers. Bear Dog is a favorite with guests and he is more than willing to act as a tour guide on the wooded paths. Willing, that is, until an opossum or deer goes by and then you're on your own. Bear Dog never

catches anything; he seems to understand that he's not supposed to. But he still loves to play the game of hide and seek. Tantoe Cat, a small stray with one tan toe, Paul Newcat, a large Siamese and Sam, the brown-headed South American parrot, round out the staff at Apple Hill Farm.

While some bed and breakfasts serve nothing but casseroles, Apple Hill Farm does a modified country-style breakfast. They bake a variety of different flavored scones—lemon, peach, etc. There's also fresh fruit such as spiced apples to accompany eggs Benedict or pancakes with shredded apples, cinnamon and pumpkin spices on top. There's enough variety to meet just about anyone's tastes in breakfast. Dot can even cater to special requests with enough advanced notice.

The farm sits at about a 700-foot elevation and the mountains along the Skyline Drive are at about 2,300 feet. Wayne and Dot can prepare a picnic lunch for guests complete with champagne or fresh wine and drive you to the top of the mountain. The ten-mile hike down to Piney Branch Creek just below the house takes about four to four-and-a-half hours.

Of course, the Sperryville Emporium is well worth a bit of time to explore. I don't think I have ever seen so many antiques in one place in my life. There's also Washington, Virginia just down the road. It was the first community to be named after our first president, who completed the first survey of the town when he was still in his teens.

Apple Hill Farm Bed & Breakfast
117 Old Hollow Road; Sperryville, VA 22740
(800) 326-4583; (540) 987-9454; Fax: (540) 987-3139
Innkeepers: Wayne & Dot Waller
E-mail: dotsway@aol.com
Rooms: 4; All Private Baths; Rates: $$ - $$$
Affiliations: IIA, PAII

Payment: Amenities:

The Bailiwick Inn
Washington, DC Area (Fairfax)

Part of enjoying Washington, DC is having the right accommodations. The Bailiwick Inn in Fairfax has always met my expectations. It's conveniently located only 15 miles from the heart of Washington and near all the attractions of Northeastern Virginia.

The term "bailiwick" is an old English word that originally meant "the area around the court." It's aptly applied in this case as the Bailwick Inn is located directly across the street from the Fairfax Courthouse. The courthouse, by the way, is where George and Martha Washington's wills are on file.

Over the years the Bailiwick has played its part in American history. On the lawn of the Bailiwick the first Confederate officer was killed during the Civil War. Confederate spy Antonia Ford, a native of Fairfax, was one of the house's many guests. Colonel Robert Johnstone, Union Cavalry Commander, avoided capture by Confederate raider John Mosby by hiding in the privy, while his wife successfully defended the house with a broomstick.

Today the Bailiwick is one of America's premier bed and breakfasts. Seven of Washington, DC's top decorators were given the task of creating guest rooms honoring the lives of 14 prominent Virginia leaders. The rooms are literally a Who's Who of Virginia: Thomas Jefferson, James Monroe, George Washington, Patrick Henry, as well as George Mason and James Madison. The ladies of the Virginia are represented as well in the Nellie Curtis Room and the Antonia Ford Bridal Suite. The Thomas Jefferson Room, for example, is modeled after his bedroom at Monticello with Jefferson's favorite red and gold theme. The Washington Room, in his favorite dark green, will remind you of Mount Vernon.

Tea time at the Bailiwick is a grand affair with silver plates heaped with smoked salmon finger sandwiches, chocolate chip cookies, and sweet cakes. Because the Bailiwick is a true inn, it serves *prix fixe* four-course meals

that were some of the best dinners we had anywhere in Virginia. While menus change monthly at the Bailiwick, guests will find a variety of entrées that will please anyone's palate.

After dinner we took a walk through the small shops just around the corner. When we returned to our room, our bags had been put away, the bed turned down, gourmet chocolates placed on the pillow and a fire lit in the fireplace.

While elegance is the standard of excellence at the Bailiwick, it is surprisingly casual. During our stay I saw guests arrive in a Rolls Royce carrying a backpack, and another couple in a minivan arrive in formal attire. Both couples were treated as friends or family arriving for the weekend.

There's much to recommend at the Bailiwick: queen-sized beds, private phones and TVs on request. It's no wonder that it has made the top 12 inns in America list several times. My hat is off to innkeepers Bob and Annette Bradley.

When you're ready to explore the Washington area you will find your hosts and their staff knowledgeable about restaurants, museums, and shopping. One of their recommendations is to take the restaurant cruise ship, the Dandy. It's the best way to enjoy the Potomac River as you cruise past the nation's historic monuments such as the Jefferson and Lincoln Memorials, the Kennedy Center and the Washington Monument.

The Bailiwick Inn
4023 Chain Bridge Road; Fairfax, VA 22030
(800) 366-7666; (703) 691-2266; Fax: (703) 934-2112
Innkeepers: Bob & Annette Bradley
Rooms: 14; **Suites**: 1; **All Private Baths**; **Rates**: $$$
Affiliations: ABBA, IIA, PAII, Mobil, BBAV, Fairfax City Chamber
Payment: $$$ CHECKS M/C VISA AMEX
Amenities: ♿ ✂ ✎ ▭ VCR ♨ ♣♣ ⊘

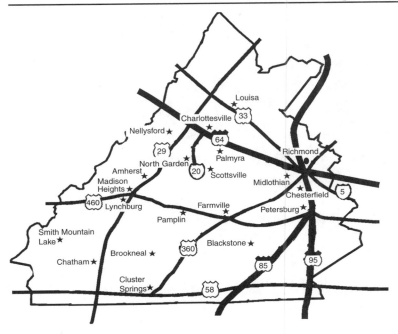

Central Region

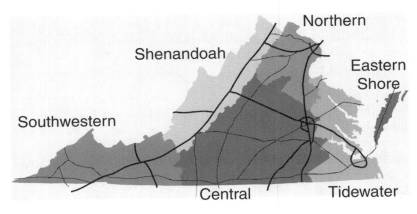

Sleepy Lamb Bed and Breakfast
Appomattox Area (Pamplin)

I spent most of my early years growing up on my grandparents' farm in the Midwest. Our trip to Sleepy Lamb, a turn-of-the-century Victorian home located on a 45-acre farm, felt just like a trip to Grandma's house. There was even the smell of homemade cookies coming from the kitchen when we arrived.

Our room on the second floor had its own deck from which we could look down on the farm animals. About two-thirds of the 45 acres is timber, while the rest is pasture for the eight dairy goats, 16 sheep, some cows, a miniature donkey and two horses. Like any farm, there are outdoor cats (seven of them), and a dog with her own pen. If you arrive in the spring, you might see the sheep being sheared.

Guests are welcome to help at feeding time or when its time to milk the goats. Kids love to come to Sleepy Lamb for just that reason. Unlike many bed and breakfasts, children are welcome. In fact, inn-keepers Ron and Judy Bernaldo are "tickled to death" to have children and families. Judy has children help with feeding, water-ing and milking the goats and Ron has them help in the kitchen. (See, I told you it was just like a trip to grandma's house. You could *never* get the kids to do all of that at home.)

Ron left his own home building business in New Jersey to come to Virginia. A bed and breakfast had been a dream of his and Judy's for a long time. The dream started with "inn sitting" for friends who owned a place at Cape Cod. On a trip to Virginia to visit their daughter, they found what would become Sleepy Lamb. However, the house required much work before it could accommodate guests. It needed baths for each of the guest rooms, new windows throughout the house and heat added to the second floor. The hard work ended when whole-house air conditioning was finally installed.

When the restoration was complete, they added family heirlooms, locally-purchased antiques and their own personal collections. One collection is the statues of horses around the house. The oldest is Tonto, which Judy has had since she was about eight years old. The other major collection is the Hummels which were handed down to Ron from his father. There are more than 200 pieces in the collection.

A few miles west of Sleepy Lamb, on April 9, 1865, General Robert E. Lee surrendered his men to Ulysses S. Grant. At Appomattox Courthouse, the Civil War that had ravaged our country ended. Today, the National Park Service maintains the site as a historical park.

The entire area around Sleepy Lamb is rich in Civil War history. To the east is Petersburg where a ten-month siege of the city by Union forces was the beginning of the end of the Confederacy. Lee and his troops began a retreat across Virginia with Union soldiers close behind. Just east, near Farmville, the last major battle of the Civil War took place at Sailor's Creek. More than 7,700 men and eight generals were captured by Union troops. Seventy-two hours later, Lee surrendered. Several historic sites similar to Appomattox and Sailors Creek are also open to the traveler.

Sleepy Lamb Bed & Breakfast
HCR 1, Box 34; Pamplin, VA 23958
(804) 248-6289
Innkeepers: Ron & Judy Bernaldo
Rooms: 3; All Private Baths; Rates: $$
Affiliations: BBAV, Appomattox Chamber
Payment:
Amenities:

Epes House Bed and Breakfast
Blackstone

There are some places you visit where you feel like a part of the family the moment you walk in the door. For us, Epes House was like that. Part of it was just good Southern hospitality but, even more, it was a case of innkeepers who really enjoy their guests.

Jim and Connie Barfell have created a haven for travelers in the small community of Blackstone, just 35 miles southwest of Petersburg. Blackstone's history dates back to pre-Revolutionary War days when two rival taverns sat at the intersection of three stagecoach routes. The first was the Schwartz (German for black) Tavern and the second the Whites Tavern. The village that formed around the crossroads was called Blacks & Whites for the two taverns until 1885. Whites Tavern is no longer standing. However, Schwartz Tavern, Blackstone's oldest building, has been fully restored.

The area around Blackstone is rich in history although it missed being involved in the Civil War by just a few miles. After a ten-month siege at Petersburg by Northern troops, the Confederate Army began a westward retreat across Virginia. The troops, led by General Robert E. Lee, followed a route to Appomattox Courthouse where they surrendered on April 9, 1865. For those interested in following the Civil War, the Epes house is centrally located to many of the historic sites.

The house that Jim and Connie chose to be their bed and breakfast was built in 1890 for Sidney P. Epes. Just five years later, Epes was elected to the U.S. Congress where he served until his death in 1900. History has remembered Epes as being a great Virginia gentleman and his eulogy at the Capitol required half a day.

When Jim and Connie found the grand Victorian house that they named in Epes's honor, some restoration work had already been started. However, it still required 18 months of work before the house was ready for

guests. Connie's work as an interior decorator shows throughout the bed and breakfast she has carefully decorated in the style of the late 1800s.

Assisting Jim and Connie in the roles of assistant innkeepers are Baron, a standard French poodle, Amber, a Sheltie and two cats named Sir Edmund Hillary and Chocolate. While they are generally confined to the innkeepers' quarters, Angel was able to entice them out to play.

Comfortable rooms decorated with family heirlooms and handmade quilts await the traveler who stops at the Epes House. Each of the rooms is quite large considering that while most sizable homes of the period had quite a number of rooms, bedrooms were typically small. An added benefit is that each of the three guest rooms has its own private bath.

A full breakfast greeted us after a pleasant night's sleep. Local ham, bacon or sausage accompanied by eggs, pancakes or waffles plus fresh fruit and cereals reminded me of the breakfast I had growing up on grandma's farm. On Sunday mornings, a complete buffet-style breakfast is served.

Blackstone has nearly 400 buildings in its historic district, and the Chamber of Commerce can supply information for a walking tour of the community. In addition to its proximity to historic battlefields, the area is rich in outdoor opportunities. There are a number of places in the area where you can hike, fish or spend a day on the water.

Epes House Bed & Breakfast
210 College Avenue; Blackstone, VA 23824
(804) 292-7941
Innkeepers: James & Connie Barfell
Rooms: 3; All Private Baths; Rates: $$
Affiliations: BBAV, Blackstone Chamber
Payment:
Amenities:

Staunton Hill
Brookneal

We were unprepared for Staunton Hill, but it was one of the most pleasant surprises on the entire tour of Virginia. The house of Bruce, while built in 1848, does not follow the traditional style of most colonial plantation homes. Instead it is patterned more after a European castle.

Charles Bruce hired John Evan Johnson to create a home on his 5,000-acre estate, high above the Staunton River. Bruce's instruction to Johnson was to spend no more than $25,000 on house and furnishings. Charles then went off to Europe for a year while the mansion was under construction. Johnson, a graduate of West Point whose training was that of a Civil War engineer, created a castle-like structure complete with battlements and turrets. The final cost of construction was $75,000, yet Charles Bruce was never known to complain about it.

Today, the fourth generation of the Bruce family, great-grandson David Bruce, lives at the end of the mile-long drive on 275 acres. The private road leading to Staunton Hill is lined by magnolias while the rest of the estate is covered with red and white oaks, dogwoods, cedars, beech, and hemlock. There are flowers almost everywhere you look. A magnificent formal garden with a boxwood maze lies between the mansion and the pool. While there isn't a moat, a mile-long stone wall encircles the house. You'll find miles of trails for hiking and bird watching. Besides the pool and hot tub there are tennis and racquetball courts as well as an exercise room. Hungry? You won't need to leave the property. The Bistro, located down the drive from the main house in the conference center, serves lunch and dinner by reservation to inn guests during the week and is open to the public on weekends.

Yes, we were very pleasantly surprised by Staunton Hill; not just by the surroundings and the imposing castle, but by our room as well. The rooms are not in the main house but in the wings that were added to the mansion by our innkeeper's father just after World War II. The senior Bruce, who served as the European chief of the Office of Strategic Services (OSS) during World War II, later served as Ambassador to France, Germany and Great Britain. In the 1970s, he became the first United States liaison officer to China. His last position was that of Ambassador to NATO. The wings were built to house guests and friends who would often visit Staunton Hill. Befitting the guests of an Ambassador, the rooms are large and airy and filled with antiques and treasures from around the world. Other accommodations include three Gothic-style cottages on the property.

For all of its history and splendor, there is a laid back atmosphere to Staunton Hill that makes it relaxing, not overbearing. Much of this is due to David, his artist wife, Janet, and their efforts to make Staunton Hill not a typical bed and breakfast but a mini-resort and conference center.

Because there is so much to do at Staunton Hill, we spent little time exploring the area. However, just a mile or so away is Red Hill, the last home and burial place of the patriot, Patrick Henry.

Staunton Hill
RR 2, Box 244B; Brookneal, VA 24528
(804) 326-4048; Fax: (804) 376-5929
Innkeepers: David & Janet Bruce
Rooms: 20; **Cottages**: 2; **With Private Baths**: 10; **With Shared Baths**: 12; **Rates**: $$ - $$$
Affiliations: ABBA, BBAV
Payment: MC VISA
Amenities:

The 1817 Historic Bed and Breakfast
Charlottesville

They say that with any business, location is everything. For the 1817 Historic Bed and Breakfast, this is definitely true. It's located just a block from the University of Virginia on Main Street. Along the street are a number of small bistros and shops. The center of the downtown is within walking distance. However, the moment you walk through the front door of this Federal style townhouse, all the sounds of the city disappear.

The carefully designed construction of the townhouse is due to the efforts of Thomas Jefferson's master craftsman, James Dinsmore, an Irishman who came to America in 1789. Dinsmore's work can also be seen at Poplar Forest, Jefferson's retreat near Lynchburg, at Monticello, Jefferson's home just outside Charlottesville and at Montpelier, James Madison's home near Orange.

Actually, the 1817 isn't one townhouse, but two that sit side-by-side. The first is one of the finest antique shops in the heart of Charlottesville. The second townhouse (and much of the second floor of both) is a very comfortable bed and breakfast, both owned and operated by innkeeper Candace DeLoach.

Candace grew up in Savannah, Georgia, where her parents are in the antique business. After attending school in South Carolina, she moved to New York City where she worked in the highly competitive business of interior design. As you walk through her inn, it becomes obvious that she became a master at not only antiques and design, but also the role of innkeeper. She makes guests feel right at home.

Owning your own antique shop helps when you begin to decorate thousands of square feet as a bed and breakfast. Not all of the furnishings are antiques: you will find an eclectic blend of furnishings and accessories that work amazingly well together. As you would expect, each room at the 1817 is decorated with entirely different themes and since the an-

tiques are for sale, the rooms change from time to time. This makes each return trip to the 1817 as exciting as the first. Another advantage is that since the antiques are for sale, that wonderful bed in which you rested so well can go home with you!

A third business operates out of the townhouse, The Tea Room Café at the 1817. Carefully prepared lunches are served each day for locals and tourists alike. The menu ranges from the Grand Café Salad to Mom's Meatloaf Sandwich. The Café and its offerings fit right into the informal but elegant atmosphere you will find at the 1817.

Charlottesville has much to offer since it sits near the Blue Ridge Mountains: there is a world of outdoor activities. Yet the city has a very upscale metropolitan flavor in a historical setting. The Historic Michie Tavern and nearby Monticello give visitors a glimpse of late eighteenth-century life from two uniquely different perspectives; the first of the common man or woman of that age, and the latter of our early American elite.

Of course there are also theaters, wineries, museums and the University of Virginia to explore. Shopping opportunities abound in the area as do good restaurants. The Tea Room Café at the 1817 doesn't serve dinner, but there are a number of places nearby which do. We tried the Metropolitain and found both the food and the service to be excellent. The menu changes daily, but the high quality does not.

The 1817 Historic Bed & Breakfast
1211 West Main Street; Charlottesville, VA 22903
(800) 730-7443; (804) 979-7353; Fax: (804) 979-7209
Innkeeper: Candace DeLoach
Rooms: 3; **Suites**: 2; **All Private Baths**; **Rates**: $$ - $$$$
Affiliations: BBAV, Charlottesville Chamber, American Historic Inns
Payment:
Amenities:

The Inn at Monticello
Charlottesville

There is little doubt that Charlottesville is "Thomas Jefferson country." His home, Monticello, and the school he created, the University of Virginia, are both located here. They are a testimony to his creative genius and to the vast range of his interests.

In a small valley, just two miles from Jefferson's home, is the Inn at Monticello, an 1850s manor house. The five rolling acres are shaped like a pie wedge with the Inn at the tip so the bed and breakfast sits well back from the highway. The drive up the lane takes you past a well-manicured lawn dotted with dogwoods, boxwoods and azaleas.

Once part of a large farm that raised cattle and tobacco, the property around the Inn has only recently been divided. Although Charlottesville is only a few miles away, there is still the feeling of being far out in the country. You can sit on the front porch during the evening and hear sounds of night owls or watch a variety of local wildlife wander the grounds.

Past owners have respected the historic significance of the house. While amenities like air-conditioning have been added, there is still the feel of a nineteenth-century manor house. The Jefferson influence of clean lines and functional style are evident throughout the house as well. While the five guest rooms have been carefully decorated with antiques and period reproductions, your comfort and relaxation have been the first considerations.

Two of the guest rooms have working fireplaces while one has its own private screened porch. Four-poster canopied beds are found in two of the rooms and all feature hand-ironed sheets and down comforters on queen-sized beds.

Favorite gathering spots for inn guests are the living room with fireplaces

at both ends, and the porch facing the mountains. During good weather, breakfast is often served on the porch.

A full breakfast includes fresh baked breads, fruit and juice and an entrée with breakfast meat, served at guests' convenience. The innkeepers have no problem dealing with a variety of dietary restrictions if the need arises. Evening refreshments are often served on the porch as well. When the weather is cool, they are served in front of the fireplaces.

While the property has been a bed and breakfast for a number of years, innkeepers Rebecca and Norm Lindway are new to the area. They came from Cleveland, Ohio where they retired as school counselors. It wasn't until their youngest son graduated from college that they started staying in bed and breakfasts. They found that they enjoyed the experience so much, they wanted to share it with others. Their original goal was to start a bed and breakfast further south, but one taste of all that Charlottesville had to offer changed their minds.

This area was not only home to Thomas Jefferson but also to James Monroe, father of the Constitution and James Madison, the fifth president. Monroe's home, Ashlawn-Highland and Madison's home, Montpelier, are open to the public. Another major point of interest in the area is Historic Michie Tavern, which gives visitors an excellent view of eighteenth-century travel accommodations in America as well as serving a fine lunch.

The Inn at Monticello
Highway 20 South, 1188 Scottsville Road; Charlottesville, VA 22902
(804) 979-3593; Fax: (804) 296-1344
Innkeepers: Rebecca & Norm Lindway
Rooms: 5; All Private Baths; Rates: $$$
Affiliations: PAII, Mobil, BBAV, Charlottesville/Albemarle Chamber
Payment: $$$ CHECKS MC VISA
Amenities: A/C 🔥 ✉

The Inn at Sugar Hollow Farm
Charlottesville

My strongest memory of the Inn at Sugar Hollow Farm will always be sitting on the deck watching the deer cross the yard. It was early evening just after dinner. The sun was just starting to set, still plenty of light, when the first doe stepped out of the bushes and slowly began to wander across the yard. In a matter of moments, two more appeared and finally two young fawns. They must have been visible for a good five or six minutes before disappearing into the trees at the opposite side of the yard.

Naturally, I asked the innkeepers if the show had been planned for our benefit. Like good hosts, they informed me that it had. However, the truth is that guests often seen deer, wild turkey, fox and even a bear or two. With the Blue Ridge Mountains just a few miles away, wildlife is abundant in the area. Of course, sitting on 70 acres of land (with 50 of those in woods where hunters aren't allowed) helps to draw the wildlife, too.

Innkeepers Dick and Hayden Cabell became interested in opening a bed and breakfast or inn after staying at Mast Farm Inn in North Carolina. They looked for nearly three years around Asheville and Western North Carolina but couldn't find just the right setting. They wanted to be near the mountains with plenty of land and streams, yet close to a major community. When North Carolina didn't seem to have the right combination, they began searching Virginia. Sugar Hollow, with views to the Blue Ridge, just 13 miles west of Charlottesville between Pasture Fence Mountain and Buck's Elbow Mountain, was just what they were looking for.

Their first plan had been to restore the old farmhouse. A bit of research revealed that new construction would be better. It took months of interviewing builders to find the right one and then more time to finalize the house design. A butler's pantry, large dining room, self-

contained kitchen, rooms with fireplaces, and great views from all the rooms, were included on the list. The final design is a modern version of a Virginia farm house with 5,100 square feet of space. The large common areas allow them to host a variety of functions and to serve dinner to inn guests on weekends.

Dinner, like breakfast, could best be described as country cooking with a cosmopolitan flair. Breakfast brings egg dishes, pancakes, French toast or waffles with country ham or locally produced sausage or bacon. The weekend dinners offer boneless chicken breasts, steak or boneless center-cut pork chops in a sherry sauce. Then there are potatoes, fresh garden vegetables, wild rice and homemade bread. Basic country cooking, but so good.

There are riding stables located near the property. The new White Hall Winery is also just a few miles away. For hikers, the Appalachian Trail is nearby. The Moorman River Valley, where the inn is located, is right at the edge of the Shenandoah National Park. Of course Charlottesville, where you will find the University of Virginia, Monticello, Ashlawn-Highland and Historic Michie Tavern, is an easy drive. Charlottesville offers a nice blend of country charm and big city excitement. There's theater, fine dining and excellent places to shop for antiques.

The Inn at Sugar Hollow Farm
P.O. Box 5705; Charlottesville, VA 22905
(804) 823-7086; Fax: (804) 823-2002
Innkeepers: Richard & Hayden Cabell
E-mail: theinn@sugarhollow.com
Rooms: 3; Suites: 2; All Private Baths; Rates: $$ - $$$
Affiliations: PAII, BBAV, Charlottesville/Albemarle Chamber
Payment: Amenities:

The Quarters
Charlottesville

Everything about the Quarters is unique. I think that is why I enjoyed it so much. To begin with, you would technically have to the say that the Quarters is a homestay as it has only one guest accommodation. However, the accommodations at the Quarters are a full two-bedroom suite with its own sitting room, private bath and private entrance. As a result, you have much more privacy at the Quarters than you might find at most bed and breakfasts.

Another difference about the Quarters is its history. About 1814, John Kelly, a well to-do Charlottesville merchant, owned about 500 acres of land just west of what was then the heart of Charlottesville. The property was so valuable that Thomas Jefferson tried to acquire the land to build his "Academic Village." Kelly, not caring for Jefferson's politics, refused to sell, so Jefferson had to settle for "second best." An adjacent farm thus became the University of Virginia.

The exact date that the Quarters was built is uncertain, but it was between 1815 and 1830. It served as quarters for slaves who worked on the Kelly's farm. Later, when the property changed hands, the building became the kitchen and servants' quarters for the Preston Manor house constructed next door. On the property, where an ice house once stood, Mary Hill Caperton's wildflower garden now flourishes.

The academic community of the University of Virginia has grown up around the Quarters. Many of the buildings in the area serve as homes for both professors and students. In fact, many of the guests at the Quarters are parents and prospective students coming to visit the University, or to attend one of the school's many functions. However, the Quarters is also a great hideaway in the center of Charlottesville whether you're on a getaway or a business trip.

Mary Hill has restored the property, decorated it with family heirlooms and turned it into first class accommodations. The yard is covered with a

variety of flowers, shrubs and herbs. No house in the entire neighborhood has more old trees to help add to the privacy. A trip up the hidden stairway to the second floor brings you to a very comfortable sitting room with working fireplace and cable television. The smaller of the two bedrooms is available for a child, or more likely a young adult, traveling with parents and looking for the right school. The larger bedroom features a king-sized bed, a guest cupboard well stocked with soft drinks and a bookcase with a number of recent books.

A full breakfast is served in the formal dining room or in the large kitchen overlooking the garden. It is the dining room with which I really fell in love. I looked for ways to bring it home, but Angel was wise enough to know it wouldn't fit in the van. All the furnishings of this room reminded me of some of the restored homes I saw in Colonial Williamsburg. The planked door with its wrought iron hinges and the stone fireplace with a massive single-beam mantle just added to the ambiance of the room. The country-style breakfast seemed to fit the room as well.

There is one last thing that makes the Quarters unique. Besides operating the Quarters, Mary Hill owns and manages a very successful reservation service for bed and breakfasts throughout the area. While these properties are typically homestays and not members of the state's bed and breakfast association, each has been personally inspected by Mary Hill to meet her rigid requirements.

The Quarters
611 Preston Place; P.O. Box 5737; Charlottesville, VA 22903
(804) 979-7264; Fax: (804) 293-7791
Innkeeper: Mary Hill Caperton
E-mail: Guesthouses_bnb_reservations@compuserve.com
Suites: 1; All Private Baths; Rates: $$$
Affiliations: BBAV, Charlottesville Chamber
Payment: VISA AMEX Amenities:

Ginger Hill Bed and Breakfast
Charlottesville Area (Louisa)

Now, in my opinion you come to Ginger Hill for three reasons. The first is location. With Civil War sites, Richmond and Charlottesville all nearby, there are many opportunities for sightseeing. The other two reasons are just as high on the list: great food and the boat ride on Lake Anna. (Dinners and boat rides must be scheduled in advance.)

Ron and Ginger Ellis have more than 14 acres just outside Louisa that they purchased with the idea of building a small intimate bed and breakfast. Since they both have jobs, they limited it to just two guest rooms. This adds to the feeling of being a part of the family. Ginger, by the way, works for the U.S. Department of Housing and Urban Development while Ron is a graphic artist with his own publishing business.

The house is what I would call a country cottage and there are those who will be able to see a Florida influence in its style. Furnishings are a blend of antique and modern and the two guest rooms are comfortable, although the master guest room is the larger of the two. Both have private baths, and TV in the room is available on request.

Guests are greeted with afternoon refreshments that include Ginger's award-winning lemon-sugar cookies. Iced teas and soft drinks or, during cooler weather, hot tea, coffee and hot chocolate are available throughout the day.

Ginger Hill is one of the few bed and breakfasts that permit guests to bring the family dog by prior arrangement. The kennel is 6- by 8-foot with an igloo-shaped dog house. Since it is located on the same side of the house as the guests would stay, you can even open the window and speak to the dog. Fido won't feel quite so alone that way.

There's a two-and-a-half-acre pond and a canoe for the guests to use and there are rods and reels if you would like to fish. You'll find the

pond stocked with blue gill, crappie, large mouth bass and catfish. If you would like to picnic, there's even a grill by the pond. Two other ponds on the property really belong to the beavers so there's no fishing there.

While Ginger Hill is really a bed and breakfast and not an inn, by arrangement (at least a couple of days) they will prepare a four-course candlelight dinner or a three-course light supper. The four-course includes homemade broth, salad and treats such as Cornish game hens with a green vegetable and wild rice. They top off the dinner with a dessert such as a grasshopper parfait made with Oreo cookies and *crème de menthe* ice cream with chocolate frosting.

At breakfast, Ginger does the baking and Ron handles the cooking. Together they do a little bit of everything. Some mornings bring grilled pork chops, poached eggs and hash browns while other mornings might bring a farmer's basket. This is a pastry that's baked and comes out like a bowl or basket. To this, Ron adds ham, tomato, cheese, spinach and a poached egg on top.

Ron will take guests out on Lake Anna by prior arrangement for fishing, swimming or sightseeing in a 20-foot Procraft 200. You can even take along a picnic lunch with fresh bread, smoked chicken breast, salad, and a chocolate dessert.

Ginger Hill Bed & Breakfast
47 Holly Springs Drive; Louisa, VA 23093
(540) 967-3260; Fax: (540) 967-2555
Innkeepers: Ronald A. & Virginia F. Ellis
E-mail: raegraph@mnsinc.com
Rooms: 2; **All Private Baths**; **Rates**: $$ - $$$
Affiliations: BBAV, Louisa Chamber
Payment:  **Amenities**:

Inn at the Crossroads
Charlottesville Area (North Garden)

In the late eighteenth and early nineteenth centuries, the *ordinary* (a tavern or inn) served much the same purpose as a present-day community center. It was a meeting place, polling center, post office and trading post. For the travelers, it provided not only safe haven for the night, but a place where they could get a meal and exchange news with townspeople and other travelers.

The Inn at the Crossroads, once such an ordinary, has been preserved with only minor changes over the years. Today it serves travelers as a bed and breakfast. The furnishings of the bed and breakfast are much nicer than the typical ordinary would have had but many of the pieces are from the period and have been refinished by the innkeepers.

The Morris family built the Inn at the Crossroads in about 1820 on the old Scottsville Turnpike, the link between the James River Canal and the Shenandoah Valley. A second turnpike, the Staunton/James River Turnpike, commissioned in 1818 and completed in 1827, created the crossroads.

Built in the Federalist style, the inn is a four-story building with timber framing and an English basement. A summer kitchen located just behind the inn has been converted into a guest suite. While there was a brief period when the property was vacant, it has served as overnight lodging since it was constructed.

Innkeepers John and Maureen Deis had their first taste of running a bed and breakfast a few years ago. They had talked about owning a bed and breakfast for years. When the company John worked for, Pan Am, filed for bankruptcy, it seemed like the perfect time to make the change. After a number of seminars on running a bed and breakfast, they leased one on Deer Isle on the Maine coast. Their experience taught them two things: they wanted their own bed and breakfast and they wanted to move farther south.

Central Virginia has proved to be the perfect location for their dream and the Inn at the Crossroads has benefited from their previous experience. They have added important features such as private baths for each guest room and are converting the non-working fireplaces to working gas logs. A full breakfast is served in the original keeping room on a harvest table that dates back to the early 1800s.

Given the history of the area, I think staying at an "ordinary" is a perfect choice for the history buff. Monticello, home of President Thomas Jefferson, Ashlawn-Highland, home of President James Monroe and Montpelier, home of President James Madison, are all within a short drive. Located just nine miles south of Charlottesville, at the crossroads of Routes 29 and 692, the Inn is close to the University of Virginia and Charlottesville's historic district. Historic Michie Tavern is also only a few miles from the Inn at the Crossroads. Here you can see how a true tavern operated in Colonial America and try an "ordinary" meal as it would have been served in that period.

Of course, a visit to Charlottesville isn't just for the history. Charlottesville is a modern city with the diversity of any metropolitan community. You'll find fine dining, theater and major shopping districts that combine with its academic heritage as the home of the University of Virginia.

Inn at the Crossroads
5010 Plank Road; Routes 29 & 692; North Garden, VA 22959
(804) 979-6452
Innkeepers: John & Maureen Deis
Rooms: 4; **Suites:** 1; **Cabins:** 1; **All Private Baths; Rates:** $$ - $$$
Affiliations: BBAV, Charlottesville/Albemarle Chamber
Payment:
Amenities:

Palmer Country Manor
Charlottesville Area (Palmyra)

The moment we pulled into the drive the place seemed familiar. In fact, it is so close to my idea of how I would operate an inn that I wondered if Gregory and Kathy Palmer had been sitting in on some of my personal goal-setting sessions. However, I know that can't be the case because their inn was built before I became interested in owning my own inn.

To explain my ideal inn, I want a large farm near major points of interest with a historic building located on the property. To this I want to add five or six new duplex units that will allow me to create ten to twelve suites. It will have a pool and a formal dining room that will serve award-winning dinners and true country-style breakfasts.

Gregory and Kathy have taken a 200-acre farm with a historic home built in the early 1800s and created my ideal country inn. They have completely restored the manor house, created two very nice guest rooms, a comfortable common room and a more formal parlor. With a great deal of effort, they dug a basement under the manor house, created a true chef's kitchen and an award-winning dining room that is open to guests and the general public by reservation. Their wine cellar has won numerous awards for being one of the finest in the state.

The five very modern cabins are each 12- by 70-feet. This allows two 400-square-foot 12 by 35-foot mini suites per cabin complete with fireplace, large private bath, private deck and sitting room for each suite. Gregory and Kathy feel that people want comfortable rooms that are secure, private and functional, and I agree. The units sit in a half-circle around a very large pool and are just a short walk from the manor house where breakfast is served.

Since Palmer Country Manor is on a farm, it's only fitting that there are farm animals around. You'll find Black Angus cattle, a pot-bellied pig (the family pet named Arlene Bacon) and a number of Rhode Island Red chickens. A more exotic addition to the farm is the three peacocks. Like any good farm, there are children to enjoy it all, five in fact, ranging from grade-schoolers to high-schoolers.

While I thoroughly enjoyed Palmer Country Manor and was amazed at how closely it resembled my future plans, it was dinner that impressed us the most. Naturally, I had to try the ten-ounce filet mignon and I can assure you that I was not disappointed. Of course, they have other selections ranging from roasted breast of chicken to shrimp or beef tenderloin. I would suggest making your reservation for dinner in advance.

If you tire of swimming, hiking, hot air ballooning, fishing and biking, you might want to make the drive to Charlottesville. All of its attractions are only a short drive away. Some of your stops might include Thomas Jefferson's home at Monticello, Ashlawn-Highland, the home of James Monroe, and Historic Michie Tavern.

Of course Charlottesville has many other things to offer including excellent restaurants, shopping, antique centers, an ice-skating park open year round and the University of Virginia. There are plays to attend, area vineyards to see and wineries to tour all within an easy drive of Palmer Country Manor.

Palmer Country Manor
Route 2, Box 1390; Palmyra, VA 22963
(800) 253-4306; (804) 589-1300; Fax: (804) 589-1300
Innkeepers: Gregory & Kathleen Palmer
E-mail: palmermanor@symweb.com
Rooms: 2; **Cottages:** 10; **With Private Baths:** 10; **With Shared Bath:** 2 **Rates:** $$$
Affiliations: BBAV, AAA◆◆◆, Charlottesville Chamber
Payment: $$$ CHECKS M/C VISA AMEX DISCOVER **Amenities:**

High Meadows Inn & Mountain Sunset Inn
Charlottesville Area (Scottsville)

It's quite a career change from submarine commander to innkeeper, but Peter Sushka has made the transition very well. He and his wife, Mary Jae Abbitt, have created a unique inn 17 miles from Monticello, Thomas Jefferson's home just outside Charlottesville.

Part of what makes the inn unique is its duality. It is both a country inn and a vineyard. While they do not have their own winery (the grapes are taken to the Jefferson Winery at the foot of Monticello), they do have their own private label that is gaining popularity. They planted the grapes in the fall of 1984 and had their first harvest in 1988. One of their wines is a Vingris de Pinot Noir and there are only two other places in the world make it; one in Italy, and the other in Oregon.

The main Inn also has a dual personality. The older part is Colonial in style and was built in the 1830s by Peter White. Peter lived there until he died in the 1870s. The second owner, named Harris, wanted a new house. He picked a spot just ten feet away from the first and began construction of a new Italianate/Victorian style home. He intended to take down the White house, but his wife who was pregnant with their sixth child intervened. The couple fought over this until 1887, when the seventh child was born. Finally, Mr. Harris agreed that they needed all 17 rooms. The White house was renovated from top to bottom and a grand breezeway between the two houses was created.

The innkeepers spent many years with a diplomatic liaison team to the British Navy in England. When they returned to the U.S., they brought back more than 450 pieces of antique British furniture. Peter, not choosing to follow in the path of many retired officers, wanted to do something different. The creation of an inn gave them a chal-

lenge they could both enjoy. Their collection of antique furniture found a new home at the inn.

A second building, the Mountain Sunset, is located across the road and was added to the property in 1990. This house is a Queen Anne style manor house built in 1902. It added four guest rooms and quarters for the inn manager. Two additional suites on the property are the Glen Side cabin and the Carriage House.

A highlight of any stay at High Meadows is dinner. A full six-course dinner is prepared on Saturday night. A bistro style dinner is served Thursday, Friday and Sunday. Monday through Wednesday nights, a European basket of hot and cold foods is prepared. The dinner basket is served in your room, or can be served on the porch or in the gazebo. While all the menus change daily, our basket included iced cucumber soup, and either flank steak pinwheels or crab cakes. The European basket was the highlight of our stay.

There are two half-acre ponds on the property and the vineyards to explore. Callie the golden retriever is the official guide and will take you around the property. Along the way you will meet Sioux, an 18-year-old pony, Pooh Bear, a male golden retriever, and 23 ducks.

High Meadows Inn & Mountain Sunset Inn
High Meadows Lane; Scottsville, VA 24590
(800) 232-1832; (804) 286-2218; Fax: (804) 286-2124
Innkeepers: Peter Sushka & Mary Jae Abbitt
Rooms: 7; **Suites**: 4; **Cottages**: 2; **All Private Baths**; **Rates**: $$$
Affiliations: IIA, PAII, BBAV, Charlottesville Chamber, Scottsville Chamber
Payment:
Amenities:

Eldon—The Inn At Chatham
Chatham

In 1996, the Virginia Cattle Industry Board sponsored its yearly cook-off. Joel Wesley, the chef at Eldon, pressed for time, "whipped up a little something" and took second place. The night we visited and had dinner, he had more time to prepare and our dinner would have taken first place in any contest. When you visit Eldon, be sure to have a hearty appetite.

Food isn't the only reason to visit Eldon, just one of the best. Other reasons include hospitality, beautiful accommodations and a historic location. Like innkeepers Joy and Bob Lemm, we found the 13 acres of woods, gardens and orchards a perfect setting for this restored 1835 plantation manor home. The manor was built for James Murray Whittle, a prominent Confederate attorney, and named for British jurist, Lord Eldon.

Whittle was the first of several important owners over the years. Claude Swanson, a former Virginia governor and secretary of the Navy in the early 1900s under President Theodore Roosevelt, also owned the home.

The Lemms actually came to Eldon to fulfill the dream of their son, Joel. For as long as Joel can remember, his mother wanted to own a country inn. The dream included Joel having his own restaurant as a part of the inn. An accomplished chef who has cooked for celebrities such as Lucille Ball and Frank Sinatra, Joel convinced his family that an inn could work.

The idea was contagious and led to a five-year search. The final six months were spent with Joy and Bob driving throughout the South. The search ended at Eldon. It was the stately columns and old magnolias that first attracted them. Unfortunately the house had been neglected in recent years and it took eight months to refurbish the

interior. During the same time, Joel with his wife, Peggy, began the process of furnishing a kitchen and decorating a dining room. Interestingly, while Joel spent six months searching for his dream location, Peggy attended cooking school in Chicago. Now, as pastry chef, her creations top off the evening meals.

While the whole house has been carefully restored and decorated with antiques and Oriental rugs, the rooms are really special. Each of the three guest rooms and one suite is tastefully decorated and larger than those in most bed and breakfast accommodations. The James Whittle room and the Governor Swanson room each have a fireplace. The Whitehead suite is two connected rooms that share a large bath, and the Elliott Garden room has French doors that open onto its own secluded garden. Part of what helps to make your stay so pleasant is that you get all of this for rates far below what you would expect.

Chatham was founded in 1777 and is just north of Danville, the last Capital of the Confederacy. The area is rich in history, but it's also a treasure trove for the antique buyer. Both the Blue Ridge Parkway and Smith Mountain Lake are nearby for outdoor enthusiasts. Or perhaps you will want to just sit in Eldon's garden with a good book or take a dip in the swimming pool. Whatever your choice, Eldon is a great place to start your adventures.

Eldon—The Inn at Chatham
1037 Chalk Level Road; State Road 685; Chatham, VA 24531
(804) 432-0935
Innkeepers: Joy & Bob Lemm
Rooms: 3; Suites: 1; With Private Baths: 3; With Shared Baths: 1; Rates: $$ - $$$
Affiliations: BBAV, Pittsylvania County Historical Society, Pittsylvania County Chamber

Payment:

Amenities:

Oak Grove Plantation Bed & Breakfast
Cluster Springs

Often you will find that bed and breakfasts prefer to not have younger children as guests. Granted, this isn't always the case, but often enough that many think of a bed and breakfast as strictly an adult getaway. Oak Grove Plantation is an exception to the rule. So much so that innkeeper Pickett Craddock even has summer getaways aimed at children from ages four to twelve.

Parents can bring the children, spend the weekend with them, and then leave the children for the week. The kids have a 400-acre farm to explore, can eat watermelon under the oaks, play with the Dalmatian, and take supervised field trips. By the time the parents return the next weekend, the children will have taken a trip to the firehouse, toured llama and dairy farms and gone swimming in the lake. Having been raised on a farm, I thought about signing up for this myself.

Five generations of Pickett's family have lived at Oak Grove, the first being Thomas Easley, who built the manor house in the 1820s. The house was constructed with timber cut on the farm and brick that was made on the farm by slaves. Since the original plantation encompassed nearly 1,000 acres, it took a number of slaves to help maintain the property. Children have always been a part of Oak Grove. Thomas started the tradition with nine of his own. The second Easley generation to live on the farm had eleven children.

The manor house sits on the crest of a hill and is bordered by boxwoods in the center of a 200-year-old grove. Typical of many homes of that era, the house has been added to a number of times. However, you can still see the touches of the original work. The parlor and upstairs bedrooms are all part of the construction completed by Thomas Easley. Many of the antiques throughout the house are family

heirlooms that date back to the different families that have lived at Oak Grove Plantation. However, Pickett has child-proofed the house.

Oak Grove is only open during the summer months since Pickett has a full-time business. She operates a preschool in Washington, DC and returns to Cluster Springs to open Oak Grove early in May for weekends, and then full time in June, July and August. The week-end-only schedule begins again in September.

While Cluster Springs is a small town, to the north is the community of South Boston. Here you will find plenty of places to explore and places to enjoy casual dining or a candlelight dinner. We chose the more casual approach and visited the local pizza parlor.

Staunton River Battlefield Park and Museum is a unique museum just outside South Boston. To the left as you enter the museum are exhibits describing the Clover Power Station and the role of electricity in our modern world. To the right are exhibits on the Civil War battle of Staunton River Bridge. Another museum in the area is the South Boston Historical Museum containing area memorabilia.

West of South Boston is Danville, the last Capital of the Confederacy. It has a Museum of Fine Arts & History and an excellent Science Center located in a historic train station. The Prestwould Plantation is also in the area. It is one of the largest plantation houses in Virginia and it was built just after the Revolutionary War.

Oak Grove Plantation Bed & Breakfast
1245 Cluster Springs Road; P.O. Box 45; Cluster Springs, VA 24535
(804) 575-7137
Innkeeper: Pickett Craddock
Rooms: 3; With Private Baths: 1; With Shared Baths: 2; Rates: $$
Affiliations: BBAV

Payment: $$$ CHECKS

Amenities: A/C

"Linden" Bed & Breakfast
Farmville

After the ten-month siege of Petersburg, the Confederate army, led by General Robert E. Lee, retreated across Virginia. The last major battle of the Civil War took place, just seventy-two hours before Lee surrendered at Appomattox. Here at Sailor's Creek, just a few miles from "Linden" Bed and Breakfast, more than 7,700 men and eight generals were captured by Union troops. Lee's response was, "My God! Has the army been dissolved?"

Granted, not everyone who comes to Farmville is interested in Civil War history or even American history, but it is a good reason for coming. Petersburg, which withstood the longest siege of any American city, is to the east. Appomattox, where the war ended, is just a short distance to the west. In the center is Farmville, directly on the line of Robert E. Lee's retreat.

Of course, many come to stay at "Linden" Bed and Breakfast while visiting Farmville's historic district and shopping for Oriental rugs and furniture at the Green Front Furniture complex along the Appomattox River. Farmville is a college town, and Longwood and Hampden-Sydney Colleges schedule art exhibits, concerts, theater productions and athletic events. If you fish, you might want to try your luck at Briery Lake, a large Virginia Game Commission lake that's home to trophy-size bass and right across the road from "Linden."

History, though, just seems to fit with this house built in the early 1800s on a 1,500-acre tobacco plantation once owned by the first president of Hampden-Sydney College. Innkeepers Gretchen and Bob Rogers have lived in the house for nearly 22 years. They have not only carefully restored the property, they have added a few special touches of their own. Wait till you see the bath.

Antiques hold a special place at "Linden" because many are family heirlooms. Others, such as the dining room furniture, were given to them in the early 1960s by an 85-year-old lady who lived next door to Gretchen when she was growing up. This furniture was made from walnut trees on her grandmother's farm in Ohio.

Because "Linden" is located on six acres, there is plenty of room for a garden. You will find that much of breakfast comes from right on the property. There's a 200-year-old pecan tree that still provides pecans, and a hickory tree that provides some of the ingredients for Gretchen's Hickory Cake. There are apples and blueberries that they use as well. Even the eggs come from their own chickens. Many of Gretchen's breakfasts are seasonal such as the pumpkin pancakes in the fall.

With only two rooms, "Linden" is another homestay where you will find yourself quickly becoming a member of the extended family. Maybe it comes from flying kites, playing croquet, or just curling up with a good book in front of the fireplace. Personally I think that it's just the feeling of hospitality that we enjoyed at "Linden."

You'll find a number of very good restaurants in Farmville. At the recommendation of the innkeeper we tried Charley's Waterfront Café. (Yes, I had the peppercorn filet mignon.) The food was exceptional and the atmosphere cordial.

"Linden" Bed & Breakfast
Route 5, Box 2810; Farmville, VA 23901
(804) 223-8443
Innkeepers: Gretchen & Bob Rogers
Rooms: 2; With Private Baths: 1; With Shared Baths: 1; Rates: $$-$$$
Affiliations: BBAV, Farmville Area Chamber

Payment: $$$ CHECKS

Amenities:

Federal Crest Inn
Lynchburg

From the mid-nineteenth to the early twentieth centuries, an address in the Federal Hill district of Lynchburg assured you of being included among the "movers and shakers" of the community. The first area in Lynchburg to have gas lighting, it was on these slopes that Lynchburg's first millionaire built his home.

In 1909, a prominent Lynchburg attorney, David H. Howard, hired architect Aubrey Chesterman to design a Georgian Revival mansion. The site would be the corner of Federal and 11th Streets, which Howell considered to be best location in the district. The lot already contained an Italianate villa constructed in 1858. To build his home, Howard had to pay top dollar for the house and property and then have the villa torn down.

Howard spared no expense in the construction of his 8,000-square-foot home. Flemish bond brickwork on the outside and natural finish mahogany throughout the interior are just a few examples of the artistry that went into the construction. Elaborately hand-carved mahogany was used to create built-in bookcases and pocket doors. A grand central staircase leads up to a very large mezzanine, also constructed of hand-carved mahogany as were the moldings and trim work throughout the house.

Howard wanted his children to be able to write and present plays, so on the third floor he had a 1,300-square-foot room built with its own stage. Here, family, friends and neighbors would gather to watch the productions. Today, innkeepers Phil and Ann Ripley use the room as a meeting place for small groups.

Phil and Ann's backgrounds were in education before coming to Lynchburg; Phil as a publisher of educational materials and Ann as a teacher. When they decided to make a change in their lifestyle, they

spent two years looking for a place that could be both home and bed and breakfast. Federal Crest was a perfect choice.

The bed and breakfast appears to be very formal, yet Phil and Ann's easy-going manner has created a place where guests feel comfortable enough to prop up their feet. The house is large enough that there isn't a feeling of being confined and there are plenty of common areas in which to relax. The guest rooms are located on the second floor and all have private *en suite* baths. Rooms are named for trees that are native to Virginia and each is decorated to reflect its name.

Two of the rooms have adjacent sitting rooms with TV and three have in-room gas log fireplaces. Rooms feature queen-sized beds (two with canopies), antique and reproduction furniture and offer amenities such as down comforters, luxurious sheets and thick terry bathrobes. There are homemade treats and beverages in the room upon arrival and again at night. A snack basket is also found in each room.

"Early bird" coffee and juice are available before breakfast and the breakfast schedule is very flexible. A favorite at the inn is "message" muffins (muffins with inspirational messages) served each morning. Seasonal fruit or a homemade baked apple crisp, Federal Crest casserole, omelets with your choice of ingredients, French toast, waffles, pancakes, bacon, and sausage (or turkey bacon), are all a part of the excellent breakfast we had at Federal Crest.

Federal Crest Inn
1101 Federal Street; Lynchburg, VA 24504
(800) 818-6155; (804) 845-6155; Fax: (804) 845-1445
Innkeepers: Phil & Ann Ripley
Rooms: 2; **Suites**: 3; **All Private Baths**; **Rates**: $$ - $$$
Affiliations: PAII, BBAV, Lynchburg Chamber
Payment: VISA
Amenities:

Lynchburg Mansion Inn Bed & Breakfast
Lynchburg

The mansions in the Garland Hill Historic District are some of the finest you will find in the entire state of Virginia. Lynchburg Mansion Inn is the city's crown jewel. With 9,000 square feet, it is one of the largest on a brick street once known as Quality Row. As is fitting in a palace such as the Lynchburg Mansion, prepare to be pampered by innkeepers Bob and Mauranna Sherman.

The structure was built in 1914 for James R. Gilliam, Sr. at a cost of more than $86,000. When you consider that a family could live comfortably on an income of $1,000 a year, that was a princely sum. Gilliam was the president of five coal companies, the Lynchburg Shoe Company and six banks throughout the state. In 1913, his personal income for the year was $48,000, the highest in the city.

The mansion, located on just over half an acre, is surrounded by a six-foot-high iron fence with three separate entrance gates anchored in massive concrete piers. The roof of the 105-foot Spanish tiled veranda is supported by twenty-two massive columns. A columned *porte-cochère* provides covering for arriving guests.

Entering though the double doors, you step into a fifty-foot grand hall with wide cherry columns and cherry paneled wainscoting. The oak and cherry main staircase before you has 219 balustrades and winds up three stories. Seldom have I seen woodwork more detailed or more beautiful. Yet the lavishness of Lynchburg Mansion Inn does not stop with its woodwork.

This beautiful structure had been converted into apartments back in 1959. It took six months and twenty-five people per day working to restore it to its former glory. More time was required to carefully decorate it with the finest in antiques and period reproductions. The result is lavishly furnished and beautifully decorated guest rooms and suites with central air conditioning. Rooms feature king- or queen-sized beds, 200-thread count sheets,

private *en suite* baths and cable TV with six premiere movie stations. The list of amenities goes on and on, such as working fireplaces and a five-person spa on the rear veranda. In addition, there are complimentary sodas, coffee, tea, juices and popcorn in the suites.

At this writing I have stayed at more than 300 bed and breakfasts. Lynchburg Mansion Inn is at the top of my list for both quality and amenities. Of course, its setting in Lynchburg is also an advantage. We met some of the most delightful people in Lynchburg: from the staff at the Visitors Center to chefs at the restaurants we visited, everyone tried to make our stay as pleasant as possible.

You will find that Bob and Mauranna are very knowledgeable about the area and can help with recommendations of things to do, places to shop and restaurants to visit. Two of our favorite places to eat are Sachiko's and the new Meriwether's. During the week we spent in the area, we visited both restaurants several times and always found the food and service to our satisfaction.

While in the area be sure to visit Thomas Jefferson's home at Poplar Forest. It was designed as his personal retreat. Other historic sites you might consider visiting are Fort Early, Point of Honor and Anne Spencer's Home and Gardens. Walking tours of the gardens and mansions in the historic districts are also worthwhile for the history buff.

Lynchburg Mansion Inn Bed & Breakfast
405 Madison Street; Lynchburg, VA 24504
(800) 352-1199; (804) 528-5400
Innkeepers: Bob & Mauranna Sherman
Rooms: 3; **Suites**: 2; **All Private Baths; Rates**: $$ - $$$
Affiliations: PAII, Mobil★★★, BBAV, Lynchburg Chamber
Payment: $$$ CHECKS MC VISA AMEX Diner's Club
Amenities: A/C 📠 💻 🎖️ 🧳 ⊘

The Madison House Bed & Breakfast
Lynchburg

Located on the banks of the James River, Lynchburg is known as the City of Seven Hills. A short drive to the west will take you to the Blue Ridge Mountains and Parkway while to the east is Appomattox where the Civil War ended. There are so many historical sites in the area that it would take a week to visit them all. There are a number of museums including the Pest House Medical Museum and the Old Court House. If you enjoy historic architecture, you can take a driving or walking tour of five historic districts such as the Garland Hill area.

Garland Hill was named for a family who lived there for more than 100 years. Garland, a wealthy lawyer, built his home in 1846. By the 1880s the area was considered one of Lynchburg's most prestigious districts. That was when the Fleming family built what is now known as Madison House Bed and Breakfast. The family's descendants lived here until 1962.

Lynchburg was a major port for tobacco being shipped down the James River. Fleming's tobacco warehouse was one of the most important. Although Fleming contracted and supervised the work on the house himself, he hired architect Robert Burkeholder to design it. One of its more notable features is the cast-iron front porch. During construction, one unlucky worker must have put his pay packet over a door jamb which another worker then plastered over. During restoration, the innkeeper found a pay packet containing two dollars and thirty-five cents in silver coins dated 1864, 1874 and 1880. In the 1880s, this would have been a week's pay for a carpenter's assistant.

Innkeepers Irene and Dale Smith have worked carefully to preserve the Victorian flavor of the house. Wallpaper, drapes, antiques

throughout the house, the chandeliers and even the colors used for paint are strictly from the Victorian period of the 1880s.

In keeping with the Victorian era, the Madison House is the only bed and breakfast in the Lynchburg area that serves afternoon English tea. While tea is mainly for guests, it is not unusual to see locals stop by for English scones, oatmeal cake, hot milk cake, applesauce raisin cake, finger sandwiches, or one of the many other treats that Irene prepares.

One of the highlights at the Madison House is the Civil War library which contains a number of Civil War artifacts and more than 100 books plus magazines and newspapers. A professor from the University of North Carolina doing research on the Western Theater said it was one of the finest collections available.

Breakfast is served around the guests' time table instead of at a set time. The hosts have even served a full breakfast at six in the morning because guests had to leave early. While they can accommodate anyone's dietary restrictions, they serve a variety of items such as baked blueberry pancakes, eggs Benedict, oven omelets, egg popovers and ham and apple pie with cheese. Dinners, too, can be served on request. The Madison House also features The Good Knight Pub where guests can enjoy wine, beer or cocktails in front of a suit of armor.

The Madison House Bed & Breakfast
413 Madison Street; Lynchburg, VA 24504
(800) 828-6422; (804) 528-1503; Fax: (804) 528-4412
Innkeepers: Irene & Dale Smith
E-mail: madison@lynchburg.net
Rooms: 3; Suites: 1; All Private Baths; Rates: $$ - $$$
Affiliations: NBBA, Mobil, BBAV, Lynchburg Chamber
Payment:    Amenities:

Dulwich Manor Bed & Breakfast Inn
Lynchburg Area (Amherst)

Herman Page, an Englishman, built the house in 1912, a copy of his uncle's home in Dulwich, England. Located on a 1,250-acre working estate, it was his summer home while the family's main residence was in Norfolk. Dulwich Manor remained in the family until the early 1960s. A local millionaire bought the home, not to live in but to use as a school. He wanted his children in a private school so he established the Amherst Academy.

Innkeepers Bob and Judy Reilly spent most of there lives in professional theater. Bob was a photographer for 21 years. When in his 40s, he turned to acting. Over the years, he sang with the Buddy Rich Band and the Ray Charles singers. He performed on stage for more than 15 years. Judy, however, was in the business end of the theater in marketing and public relations. They met in the theater. In a way, they now own their own theater, a beautiful bed and breakfast, where the guest writes the script. The show Bob and Judy perform is a getaway adventure story.

A quarter-mile driveway leads to the 7,800-square-foot house on five acres of land. Dulwich Manor is an imposing site with its Flemish bond brickwork and fluted columns. Within its twenty rooms you'll find six comfortably large guest rooms each reminiscent of those in an English country home. Some rooms feature fireplaces while the Scarborough Room includes a whirlpool tub. All but one of the rooms have queen-sized beds and private baths. A house of this size required a great deal of work to restore and redecorate. Plastering, painting and papering every wall and refinishing the floors were all done within just four months, in time to open for the first guest to arrive.

Mornings bring the aroma of breakfast, which you will find on chafing dishes and warming trays on the long sideboard in the formal

dining room. As guests are free to have breakfast on their own time table, you will generally have all the privacy you might want. Fresh fruits, inn-baked hot breads, country sausage or bacon along with the innkeeper's own special entrées, help to start off a day of exploring.

With Lynchburg just 14 miles to the south and the Blue Ridge Mountains to the west, there is enough to hold your interest for days while staying at Dulwich Manor. Appomattox Courthouse, where the Civil War ended, is also nearby. While most of us are familiar with Monticello, the home of Thomas Jefferson, there is another Jefferson home: Poplar Forest was designed and built by Jefferson as his family retreat. It's located just southwest of Lynchburg.

With five historic districts in Lynchburg and a number of museums, Fort Early and Point of Honor (the restored home of Dr. George Cabell), Lynchburg is a great site for the historian. One of the more interesting stops in the area is known as Walton's Mountain Museum. Here, north of the Dulwich Manor, the creator of the popular television series grew up. The school he attended has been turned into a museum honoring the creator of the series. Within minutes of Dulwich Manor you will also find a number of good places for dinner. Bob and Judy can help with recommendations and reservations.

Dulwich Manor Bed & Breakfast Inn
550 Richmond Highway; Amherst, VA 24521
(804) 946-7207
Innkeepers: Bob & Judy Reilly
Rooms: 6; **With Private Baths**: 4; **With Shared Baths**: 2; **Rates**: $$
Affiliations: Mobil★★★, BBAV, Lynchburg Chamber, Amherst Chamber
Payment:
Amenities:

Fair View Bed & Breakfast
Lynchburg Area (Amherst)

Fair View Bed & Breakfast is located on six acres surrounded by a 240-acre farm. From the house there is a panoramic view of the mountains 12 miles away. Directly to the west is Mount Pleasant at a 4,000-foot elevation, also the peaks called Priest, Little Friar, Big Friar, and Devils Knob.

The Italianate style house was built in 1867, just two years after the Civil War, by Nathan Taliaferro, a doctor from New York City. The walls of this grand house, both exterior and interior, are nearly 12 inches thick. Most of the original glass is still in the house and you can see the bubbles and waves created in the handmade windowpanes.

Our hostess, Judy Noon, opened her first bed and breakfast, the Palmer House, in Columbia County, New York. Then along came her high school sweetheart, Jim. Twenty-three years after their high school romance, they made it to the altar. Since Jim's territory as a salesman for a safety equipment firm was in Virginia, the couple decided to search the back roads near the mountains for the perfect site for a new bed and breakfast. It took about eight months of exploring the mountains to find Fair View.

At Fair View, the Noons have created a very comfortable homestay that is family oriented. The house is decorated with family heirlooms, antiques and original art. A collection of stuffed bears sits on the winding staircase to guest rooms on the second floor. Old photos and Judy's paintings cover the walls. The three guest rooms, the Victorian, the Southwest and the Stockbridge, have their own distinctive personalities.

The Victorian, which we stayed in, had a four-poster bed, a handmade quilt, and a fireplace that will soon be converted to gas logs. The Southwest Room reminded me of the old Saturday morning horse operas I watched while growing up. It was decorated in browns, burgundies and

desert shades of off-white and the mountains were visible outside the windows. My favorite room was the Stockbridge, for it is a tribute to Judy and Jim's hometown of Stockbridge, Massachusetts. It is really a tribute to another Stockbridge resident, one of Judy and Jim's neighbors, Norman Rockwell. You will find a number of signed Rockwell prints on the walls. One is Rockwell's tribute to the Boy Scouts of America's 50th anniversary. Look closely, the scout in the middle is Jim.

Judy and Jim invite you to explore the property. The creek, just a short walk from the house, is a good site to watch for beaver. There's always bird watching or hiking. You can borrow an inn bicycle or canoe and take a ride, or just sit back on the porch swing and watch the endless show of shadows on the mountains. There is so much to do around Fair View that we didn't have the time to visit all the other places we wanted to see.

Outdoor enthusiasts will enjoy the 1,200-foot cascades of Crabtree Falls. Historians will enjoy the 200-year-old Woodson's Mill located just a few miles away. Other attractions within an hour's drive or less include Lynchburg's five historic districts and Appomattox Courthouse, where the Civil War ended. There's also Poplar Forest, designed by Thomas Jefferson as his family retreat. The Blue Ridge Mountains and Parkway are also just a short drive away.

Fair View Bed & Breakfast
2416 Lowesville Road (Rt. 778); Amherst, VA 24521
(804) 277-8500; Fax: (804) 277-8311
Innkeepers: Judy & Jim Noon
Rooms: 3; **All Private Baths**; **Rates**: $$
Affiliations: BBAV, Lynchburg Chamber, Amherst Chamber

Payment: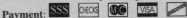

Amenities:

Winridge Bed & Breakfast
Lynchburg Area (Madison Heights)

Winridge offers the best of both city and country. Lynchburg, where you will find historic sites, shopping and excellent restaurants, is only a few miles to the south. Yet Winridge is a stately grand colonial southern home that is surrounded by acres of country meadows. The Blue Ridge Parkway is only 14 miles to the west and the second story porch across the back of the house offers a great view of the mountains.

Innkeepers LoisAnn and Ed Pfister and their two assistant innkeepers, Frances Katherine and Elizabeth Ann, have made a very comfortable retreat at Winridge, a one where you will feel completely at home. In fact, guests feel so much at home they often help in the gardens around the house. Along with their role as innkeepers, the Pfisters' have a very successful landscaping business that emphasizes floral and water landscaping. Helping in the garden is a great way to learn tricks you can use at home.

The house was built in 1910 for Wallace Taylor, inventor of the Piedmont Automobile. Taylor was only able to produce it for about four years, since during World War I, parts were too difficult to obtain. What parts he could get were just too expensive so Taylor moved back to Atlanta.

While the Pfisters' have restored the house and decorated it with a mix of antiques and modern furniture, it's the grounds that guests remember. You're welcome to explore the meadows, have a picnic under the trees or sit in the rockers on the veranda. There are hundreds of varieties of shrubs, flowers and trees. The frogs in the lily pond will lull you to sleep at night.

Both Ed and LoisAnn worked for Mariott before opening a bed and breakfast. They have been in the hospitality business for a long time

and it shows. They have learned the art of making people feel comfortable. It even shows in their morning breakfast. Guests pick the breakfast time, and they arrive to everything fixed freshly that morning. While the morning meal varies, there's stuffed French toast with apricot sauce, maple syrup muffins, gingerbread waffles, sourdough pancakes, or farm fresh eggs, hash browns, grits, sausage, bacon and biscuits.

Lynchburg is one of my favorite cities in Virginia. From the volunteers at the Welcome Center to JoAnn, our tour guide who showed us the sights, everyone we met seemed to go out of their way to make us feel welcome. Even the staff at the various restaurants we visited really cared that we had a good time. We did find a couple of places for dinner that we visited several times. The first, Meriwether's, was an experience in fine dining, while Cattle Annie's is a modern honky-tonk offering line dancing for entertainment and great steaks for dinner.

There's no limit to the number of historic sites in the area to visit: five historic districts, Poplar Forest, the retreat built by Thomas Jefferson, and Appomattox Courthouse where the Civil War ended. The James River flows through the middle of Lynchburg and offers opportunities for boating and fishing. Shopping opportunities abound, from antique shops to small out-of-the-way gift shops.

Winridge Bed & Breakfast
Winridge Drive; Route 1, Box 362; Madison Heights, VA 24572
(804) 384-7220; Fax: (804) 384-1399
Innkeepers: LoisAnn & Ed Pfister & Pfamily
E-mail: pfisterpfamily@juno.com
Rooms: 3; **With Private Bath**: 1; **With Shared Baths**: 2; **Rates**: $$
Affiliations: BBAV, Amherst County Chamber
Payment:  **Amenities**:

Mayfield Inn
Petersburg

This beautiful bed and breakfast was nearly lost in 1969 to developers who wanted to tear it down. Fortunately a group of concerned individuals and local preservation groups, with help from several state agencies, saved the house. The 300-ton house was moved intact to the four-acre site where it sits today.

Careful restoration of the foundation brickwork and the shingling was completed after the move. The house then sat empty for more than ten years. It was sold twice, but no one wanted the massive task of restoring the grand old lady. In 1979, local businessman Jamie Caudle and his wife, Dot, purchased the property with a determination to authentically restore the house. Their success was formally recognized in 1987 by the Association for the Preservation of Virginia Antiquities.

While it isn't certain who built Mayfield, it is known to be the oldest existing brick house in the county. Historians believe that it was Robert Ruffin. We do know that Ruffin, a member of the Virginia House of Burgesses, lived in the house from about 1750 until he moved from the county in 1769. At one time the house was owned by Captain Thomas Whitworth, the great-grandfather of Joseph Cotten, a noted movie actor, originally from Petersburg. During Robert E. Lee's final attempt to defend Petersburg in 1865, two defense lines were maintained on the property, Fort Whitworth and Fort Gregg. They fell to Union troops on April 2, 1865, while Lee watched from near the home.

The house is one-and-a-half stories over a raised English-style basement and constructed of Flemish bond brick. The roof, with five dormers at the front and rear, is wood-shingled. When the house was moved and the new shingles added, the workmen utilized eighteenth century tools and techniques under the supervision of the Virginia Landmarks Commission. Two interior chimneys are shared by seven fireplaces in the

house. The landscaped grounds include a gazebo and an award-winning herb garden as well as a 40-foot long swimming pool. The innkeepers have also paid a great deal of attention to detail throughout the house, using period antiques and the highest quality reproductions.

As would be fitting in a bed and breakfast with this rich history, breakfast is a true Virginia country-style feast with fresh fruit, eggs, bacon, sausage and hot biscuits. They try to serve a cooked-to-order breakfast as frequently as possible, working with the guest's schedule, not their own.

Petersburg's history goes back nearly three centuries to the mid-1600s when a garrison was built on the Appomattox River. Yet most will remember it from their history books in school as being the city that withstood the longest siege of any American city. Its history can best be understood by visiting the six Petersburg museums. Two of the most interesting are the Siege Museum and the Trapezium House. At the Siege Museum you will learn the story of how the citizens lived before, during and after the Civil War. The Trapezium House was built in 1817 without a parallel wall because the builder was told that such a house could not harbor evil spirits.

There are plenty of great restaurants in the area and your innkeeper can help with reservations. However, if you like good old fashioned bar-b-que, I recommend Kings, just down the street from Mayfield. It's owned by Jamie and Dot Caudle.

Mayfield Inn
3348 West Washington Street; P.O. Box 2265; Petersburg, VA 23804
(800) 538-2381; (804) 861-6775; Fax: (804) 863-1971
Innkeeper: Cherry Turner
E-mail: mayfield@ims-usa.net
Rooms: 2; **Suites**: 2; **All Private Baths**; **Rates**: $$
Affiliations: BBAV, Petersburg Chamber
Payment: Amenities:

Bellmont Manor Bed & Breakfast
Richmond Area (Chesterfield)

Antique lovers beware: you may have a hard time leaving Bellmont. There's just so much to see here and it starts with the house.

Bellmont is located on five acres and was originally called Locust Grove when it was constructed in 1726. It wasn't until the late 1790s that the name was changed to Bellmont. In the 1830s, new construction almost doubled the size of the house. In 1989, when Uly Gooch and his partner, Worth Kenyon, bought the property, they added to the house again. Today there is nearly 6,500 square feet of floor space and every foot is decorated with antiques and collectibles. The amazing thing is that all the antiques and collectibles seem to belong together, unlike many places where they seem out of keeping with the building or each other.

Almost all the antiques in the house are family heirlooms that Uly has inherited through the years. He has been collecting antiques all of his life. One of his most interesting collections is the 64 clocks throughout the house. Uly also runs an antique shop, "The Silver Rooster," on the grounds. Uly, by the way, is a retired priest, while his partner is still a social worker for the Veterans Administration Medical Center.

Chesterfield is more a rural area than a suburb, yet you're located just ten miles from the State Capitol in downtown Richmond. Driving down Belmont Road, there are still a number of small farms around the bed and breakfast, giving Bellmont Manor more of a country setting. Yet the property is protected by gates and two other members of the family, Miss Belle and K.G., German Shepherds who add to the feeling of security.

Meals at Bellmont are an experience, as one of your hosts is a "country gourmet" cook. You can look forward to a true example of a Virginia county breakfast. It can even be delivered to your door on the finest of silver service. The breakfast menu includes sausage, bacon, fried apples,

applesauce, grits, eggs, and always, fresh baked hot bread. Other meals can also be served with prior arrangement, and there is almost always a full cookie jar around. If you need something to hold you between meals, you can help yourself in the kitchen and pantry.

While Bellmont is off the beaten path, you can reach downtown Richmond in about 20 minutes and Interstate 95 in only five minutes. To the south is Petersburg where the longest siege of any American city took place during the Civil War. Richmond, of course, was the Capital of the Confederacy and historic points of interest are located throughout the city.

For the Civil War buff a trip to Richmond National Battlefield Park and Visitor Center should be one of your first stops when visiting the city. Here you have an overview of Richmond's Civil War battlefield. Another stop is the Museum and White House of the Confederacy. This comprehensive collection of military, political and domestic artifacts of the Confederacy is one of the finest in the country. The house was also Jefferson Davis's home during the war.

Of course, there are more than a dozen other museums from the Black History Museum to the Edgar Allan Poe Museum as well as botanical gardens, and a zoo. There's also Maymont, a 33-room Victorian Romanesque mansion with formal Italian and Japanese gardens near the heart of the city.

Bellmont Manor Bed & Breakfast
6600 Belmont Road; Chesterfield, VA 23832
(800) 809-9041 (PIN Code 69); (804) 745-0106; Fax: (804) 745-0740
Innkeepers: Uly Gooch & Worth Kenyon
E-mail: bellmont@aol.com
Rooms: 4; With Private Baths: 2; With Shared Baths: 2; Rates: $$
Affiliations: BBAV
Payment: Amenities: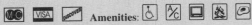

Uli Manor
Richmond Area (Midlothian)

The beautiful 6,200-square-foot home of Bill and Jennifer Chvala is located in a private community on the shores of the Swift Creek Reservoir. Since it's just a few miles outside Richmond in the suburb community of Midlothian, Uli Manor offers you easy access to the entire metropolitan area.

Uli Manor has only two guest rooms so it's more like visiting close family than staying at a bed and breakfast. That, however, is part of its charm and part of Bill and Jennifer's goal. They knew they had a place where guests could relax away from the hustle of Richmond, so they opened their home to guests shortly after construction was completed in April of 1995.

Bill and Jennifer have decorated their modern home with quality antiques and reproductions which fit nicely into the design of the house. Our room was very large and included its own TV. The gas fireplace added just the right ambiance to the room.

From the billiard room on the lower level to the screened porch overlooking Swift Creek Reservoir, your innkeepers want you to feel at home, and we did. Borrowing their canoe for a ride across the lake to Sundays Waterfront Restaurant helped.

I'll admit it didn't look quite so far across the lake on the map. We were however, ready for a good dinner when we arrived and we weren't disappointed. Sundays is where residents who live around the lake go for dinner. Just like at Uli Manor, we were made to feel a part of it all. While dining at Sundays is very casual, there is a dress code: no swim suits. You will see almost everything else. If the weather is nice, I recommend dining on the patio; the sunset was spectacular! You'll find the menu includes sandwiches as well

as pork chops with a wild mushroom sauce, farmland Black Angus strip steaks and a large variety of fresh seafood.

The trip back across the lake helped us to work off some of the calories from dessert although the chef assured us that all the desserts were calorie-free. A game of billiards, fresh popcorn and a movie on the big screen TV completed our day before we retired to our room.

The highlight of the continental breakfast is homemade cinnamon rolls. Bill will even share the recipe with you. Since your hosts are from the area, be sure to ask for suggestions on sights to see and places to visit. I also recommend picking up a copy of the *Insider's Guide To Richmond* so that you don't miss anything.

If you love early nineteenth-century architecture, be sure to add Maymont to your list of places to visit. This 33-room Victorian Romanesque mansion includes formal Italian and Japanese gardens, antique carriage rides, and a nature center. Nearby is Meadow Farm Museum, an 1860s living history farm. The Metro Richmond Zoo is also a worthwhile experience. If you decide to go to the Science Museum of Richmond, you'll drive through the historic Fan district and past the War Memorials on Monument Road. The memorials honor Virginians who have given their lives for their country. Edgar Allan Poe fans should stop at his museum which contains the largest collection of artifacts belonging to Poe.

Uli Manor
14042 Southshore Road; Midlothian, VA 23112
(804) 739-9817; Fax: (804) 639-1909
Innkeepers: Bill & Jennifer Chvala
Rooms: 2; All Private Baths; Rates: $$ - $$$
Affiliations: BBAV

Payment:
Amenities:

The Manor At Taylor's Store
Smith Mountain Lake

There is really only one way to describe the Manor At Taylor's Store: it's a "make yourself at home" type of place. The moment you're greeted by innkeepers Mary Lynn and Lee Tucker, you'll sense their easygoing hospitality. Of course, the country setting helps add to the down home feeling of the place. Even the amenities add to the general idea that you're here to make yourself comfortable.

The list of amenities seems almost endless: you'll find private porches, a billiard room, an exercise room, and even a guest kitchen. There is also a great room with fireplace, large screen TV and a good selection of movies to play on the VCR. Play the grand piano in the formal parlor. Relax in the sun room with a glass of iced tea and enjoy the plants and panoramic views of the countryside or hide away in the hot tub. Need to borrow a book? Visit the library. Are you looking for something else to do? You can take a walk over the more than 100 acres of land that make up the estate. Along the way you'll find six spring-fed ponds on the property. There are swimming docks and sun decks. You can borrow the canoe or a fishing pole to see if the fish are biting. Even a picnic lunch can be arranged to take to the gazebo. When evening comes, a European dinner basket may be ordered to enjoy in front of the fireplace in your room.

The Manor At Taylor's Store is truly a private resort yet one with a historical background. A historical marker at the road announces that this is the site of the Taylor's Store, founded in 1799 by Skelton Taylor. Mr. Taylor built a trading post that, over the years, served as ordinary and a gathering place for the community. From 1818 until 1933 it was the local Post Office. Even into the 1950s, square dances were held in the upstairs of the store. While the store was dismantled in the 1970s, the granary still stands. The massive brick columns you'll pass at the entrance were constructed with bricks from the old store.

The original manor house at Taylor's Store was built in the 1820s for the John Dewitt Booth family. Although the brick manor house was destroyed in a fire more than 70 years later, it was immediately rebuilt. The wood frame construction used timbers cut on the property. A hundred years later Dr. Henry Lee started restoration on the property which was completed by innkeepers Lee and Mary Lynn, who have carefully restored the house and decorated the main house with period antiques. But the inn doesn't end with just the three rooms and three suites in the manor house. There is also the West Lodge, a handhewn log home set in the woods, and the Christmas Cottage.

The West Lodge is decorated with antiques and includes three luxury suites that share a full guest kitchen. The great room with its stone fireplace is a favorite place to relax. The Christmas Cottage, with three bedrooms, two baths and a fully equipped-kitchen is perfect for families with children.

When the time comes that you are ready to explore the area around the inn, you might want to make your first stop the Booker T. Washington National Monument. Booker T. Washington was born here just before the Civil War. A few miles farther is Smith Mountain Lake, covering over 20,000 acres with nearly 500 miles of shoreline.

The Manor at Taylor's Store
Route 1, Box 533; Smith Mountain Lake, VA 24184
(800) 248-6267; (540) 721-3951; Fax: (540) 721-5243
Innkeepers: Lee & Mary Lynn Tucker
E-mail: taylors@sym.web
Rooms: 3; **Suites**: 6; **Cabins**: 1; **With Private Baths**: 8; **With Shared Baths**: 2
Rates: $$ - $$$$
Affiliations: NBBA, PAII, Mobil, BBAV, Roanoke Chamber, Smith Mtn. Lake Chamber
Payment: SSS CHECKS MC VISA AMEX **Amenities**: A/C ⬚ VCR ⬚ ⬚ ⬚ ⬚

The Mark Addy
Wintergreen Area (Nellysford)

The Mark Addy began in the 1840s as a simple farm house perched on a knoll. The design was typical of frontier homes: two rooms on the main floor and two rooms on the second. Somehow it managed to survive the conflict of the Civil War.

In July of 1884, Dr. John Coleman Everett came to the area to escape the wrath of both his parents and his in-laws. It seems that he had married far above his social status, and the frontier offered sanctuary. Everett and his wife purchased the house and its 680-acre farm with the goal of having the most commanding estate in the county. They began with her money and as his practice grew so did the house. A number of expansions took place over the years. By 1905, the manor house finally reached its present size of nearly 7,000 square feet.

Sitting on twelve-and-a-half acres, the Mark Addy is located in the small community of Nellysford, just 15 minutes from the Skyline Drive and only 30 minutes from Charlottesville. While the location is perfect, it took John Maddox and Saverio Anselmo nearly 18 months to find it.

The dream of owning an inn began while John was running a catering business in New York city. When he moved to Long Island, he continued catering and took over management of an antique store. As if that wasn't enough, he also was involved with the theater, both on stage and behind the scenes and finally as managing director. John was happier with these changes but, still the desire to be an innkeeper grew. It wasn't until his father passed away that he formed a partnership with his mother and began the search for just the right location. Their 18-month search brought them to Nellysford.

While the Mark Addy was operating as a bed and breakfast when John and Saverio arrived, they decided that a change in style and name was in order. The name "Mark Addy" is a tribute to John's grandparents,

Mark and Adelaide. But the style of the inn is John's. His years of involvement in the theater, his talents as a caterer and his knowledge of antiques have paid off.

The style is Victorian yet not overwhelming. Typically the Victorian style can be either dark or, more often, lacy, with stuffed pillows, ribbons and lace. Using family antiques and heirlooms and an eye for detail, John has created comfortable rooms where you're not afraid to sit down and relax. The mood is cheerful, romantic but not overpowering.

If you're fortunate enough to stay on a night when they're serving dinner, be sure to make a reservation. One of their dishes took top honors in the state-wide cook-off sponsored by the Virginia Cattle Industry.

Breakfast is also a treat at the Mark Addy. There is always a fruit course, such as honey dew, grapes, plums or broiled ginger grapefruit. The entrée always has an egg course, often a cheese soufflé, pastry cups, or eggs to order. In the winter they serve butterscotch French toast and heavier pancakes and waffles.

The area is rich with things to do, from exploring the Blue Ridge Mountains to playing golf at the world famous Wintergreen Resort. There's canoeing, rafting and skiing all within an easy drive. Of course, historic Charlottesville can keep you occupied for days.

The Mark Addy
56 Rodes Farm Drive; Nellysford, VA 22958
(800) 278-2154; (804) 361-1101
Innkeepers: John S. Maddox & Saverio Anselmo
E-mail: markaddy@symweb.com
Rooms: 9; **Suites**: 1; **All Private Baths; Rates**: $$ - $$$
Affiliations: NBBA, PAII, BBAV, Nelson County Chamber, Charlottesville Chamber
Payment: 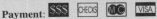 **Amenities**:

Trillium House at Wintergreen
Wintergreen Area (Nellysford)

A winding country road takes you from the valley far below up towards the Blue Ridge Parkway. Follow the road through the gates of Wintergreen into Trillium House's circular driveway. The grayed cedar exterior of the Trillium House blends so well with Blue Ridge Mountains you would think that it was a country farm house built early in this century. Yet the Trillium was built in 1983 to be a small self-contained inn in the heart of one of the finest four-season resorts in the country.

Located above 3,500 feet in the Blue Ridge Mountains, Wintergreen covers more than 11,000 acres. It's 36 holes of championship golf has earned it Golf Magazine's Silver Medal as one of the "Top Golf Resorts in the Country."

Its 25 tennis courts, pro shops and instructional programs have given it a rating as one of the top 50 tennis resorts by Tennis Magazine. Other activities include five swimming pools, a 20-acre lake for fishing, boating and swimming, stables for trail rides and more than 30 miles of marked hiking trails. Ski Magazine calls the area one of the "South's single-best ski areas." Its indoor/outdoor spa is without equal along the mid-Atlantic. All of Wintergreen is available to Trillium House guests with preferred rates for golf and tennis.

For all the amenities at Wintergreen, this is a mountain resort that has not destroyed its wilderness setting. Even the wooded acreage of Trillium House helps to create a feeling of being far from civilization, although you're really nestled into the woods just across from the 17th hole of the golf course.

Rockers on the porch at Trillium welcome you to the inn. During our short stay, I spent many hours enjoying their comfort as I watch squirrels and chipmunks scampering in the trees.

The double doors at Trillium lead you into a great room with cathedral ceiling and free-standing wood-burning stove. A stairway leads to the loft and its collection of leather chairs and good books.

Each of the ten rooms is modern in design and decorated with a blend of modern furnishings and antiques. Seven of the rooms offer queen-sized beds while other rooms include two twin beds. Two suites with queen-sized beds and separate sitting rooms are also available. The rooms all offer individually-controlled heat and air-conditioning and private baths. There's no television set to spoil the quiet mood, although one is available by request.

A full buffet-breakfast is served each morning in the dining room and on Friday and Saturday a *prix fixe* dinner is also available by advance reservation. Menus change daily but offer choices such as grilled chicken breast, beef carbonara and salmon steak.

You may find as we did that there is so much to do on top of the mountain that there is little reason to go elsewhere. However, if you are prepared to venture farther afield, both Charlottesville and Staunton are located nearby. Monticello, home of Thomas Jefferson and Ashlawn-Highland are both located in Charlottesville as is the University of Virginia. In Staunton is the Museum of Frontier Culture and the Birthplace of Woodrow Wilson, now a museum including his Pierce Arrow limousine. Just a few miles from Trillium is the Blue Ridge Parkway heading north to the Skyline Drive. To the south you can follow the Blue Ridge more than 400 miles into the Great Smoky Mountains.

Trillium House at Wintergreen
Wintergreen Drive; P.O. Box 280; Nellysford, VA 22958
(800) 325-9126; (804) 325-9126; Fax: (804) 325-1099
Innkeepers: Betty & Ed Dinwiddie
Rooms: 10; **Suites**: 2; **All Private Baths**; **Rates**: $$$
Affiliations: AAA, IIA, PAII, Mobil, BBAV, Waynesboro-East Augusta Chamber, Nelson County Chamber, Charlottesville Chamber
Payment: **Amenities**:

Shenandoah Region

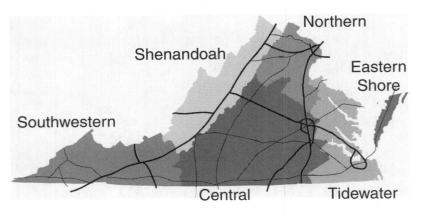

Longdale Inn
Clifton Forge

Alleghany County was mostly untamed wilderness when it was founded in 1822, but the Cowpasture River was navigable all the way to the James and on to Chesapeake Bay. Rich iron ore was found in the area and, in 1827, John Jordan and John Irvine erected the Lucy Selina Furnace along the banks of Simpson Creek. During the Civil War, the Lucy Selina Furnace was one of only 14 furnaces that supplied the Confederacy. It required three tons of iron ore to yield a single ton of pig iron, the average daily output for the furnace.

In 1870, English born William Firmstone and his partner purchased the furnace and 23,000 acres of land from Jordon and Irvine. Firmstone upgraded the furnace with new technology and within a few years, Longdale #1 (as the Lucy Selina was now known) and Longdale #2 became the most efficient furnaces in the nation. For the next thirty years, until 1911, it was a major producer of pig iron, making 70 to 120 tons a day. As workers moved in to work there, the area became known as Longdale Furnace.

In 1873, Firmstone's son, Harry, constructed a 7,000-square-foot, three-story Victorian with twenty rooms for his father just across from the furnace. William died before the mansion was completed and Harry became the master of the furnace. Here he lived as a feudal lord until his death in 1925. The home was built of the finest materials that money could buy, shipped in from all over the country by rail. The grounds were immaculately cared for and it was said that there were more varieties of trees on the grounds than any other property in the nation except the Rockefeller estate.

Nine buildings and the towering 106-foot high chimneys of the Longdale Furnace still remain. Firmstone's magnificent mansion,

listed on the Virginia Landmark Register and the National Register of Historic Places, has been restored as the Longdale Inn.

The dusty rose-colored Manor house sits on twelve acres. Within it, you will find some of the most beautiful workmanship imaginable. There are brass chandeliers that once operated on carbide gas that have now been electrified. There are also eight hand-painted marble fireplaces and 11-foot canvas ceilings embellished with hand-carved designs. The main hallway is 14 feet wide and 28 feet long and opens to a formal dining room that seats 30 people.

Eight bedrooms and one suite occupy the second and third floors. A second king-sized suite is located in a new addition on the main floor. All the rooms have been carefully restored and decorated with original and period antiques. A Victorian suite, doubling as the honeymoon suite, is done in white wicker. The Manor Room was Harry Firmstone's personal bedroom and contains several original pieces of his furniture. There's the Savannah Room with its hand-carved mantle of dogwood blossoms. There are rooms with twin beds, double beds, queen- and king-sized beds. Some rooms have views of the mountains and others have views of the grounds and gardens.

From the splendor of Longdale you can explore the splendor of the Alleghany Mountains. You might want to soak in the famed mineral baths at Warm Springs or play golf at the Homestead. There's swimming, boating and fishing at the nearby Douthat State Park.

Longdale Inn
6209 Longdale Furnace Road; Clifton Forge, VA 24422
(800) 862-0386; (540) 862-0892; Fax: (540) 862-3554
Innkeeper: Bob Cormier
Rooms: 8; **Suites**: 2; **With Private Baths**: 6; **With Shared Baths**: 4; **Rates**: $$ - $$$
Affiliations: PAII, BBAV, Lexington Chamber, Alleghany Highlands Chamber, RATHA
Payment: $$$ CHECKS MC VISA AMEX DISCOVER
Amenities: A/C

Milton Hall Bed & Breakfast Inn
Covington

The elevations of the Alleghany Highlands range from 1,000 to 4,049 feet above sea level. The mountains are covered by hardwood forests and a number of lakes and rivers dot the landscape. This is Virginia's Western Gateway. The first settlers arrived more than 250 years ago in 1746. For years they made their living as trappers, traders and farmers. In the early 1800s, the making of pig iron became the first major industry of the Highlands. By 1874, eleven iron furnaces were in existence.

Here in 1874, at the urging of her brother, Laura Marie Theresa Fitzwilliam (Viscountess Milton) built a 17-room English country manor on 130 acres for her ailing husband, Lord Milton. Lady Milton hoped that the peace and tranquility of the mountains would help return Lord Milton to health.

The brick Gothic Revival house with its gables, buttressed porch towers and 14 fireplaces sitting within an English garden was an exotic contrast to the rustic surroundings of the mountains. While great attention had been paid to construction, the interior was rather ordinary without the typical ornate woodwork generally found in the Gothic Revival style.

The house has retained its charm over the years. Within it, innkeepers John and Vera Eckert have created a restful haven for visitors to this mountain destination. The five large guest rooms and one suite have been decorated for comfort and are quite suitable for extended stays. All the rooms are large enough to accommodate an additional person. Queen-sized beds, wood-burning fireplaces and comfortable sitting areas will be found in each room. Several rooms have cable television and phone available.

Forty-three acres remain of the original estate. As you drive past the nearly three-quarters of an acre of English gardens, there is a feeling of

having been transported to another time—another country. Vera's soft British accent (she was born in Yorkshire, England) seems to add to the ambiance of the inn. Vera and John offer guests a full country-style breakfast in the formal dining room.

While Milton Hall provides a restful backdrop for a hideaway week-end, its location makes it suitable for visiting the attractions in the area. Virginia's oldest standing covered bridge is just two miles away and makes a perfect picnic spot. The innkeeper can even prepare an elegant basket lunch. For the hiker, a suitable picnic lunch can be packed to take along one of the many trails at Douthat State Park, Lake Moomaw, or to Falling Spring waterfall.

The amenities of the Homestead are available to area guests and offer a variety of activities from golf to skeet shooting. Tennis, horseback riding or carriage rides, the invigorating waters of Warm Springs and, in season, skiing and ice skating are also available. For many, the chamber music offered at the Garth Newel Music Center in Hot Springs is a must when visiting the area. You may be surprised to see international stars of screen and theater in the audience.

There are many fine dining opportunities in the area including Greenbrier and the Homestead. Places such as the Cat & Owl offer more casual dining. John and Vera can help with suggestions and reservations.

Milton Hall Bed & Breakfast Inn
207 Thorny Lane; Covington, VA 24426
(540) 965-0196
Innkeepers: John & Veronica Eckert
Rooms: 5; **Suites**: 1; **All Private Baths; Rates**: $$ - $$$
Affiliations: BBAV, Shenandoah Valley Travel Assoc., Covington Chamber

Payment:

Amenities: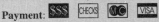

Chester House
Front Royal

Brochures on the small Blue Ridge community of Front Royal proclaim that there is no place like it on earth. I am inclined to agree. Like a magnet, the area draws you back time and again.

Front Royal has been a wellspring of hospitality in the Blue Ridge Mountains since colonial days. Its variety of activities ranges from canoeing the Shenandoah River to exploring the depths of the earth at Skyline Caverns. Here, too, is the beginning of the Skyline Drive, a 105-mile road that follows the Blue Ridge through the Shenandoah National Park.

In the heart of all this is one of our favorite places to stay, the Chester House, an architectural gem situated on two acres. The grounds include a formal terraced garden ringed by boxwoods and filled with old-fashioned wisteria arbors as well as ancient dogwoods and oaks. Stone steps and brick walks lead to a fountain hidden deep within the maze of flowers and shrubs. The Georgian style mansion, built by Charles Samuels in 1905, was created with the finest turn-of-the-century craftsmanship. No expense was spared.

Within its 5,500 square feet you will find nine decorative fireplaces with marble mantles, ceilings with superb dentil moldings, hardwood floors and ornate fixtures original to the house. To this, innkeepers Bill and Ann Wilson have added furnishings and art that blend perfectly with the style and grace of this wonderful hideaway.

Five guest rooms and one suite are located within the main house. Recently a guest cottage has been completed on the grounds. The cottage was once a two-story concrete "cow barn" that housed the Samuels' family pet cow. The suite, which overlooks the garden, includes a working fireplace, a queen-sized four-poster bed and its own sitting room. Each of the other guest rooms, the Blue Ridge, Appalachian, Skyline, Happy Creek and Chester Gap, has been carefully decorated to offer the finest in accommodations.

We found that the brochure's promise of "hand-ironed sheets, thick terry robes, soft pillows, firm mattresses and fluffy towels," was fulfilled. In fact, they were only the beginning of the care that the innkeepers bestow upon their guests. Nightly turn-down service, fresh-cut flowers, bed-side mints and a fire lit in the fireplace topped off our perfect evening at Chester House.

Sterling silver and bone china settings greeted us in the formal dining room after our night's rest. The Wilsons serve a continental-plus breakfast that includes fresh-squeezed orange juice, locally produced apple cider, a selection of cereals accompanied by fresh fruit, and homemade breads. That was more than enough to hold us until lunch at one of the few true dairy bars left in the state.

Within the city of Front Royal, you will find a variety of restaurants. They range from the local Royal Dairy Bar with its made-to-order milkshakes and thick juicy hamburgers to the Stadt Kaffee Restaurant with its authentic German dinners. Bill and Ann know the area well and can help with recommendations and reservations for just about anything your taste buds might demand.

Outdoor activities abound in the area. In addition to its natural setting against the Blue Ridge Mountains, Front Royal is rich in history. Just two doors from the Chester House is the home of Confederate spy, Belle Boyd. Here also is the Confederate Museum with its history of the Civil War and the legendary Stonewall Jackson and his Valley Campaign.

Chester House
43 Chester Street; Front Royal, VA 22630
(800) 621-0441; (540) 635-3937; Fax: (540) 636-8695
Innkeepers: Bill & Ann Wilson
E-mail: chesthse@rma.edu
Rooms: 5; **Suites**: 1; **Cottages**: 1; **With Private Baths**: 5; **With Shared Baths**: 2
Rates: $$ - $$$
Affiliations: Mobil★★★, BBAV, Front Royal/Warren County Chamber
Payment: $$$ CHECKS MC VISA AMEX **Amenities**: A/C ✍ 🖥 VCR ⛷ ♠ ☺

Killahevlin
Front Royal

For weeks before I arrived in Front Royal, I had been listening to innkeepers and travelers telling me about Killahevlin. I had heard so many stories that I finally came to the opinion that they had all kissed the "Blarney Stone." That was until I turned into the lane at Killahevlin. As I sat at the bottom of the highest knoll in Front Royal and looked up at the imposing Edwardian Mansion at the top, I knew there might be some truth to all I had been hearing.

I'm glad to say that it didn't take long to realize that for innkeepers Susan and John Lang, restoration of Killahevlin has been a true labor of love. They both have enough Irish in their blood to truly appreciate the spirit of the Irish, and, just as important, to appreciate Killahevlin's builder, William Edward Carson.

Carson, an Irish immigrant, came to America in 1885 at age 15. He graduated from the University of Virginia with a law degree and became an active figure in local, state and national politics. It was Carson who is credited with the creation of the historic roadside markers that you will find throughout the state and with the creation of the Skyline Drive that runs along the Blue Ridge through the Shenandoah. The home he built in Front Royal was a tribute to his homeland.

When Susan and John first arrived at Killahevlin, the house was in terrible shape. It was structurally sound, but years of neglect had taken its toll. They knew that purchasing the three-acre Killahevlin estate would require a deep commitment to bring it back to life. Since the day they took residence in 1990, they have made tremendous progress in their restoration work and created a haven for the traveler.

A project of this size takes time. When we were there, work was still underway on some of the public areas. With the help of a talented interior designer and several local artisans, most of the work has now

been completed. Each of the guest rooms and guest suites has been carefully restored and decorated.

One of their biggest accomplishments is the guest suites located in the historic Tower House that sits about 50 feet behind the main house. The Tower was built in 1905 as a combination guest house and water tower. Here, they have created two modern suites complete with turn-of-the-century antiques, private porches, sitting room with TV, and a special treat, double whirlpool tubs.

The Irish Pub is also a personal favorite. Here guests can belly up to the fitted oak bar with its brass foot-rail and get a complimentary Irish draft beer on tap. Some just like to sit with a cold soft drink and play a game of backgammon or cribbage.

Working fireplaces, period antiques, nineteenth-century wallpapers and beautifully restored woodwork greet the visitor to Killahevlin. However, the amenities only start there. Fresh baked cookies and evening turn-down service (complete with handmade chocolates on the pillows) add to the luxury of Killahevlin.

There was no "Blarney Stone" at Killahevlin, just a comfortable blend of Southern hospitality and Irish charm.

Killahevlin
1401 North Royal Avenue; Front Royal, VA 22630
(800) 847-6132; (540) 636-7335; Fax: (540) 636-8694
Innkeepers: Susan & John Lang
E-mail: kllhvln@shentel.net
Rooms: 4; **Suites**: 2; **All Private Baths**; Rates: $$$
Affiliations: ABBA, PAII, BBAV, Bed & Breakfast of the Historic Shenandoah Valley
Payment:  **Amenities**: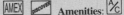

Woodward House on Manor Grade
Front Royal

One of the most scenic drives in America is the Skyline Drive through the Shenandoah National Park. Completed in August 1939, the road begins at Front Royal and follows the crest of the Blue Ridge Mountains for 105 miles. As the gateway to the Shenandoah National Park, Front Royal is a hospitable community that has welcomed millions of visitors over the years.

Just a few blocks north of the beginning of the Skyline Drive, and about the same distance from downtown Front Royal, Woodward House on Manor Grade sits high above the main thoroughfare. This Colonial-style home was built in 1910 by the Woodward family. It is the oldest, continuously operated inn located in the area. It first opened its doors as a boarding house in 1939. Germany invaded Poland, war was inevitable and the largest rayon manufacturing plant in the world opened in Front Royal. Its opening created a housing shortage and the Woodward house operated as a boarding house under the name Rambler's Rest. When the war was over, the name changed to Stony Ledge and tourists began driving the Skyline Drive. For the next 35 years Stony Ledge was a favorite stopover. The name changed again in 1975 to the Constant Spring Inn but it was still a favorite stopping place.

When Joan and Bob Kaye arrived in Front Royal in 1993, the house had been a haven for travelers for more than 50 years. The new innkeepers wanted to honor the original builders so the name was changed to Woodward House on Manor Grade. With its rich heritage as a getaway spot for travelers and a major overhaul by the new innkeepers, Woodward House was ready to serve a new generation of travelers.

The floors may creak a bit, but it's easy to see the care that has gone into making the five suites and three guest rooms as comfortable as possible. Private baths, an eclectic blend of antiques and country pieces, king- and queen-sized beds and color cable television in each accommodation will help to make Woodward House a favorite for years to come. Special touches throughout the bed and breakfast are Joan's doll collection and Bob's historic photographs.

The breakfast at Woodward House would be reason enough to stay. They serve a full country-style breakfast. First comes juice and a fruit cup. The second course is one of a variety of hot and cold cereals. The third course is a surprise course with homemade muffins. Next is the entrée that might include eggs cooked to order, cheese omelets, French toast, or pancakes. On some mornings there's hash browns with mushrooms and tomatoes. There's always coffee, tea and hot chocolate.

A new addition to Woodward House is the guest bar with its free draft beer, wine and snacks. Guests often spend part of their evenings here or in front of one of the two fireplaces in the common areas. Of course you may want to take time to explore downtown Front Royal. It's just an easy walk to the center of town.

Woodward House on Manor Grade
413 South Royal Avenue; Front Royal, VA 22630
(800) 635-7011; (540) 635-7010; Fax: (540) 635-8217
Innkeepers: Joan & Bob Kaye
E-mail: woodhous@rma.edu
Rooms: 3; Suites: 5; All Private Baths; Rates: $$$
Affiliations: ABBA, NBBA, BBAV, Front Royal/Warren County Chamber
Payment:  Amenities:

Hearth N' Holly Inn
Harrisonburg Area (Penn Laird)

Located just a few miles outside Harrisonburg, the Hearth N' Holly Inn sits on 15 acres of woods and pastures. The house, built in the late 1880s, was originally the manor house for a large farm. Like many houses of the period, it was built in the Colonial style. Its Victorian elements were added to the home during later remodeling.

On the grounds, guests will find a small pond, trails for hiking and a stream. This is a place to come and relax. Recently the innkeepers have built a large new picnic pavilion complete with hot tub, portable gas grill, picnic table and chairs and a queen-sized hammock. It's far enough away from the house for privacy but close enough that you won't mind the walk.

When innkeepers Doris and Dennis Brown decided to open their home as a bed and breakfast, they didn't have any experience at staying at bed and breakfasts. What they knew was what they didn't like about staying at motels and hotels. A friend who was an innkeeper suggested that the best way to start would be to make a list of their complaints about places they had stayed. It proved to be good advice. They started with no preconceived notions about what a bed and breakfast should or should not be. Time and experience, along with attending workshops on being innkeepers, have helped them create a very comfortable place for guests.

Three large guest rooms, each decorated with antiques, fine carpets and fabrics, are available for guests. Each room includes a private bath, an antique brass bed, working fireplace and plenty of room to relax. The rooms also have cable TV, complete with the Disney Channel, as well as a VCR and a selection of movies just in case it rains.

While there is a very comfortable downstairs living room with an old pump organ, guests find the sun porch a favorite place to relax. The sun

porch is also where breakfast is served. I would have to call it a modern country breakfast. Of course, there are breakfast meats and old stand-bys like eggs and traditional pancakes but there are also some special entrées as well. You might find yourself dining on blueberry pancakes with blueberry sauce, lemon pancakes with lemon sauce or sour cream waffles with a spiced pear sauce. On other mornings you might find soufflés, German apple pancakes or the house specialty of eggs with Monterey Jack cheese rolled and served on a bed of spinach leaves garnished with a mustard sauce. You could stay for days and never have the same breakfast twice.

Dennis does all the cooking and by prior arrangement he will prepare dinner as well, anything from beef to fish or chicken. He makes all of his own sauces and homemade breads. Like the breakfast menu, dinner can vary from day to day.

The area around the Hearth N' Holly Inn offers guests many reasons to climb out of the hammock and wander around. To the east are the 105 miles of the Skyline Drive that winds through the Shenandoah National Park. Historic Staunton, where you will find the Museum of Frontier Culture, is to the south.

In Harrisonburg, just a few miles to the west, there are James Madison University, Bridgewater College and the Eastern Mennonite College and Seminary. There are also antique shops, live theater, and a number of fine restaurants.

Hearth N' Holly Inn
Route 2, Box 655; Penn Laird, VA 22846
(800) 209-1379; (540) 434-6766
Innkeepers: Dennis & Doris Brown
E-mail: hhinn@aol.com
Rooms: 3; All Private Baths; Rates: $$
Affiliations: BBAV, Harrisonburg/Rockingham County Chamber
Payment: Amenities:

Inn at Keezletown Road Bed & Breakfast
Harrisonburg Area (Weyers Cave)

One of the great things about the Inn at Keezletown Road is that it is located close to so many major points of interest in the Shenandoah Valley. The inn is just a mile east of Interstate 81 in the small village of Weyers Cave. To the east, just twenty minutes away, are the Skyline Drive and the Shenandoah National Park. Following the interstate, Harrisonburg is only a 10-minute drive to the north while Staunton is about the same distance to the south.

Harrisonburg is a thriving city and home to more than 20 major industries. Bridgewater College, Eastern Mennonite College and Seminary and James Madison University are all located here. Further west is the George Washington National Forest.

Staunton is much different from Harrisonburg and a great place to explore Victorian architecture and museums. Antique shops, fine dining, and a number of historic sites can be found throughout the area around Staunton. The birthplace of Woodrow Wilson and the Museum of Frontier Culture are located here.

Of course, location isn't the only reason to stay at the bed and breakfast that Alan and Sandy Inabinet have created. Comfortable rooms and good food are two other excellent reasons. The Inn at Keezletown Road is located in a large Victorian house with gingerbread trim built by Dr. Sellers in 1896. Oriental rugs and Victorian wallpapers have been added to the Shenandoah antiques to create a bright and cheerful setting. Family heirlooms, the personal collections of the innkeepers and a variety of art can be seen throughout the house. Vintage ceiling fans and central air-conditioning help ensure comfort on the rare warm evening. During cool evenings, the fireplace in the common area adds to the ambiance.

Each of the four guest rooms is large enough to accommodate a sitting area complete with color cable TV. The main floor guest room includes its own fireplace. The design of the house permits each guest room to have windows on two sides. And most rooms offer spectacular views of the Blue Ridge Mountains. Most of the acre lot is covered with perennial and herb gardens that help create a pleasant atmosphere making the terrace a perfect place to just sit back and relax.

Since the Inn at Keezletown Road will prepare dinners on weekends or for special occasions, we chose to try Sandy's cooking instead of driving to one of the nearby towns. Sandy and Alan's special dinner is by advanced reservation only and I can say that it was well worth it. The *prix fixe* meal includes appetizer, salad, fresh hot bread, entrée and a selection of desserts. Dinner varies depending on the season and the guests' taste but Sandy can handle just about anything from local trout to pork or beef dishes. The portions were large, more than we would have had at most restaurants.

Sandy serves a full country gourmet breakfast each morning. The eggs couldn't be any fresher since they come from their own chickens. In keeping with their desire to pamper guests, Alan and Sandy use North Carolina sausage and ham and their bacon is from the Pennsylvania Dutch. Entrées of pumpkin or lemon pancakes, Belgian waffles or Grand Marnier French toast are a great way to start a day.

Inn at Keezletown Road Bed & Breakfast
1224 Keezletown Road; Weyers Cave, VA 24486
(800) 465-0100; (540) 234-0644
Innkeepers: Alan & Sandy Inabinet
Rooms: 4; All Private Baths; Rates: $$
Affiliations: BBAV, Inns of the Historic Shenandoah Valley
Payment:
Amenities:

Kings Victorian Inn
Hot Springs

Hot Springs captures the imagination as few areas in the country can. Most of us have read about or seen movies depicting the lifestyles of the rich and famous, such as the Rockefellers, Fords and Vanderbilts at world-class spas. At Kings Victorian Inn we have the opportunity to sample that lifestyle by staying in a grand Victorian home built in 1899. Within a stone's throw of the Inn are all the amenities of one of the world's last great spas, the Homestead.

The history of Hot Springs dates back to the Indians who found that the warm spring waters seemed to have miraculous healing powers. The first white men arrived in the area in the early 1700s. In 1760 a rustic log inn was erected and called the Homestead. By the turn of this century, a great resort spa covering nearly 15,000 acres beckoned the well-heeled from around the globe. Local doctor Henry S. Pole built his home just down from the Homestead. The house was without equal in the area with its turrets, bay windows and a veranda that extends around most of the house.

Over the years, the home had changed hands many times and served many purposes. In 1987, Liz and Richard King discovered the property while on vacation. Their vision, combined with a lot of hard work, has created one of the finest bed and breakfasts in the entire area. They have lovingly restored the great Victorian home and decorated it with country elegance.

The three-story Victorian sits back under a grove of old maple trees on three acres of land. The veranda is a favorite resting place with its wicker chairs and rockers. Inside, two parlors (one formal and one casual) are decorated with thick oriental carpets. The house is light and airy with none of the clutter and darkness that would have existed in the home during the early 1900s. Quality fabrics adorn

windows and carefully selected antique reproductions fit comfortably in the six guest rooms, cottage and common areas.

Afternoon refreshments are available upon arrival and a full breakfast is served in the formal dining room. For breakfast you might have bacon or sausage; eggs, pancakes or French toast; hash browns and homemade biscuits. This is a true country breakfast, one that will stay with you as you explore the area.

With all the amenities of Homestead available, including the waters of Warm Springs just a few miles down the road, you would be hard pressed to not find something to enjoy. Depending on the season there are skiing and ice skating, skeet shooting and tennis. There are walking trails and waterfalls to explore, horseback riding, carriage rides and trout streams that offer excellent opportunities for fishing. Of course, many come to play the three championship golf courses at the Homestead.

During its season the Garth Newel Music Chamber offers a variety of programs. I was amazed to hear about some of the internationally-known stars found in the audience. With the Homestead so near, there are a variety of dining opportunities available. You will find both casual and candlelight dining at the Homestead. There is also a historic restaurant located in an old mill at nearby Warm Springs.

Kings Victorian Inn
Route 1, Box 622; Hot Springs, VA 24445
(540) 839-3134
Innkeepers: Richard & Liz King
Rooms: 6; **Cottages**: 1; **With Private Baths**: 4; **With Shared Baths**: 3; **Rates**: $$ - $$$
Affiliations: BBAV

Payment:

Amenities:

Applewood Inn
Lexington

The drive to Applewood Inn starts on one of Virginia's most scenic highways, Route 11. It runs between Lexington and Natural Bridge, one of the seven natural wonders of the world. Just south of Lexington, state route 678 (Buffalo Bend Road) veers off to the west. For nearly a mile it follows the channel that Buffalo Creek has cut through the rock. With the rock formations on the left and the creek to the right, it's easy to imagine that you're a hundred miles from civilization instead of only five miles from Lexington.

Applewood Inn is located on 35 acres with views of House Mountain and the Short Hills. With 900 acres of the Rockbridge Hunt bordering their property, innkeepers Chris and Linda Best can assure their guests' privacy. Birds and wildlife are abundant on the property. Four llamas and a sheep have their own grazing area. You can hike, bird watch, go on a llama trek with the innkeepers or go fishing or tubing in Buffalo Creek. You can also relax on the deck or take a dip in the 20- by 40-foot oval pool.

Built at an elevation of 1,100 feet, the house at Applewood is unique in its use of passive solar technology and natural materials. Constructed in 1979, the house has three levels. The ground level opens to the front, the middle level opens onto the ends and the upper level opens to the rear. Porches are enclosed to help with solar heating. There's a little more than 4,500 square feet of space within the house. The porches are all made of natural wood and provide excellent views of the mountains.

Three guest rooms had been completed and a fourth was being remodeled when we visited Chris and Linda. On the second level is the Hillside Room with its four-poster converted rope bed and the Autumn Room which shares a porch with it. On the first level, the European Room opens onto a small porch adjoining the hot tub. The room under construction was the Quilter's Room, also located on the first level, which

should be completed by the time this book returns from the printer. The Quilter's Room includes a whirlpool tub and wood stove. The kitchen is available for all guests' use.

While Applewood Inn is new, Chris and Linda are not new to the role of innkeepers. For 18 years they owned and operated Seekonk Pines Inn in the Berkshires of Western Massachusetts. Their experience as innkeepers has helped them to create a comfortable bed and breakfast in a very natural setting.

The breakfast changes daily: most breakfasts are heart-healthy with whole-grain baked goods and fresh seasonal fruit. Hazelnut pancakes, wheat germ and cornmeal waffles accompanied by a variety of breakfast meats are just a sampling. For the early or very late riser, a continental breakfast can be easily arranged.

While you may want to just sit back, relax and enjoy the beauty of Applewood Inn's secluded acreage, the area includes a variety of activities from horseback riding to Theater at Lime Kiln in Lexington. The Virginia Horse Center is located in Lexington and a carriage ride through the historic district of the city is a delightful way to become familiar with the area. Natural Bridge and Caverns and Goshen Pass are both within an easy drive.

Applewood Inn
Buffalo Bend Road; P.O. Box 1348; Lexington, VA 24450
(800) 463-1902; (540) 463-1962; Fax: (540) 463-6996
Innkeepers: Linda & Christian Best
Rooms: 3; Suites: 1; All Private Baths; Rates: $$ - $$$
Affiliations: BBAV, PAII, RATHA
Payment: $$$ CHECKS MC VISA AMEX
Amenities:

A B&B at Llewellyn Lodge
Lexington

Recently I was asked by friends what I remembered most about Llewellyn Lodge. They were looking for a place to stay in town that would be as close as possible to Washington and Lee University. The first thing that came to mind was breakfast. It was so good that I'm glad I have a standing invitation. Of course there are many other reasons to stay at Llewellyn Lodge. Sometimes, breakfast alone can be enough, especially when the cook knows how to get the eggs just right and the waffles are light and airy.

Llewellyn is located near Lexington's historic district and only a few blocks from downtown and Washington and Lee University. It's a Colonial-style brick home built in 1947 as a tourist home. While many think that the concept of bed and breakfasts is a European import, bed and breakfasts in America actually predate the Civil War. Tourist homes were just one of the many types that existed before evolving into the present form. Most of the tourist homes in Lexington were for young ladies who came to dances at the Virginia Military Institute or for parents visiting sons and daughters at school.

The house had been converted into a single family home by the time that Ellen Roberts came to Lexington to open a bed and breakfast in 1985. Her understanding of the needs of travelers and cooking skills had been well honed during the 30 years she had worked with the traveling public at airlines, hotels and restaurants. Still, opening a bed and breakfast as a single woman required a lot of determination. Shortly after opening Llewellyn Lodge, Ellen met and married John Roberts. Together they operate one of Lexington's oldest bed and breakfasts.

Six guest rooms, all with private baths, feature extra-firm mattresses on antique beds. Each room is distinctive and designed to meet the

needs of a variety of guests. One room features a king-sized bed while another has two twin-sized brass beds. A room on the main floor was designed to accommodate a handicapped person who does not require a wheelchair. An eclectic blend of period antiques and items Ellen has collected in her travels decorate the rooms and common areas.

John is a local who knows all the best hiking trails and fishing holes in the county. Guests also find him a wealth of information on local history and Civil War sites. Occasionally John can be talked into showing you his favorite fishing hole. Ellen, on the other hand, can help with reservations for dinner or for a round of golf at the local country club. And, of course, it's Ellen who prepares that memorable breakfast about which I was telling you.

Llewellyn Lodge is one of the very few bed and breakfasts that offers a breakfast menu. A variety of juices, such as apple, orange, V8 and ruby red grapefruit, starts out the menu choices. You may have eggs any style, a choice of ham, sausage or bacon complemented with the muffin of the day, toast or English muffins. There are also Ellen's Belgian waffles topped off with Virginia maple syrup or her special made-to-order omelets. Whatever you choose, it will get you started on a day of exploring Washington and Lee University, the Virginia Military Institute or Lexington's historic district.

A B&B at Llewellyn Lodge
603 South Main Street; Lexington, VA 24450
(800) 882-1145; (540) 463-3233; Fax: (540) 464-3122
Innkeepers: John & Ellen Roberts
E-mail: LLL@rockbridge.net
Rooms: 6; All Private Baths; Rates: $$
Affiliations: NBBA, PAII, BBAV, Lexington Chamber
Payment: Amenities:

Brierley Hill Country Inn
Lexington

It was quite a change in lifestyle for Carole and Barry Speton when they moved from their home in Vancouver, Canada to the Shenandoah Valley of Virginia. A change, yes, but they couldn't have picked a better location than the side of a hill just a mile outside Lexington. From their porch they have commanding views of the Blue Ridge Mountains to the east and the Allegheny Mountains to the west.

Before coming to the Virginia, Barry was an attorney and Carole the former director of the National Canadian Figure Skating Association. However, a trip to the mountains to visit their daughter at school in Buena Vista was the catalyst to their change of lifestyles. During the trip they discovered the eight acres that would soon be their new home.

Careful planning went into the design of the bed and breakfast they would build from scratch. An English-style country home was selected as a design model. Antiques, Oriental rugs, paintings and family heirlooms brought from Canada were to fill the rooms. Carole created paper templates of her furniture and used graph paper to make sure everything would fit just right. When the 5,000-square-foot house was completed in 1993, fabrics and wall coverings by Laura Ashley were added to enhance the English country look.

The result was several comfortable common areas, five guest rooms and one suite, each with its own distinctive personality. The largest is the Rose Suite located on the lower floor. Here, guests can enjoy their own private patio, fireplace and a double Jacuzzi bath. All the rooms have been carefully designed to offer scenic views of the mountains, meadows or the flower and herb gardens.

The windows of the dining area offer an excellent view of the mountains and the fireplace adds to the overall ambiance. During most of the week Brierley Hill operates as a bed and breakfast. However on Thursday, Friday and Saturday, a four-course *prix fixe* dinner is served (by prior reservation).

Carole is a graduate of the La Varenne Cooking School in West Virginia. Her meals indicate that she must have graduated with top honors. While the menu changes daily, here are a few samples of Carole's specialties: salmon Wellington, sea scallops, roasted game hen and pork tenderloin with onion marmalade. Of course, guests have the opportunity to enjoy Carole's cooking each morning as she prepares dishes such as Grand Marnier French toast, Belgian waffles, or baked blintzes with ricotta cheese.

Looking down into the valley from the meadow above Brierley Hill, you quickly realize what brought your innkeepers from Canada's west coast to the mountains of Virginia. The view can only be described as perfect as a picture postcard. We couldn't wait to begin the adventure of exploring the valley below.

The area around Lexington is rich in history and natural beauty. World-famous Natural Bridge is considered one of the seven natural wonders of the world and lies only 15 miles from town. Swimming, tubing, hiking, picnicking, and fishing are all popular past times in the great mountain gorge at Goshen Pass.

For the historian, Lexington was the home of Stonewall Jackson, one of the Confederacy's most famous generals. Theater at Lime Kiln offers performances each summer and the Virginia Horse Center schedules a variety of horse shows, trials and auctions.

Brierley Hill Country Inn
Route 2, Box 21A Borden Road; Lexington, VA 24450
(800) 422-4925; (540) 464-8421; Fax: (540) 464-8925
Innkeeper: Carole Speton
E-mail: cspeton@cfw.com
Rooms: 5; Suites: 1; All Private Baths; Rates: $$ - $$$
Affiliations: NBBA, PAII, BBAV, Lexington Chamber, Shenandoah Valley Travel Assoc.
Payment: Amenities:

The Inn at Union Run
Lexington

In 1996, 1,500 inns competed in the Cattle Industry's yearly cook-off. Third place was awarded to Chef Brian Serens for his Union Run Bourbon Street Steak. The award came as no surprise to those who have eaten at the Inn at Union Run. The inn has developed a reputation for well-appointed rooms, friendly service and excellent food.

The creek that crosses the property was named for the Union troops that camped here in June of 1864 during and after the Battle of Lexington. The Federal-style farmhouse, thanks to innkeepers Roger and Jeanette Serens, has been carefully restored and decorated with European and American antiques from the sixteenth, seventeenth, eighteenth and nineteenth centuries. You will find collections from the estates of Winston Churchill and Henry Wadsworth Longfellow. The centerpiece of the parlor is the 101st piano made by Steinway. This room and the dining room also house collections of tobacco jars dating back to the 1690s, clocks, including one that belonged to Longfellow, and 200-year-old wine glasses which belonged to Helena Rubinstein.

Roger and Jeanette's first experiences at country inns came during an extended stay in Europe. In their travels across Germany, Holland and France they found that small inns offered a hospitality that they could not find anywhere else. There was a closeness with the innkeepers and staff that didn't exist in a large hotel setting. With those experiences came the desire to create the same elegance, atmosphere and good food in an American country inn.

It took several years of looking before selecting the area just outside Lexington. The ten-acre mountainside provided all the requirements for which they had been looking: a stream, a pond and room to expand. The simple farmhouse could be expanded without destroying the integrity of the property. What began with only three rooms when they

first opened in 1992, has now been enlarged to include eight guest rooms.

Afternoon tea, wine, beer or soft drinks available upon arrival are just the beginning of the service at the Inn at Union Run. You'll find comfortable rooms, some with whirlpool tub and private porches, and all offering views of the mountains. Our room had its own private porch and I spent a relaxing afternoon just listening to the sound of the brook and the birds in the distance. Occasionally I could hear the sounds of a bull frog or of ducks splashing in the pond. Below I could see where the creek flowed under the drive and had cut out part of the embankment during high water. The only interruption was the pleasant aroma of fresh bread baking in the kitchen.

The dining room at Union Run is open Tuesday through Saturday to guests and the general public by reservation. On Sunday and Monday it is only available by prior arrangement. Black Angus beef is the house specialty but the menu also includes a variety of fresh seafood items, center-cut pork, shrimp and breast of chicken. The Bourbon Street Steak is a large filet mignon served in a special sauce of cracked peppercorn and whiskey.

A traditional country breakfast brings eggs any style, homemade biscuits, and breakfast meats. The house specialty is Union Run Eggs McJeanette. My description could not begin to do it justice but be sure that you talk Jeanette into preparing it.

The Inn at Union Run
Route 3, Box 68; Lexington, VA 24450
(800) 528-6466; (540) 463-9715; Fax: (540) 463-3526
Innkeepers: Roger & Jeanette Serens
Rooms: 4; Suites: 4; All Private Baths; Rates: $$ - $$$
Affiliations: ABBA, PAII, BBAV, Lexington Chamber, RATHA

Payment:

Amenities:

Seven Hills Inn
Lexington

In the heart of Lexington's historic district, Seven Hills is a grand mansion built of brick with classic white columns across the front. Constructed in 1928, the building has been completely remodeled and meticulously decorated in the southern style. The Grigsbys, who own the bed and breakfast, are a local family whose roots go back to the late 1700s. Captain John Grigsby, who built Fruit Hill Farm just outside of town, was the first to arrive.

In keeping with their ancestral heritage, the Grigsby's have named each of the seven guest rooms after the eighteenth- and nineteenth-century homesteads. Fruit Hill has been restored as an owner's suite and features a private bath with Jacuzzi tub and queen-sized bed. The Fruit Hill Room may be combined with the Hickory Hill Room to create a large suite complete with parlor and porch. Either room may be rented separately. A third room on the second floor is the Rose Hill Room. Four guest rooms are on the third floor; Holly Hill, Clover Hill, Cherry Hill and Liberty Hill.

A formal parlor, library and the dining room are on the main floor. Each is decorated with period antiques, family heirlooms and accented with Oriental pieces collected on travels to Asia. A large lounge is located on the lower level, complete with fireplace, games and cable TV with VCR.

Breakfast is a delight and may include German puff pancakes with strawberries and powdered sugar, oven French toast with raspberry sauce and hot maple syrup, or a surprise honeymoon treat baked in individual casseroles. Assorted juices and fresh fruit are served in season. At check-in time, the aroma of Shirley's "Killer Brownies" or homemade cookies fills the air.

Seven Hills is one of the more elegant homes in the area. Yet, it is a place where you can relax and unwind whether you're on a business trip, holiday or just interested in wandering the sites of Lexington. Since downtown

is only a ten-minute walk from the Inn, many choose to leave their cars in Seven Hills' off-street parking area.

While Lexington is a small college town home to Washington and Lee University and the Virginia Military Institute, it is also a charming town of only 7,000 residents. Stonewall Jackson taught at VMI before going off to war, and Robert E. Lee served as president of the W&L after the Civil War. A museum on the VMI campus is dedicated to Nobel Peace Prize winner George C. Marshal.

The Theater at Lime Kiln attracts thousands each year to enjoy concerts and the outdoor drama *Stonewall Country*. The Virginia Horse Center covers 400 acres and showcases national equestrian events. Just a few miles away is Natural Bridge. Surveyed by George Washington and once owned by Thomas Jefferson, the Bridge is considered one of the seven natural wonders of the world.

One of the best ways to become familiar with Lexington is by carriage ride. During the summer season you can take the carriage that starts just across from the Visitors Center. For a totally different view of the city you might try the late night Ghost Walk which also starts at the Visitor Center.

Lexington is the home of a number of good restaurants. For fine dining try the Willson-Walker House in the heart of the Virginia Landmarks District.

Seven Hills Inn
408 South Main Street; Lexington, VA 24450
(888) 845-3801; (540) 463-4715; Fax: (540) 463-6526
Innkeeper: Shirley Ducommun
Rooms: 7; With Private Baths: 6; With Shared Bath: 1; Rates: $$ - $$$
Affiliations: BBAV, RATHA, Lexington Chamber, Lexington Downtown Dev. Assoc.
Payment:
Amenities:

Hummingbird Inn
Lexington Area (Goshen)

The drive through Goshen Pass is one of the most spectacular in Virginia. Cut by the Maury River through the Allegheny Mountains, the Pass has been a natural thoroughfare for Indians, settlers, stagecoach lines, locals and tourists. The mountains are covered with rhododendron, pines, dogwoods, and mountain laurel. The river bed is lined with massive boulders.

Twenty minutes from Lexington, just west of the Pass lies the town of Goshen. Through the 1800s, railroad cars brought coal to Goshen from western Virginia to make steel from the low-grade iron ore mined just south of town. Spas in the area brought visitors until just after World War I.

In Goshen, on Mill Creek, a tributary of the Maury, Jeremy Robinson and his wife, Diana, found the site for their bed and breakfast. After 25 years in the book publishing trade in New York City, they wanted an alternative to their fast track lifestyle. Their search for a location to open a bed and breakfast took them to more than 100 potential sites throughout the Shenandoah Valley, and ended when they found the Victorian Carpenter Gothic villa in Goshen.

Built as a store and living quarters in 1780 for its owner and family, it had been expanded to 17 rooms in 1853 by a Mr. Teter. His daughter, Pearl, became the first principal of Goshen's school, and later married Joe B. Wood, an agent for the C & O Railroad. Pearl and Joe hosted Eleanor Roosevelt's visit to Goshen in 1935. (You can stay in Eleanor's room.)

When Pearl died childless in the mid-1960s, the house fell into disrepair and decay. Structurally sound but suffering from neglect when Diana and Jeremy acquired it in late 1992, it required extensive restoration. Five new bathrooms (two with Jacuzzis) were added. New mechanical and electrical systems, an exact replacement of the original tin roof and numerous other improvements have been made.

Rooms are decorated in appropriate early country Victorian style with antiques either purchased for the inn or brought from Jeremy and Diana's previous

homes. A canopied Sheraton field bed handmade by Jeremy is the appropriate centerpiece of the room in which we've stayed many times. Like all the other beds, it is queen-sized, furnished with natural linens, and down pillows and comforter. All rooms have ceiling fans, individual air-conditioners and private baths.

The wide verandas, solarium, formal parlor and the old rustic den complete with massive stone fireplace are favorite places where guests can relax. Fresh flowers from the perennial gardens adorn every room and complement the individual dining tables.

Breakfast is served on antique Meissen china and Fostoria Americana crystal in the formal dining room. A variety of juices, fresh or cooked fruits, and entrées such as honey-cinnamon baked French toast or German puff pancakes accompany breakfast meats, homemade bread and specially blended coffee or herbal teas. Diana's dinners, served on Fridays and Saturdays, have received rave reviews from guests from Washington, New York and other major cities. The menu might include chicken breast with imported wild porcini mushrooms, filet of salmon in dill sauce, pork tenderloin in pink and green peppercorn sauce or filet mignon with port wine sauce.

Comfortable, relaxed surroundings, abounding amenities and warm, friendly hospitality—the Hummingbird Inn is a fine example of what the bed and breakfast industry is all about.

The Hummingbird Inn
Wood Lane; P.O. Box 147; Goshen, VA 24439
(800) 397-3214; (540) 997-9065; Fax: (540) 997-0289
Innkeepers: Diana & Jeremy Robinson
E-mail: hmgbird@hummingbirdinn.com
Rooms: 5; All Private Baths; Rates: $$ - $$$
Affiliations: AAA♦♦♦, BBAV, PAII, Lexington/Rockbridge Chamber, RATHA
Payment: $$$ CHECKS MC VISA AMEX DISCOVER   Amenities: A/C ▢ VCR ▧ ▲ ▜ ⬯

Oak Spring Farm Bed & Breakfast
Lexington/Staunton Area (Raphine)

We were really amazed at all there was to see and do within a short drive of Oak Spring Farm. While their address is Raphine, the bed and breakfast is just off US 11, one of Virginia's most scenic roads. Fourteen miles to the south is Lexington, eight miles east is the Blue Ridge Parkway and eighteen miles to the north is Staunton. Within a short drive you will find a variety of dining opportunities ranging from quaint small-town cafés to fine dining. Antique shops abound in the area. Staunton and Lexington have a number of museums and historic areas for you to wander. Outdoor activities in the area include canoeing, horseback riding, hiking and bird watching.

Oak Spring is a Virginia Historic Landmark and on the National Historic Register. The ten-acre farm includes five acres of pasture leased to the Natural Bridge Zoo and nearly five acres of orchard . There were a number of llamas grazing in the pasture and watering at the pond when we were there. Miniature horses and a dwarf cow were also in residence.

The 1826 plantation house has been beautifully restored and decorated with an eclectic mix of period antiques and family heirlooms. Three guest rooms, each with private bath, are located on the second floor along with two additional sitting areas. The Willow Room is named for the huge weeping willow tree by the pond. This room provides the best view of the exotic animals as they come to the pond for water. The Orchard is the largest of the guest rooms and includes a queen-sized iron bed, a large bathroom with a tub and separate shower. You'll find great views of the Blue Ridge Mountains from here. The Vineyard can be rented as a suite with its own sitting room and bedroom or as a room alone. Its queen-sized bed features a 200-year-old mantle headboard.

Innkeepers Celeste and John Wood have created a very comfortable retreat for visitors to the Shenandoah Valley. From afternoon refreshments to the upstairs guest refrigerator and the elegant country breakfast, they made

certain our stay was pleasant and relaxing. While there are a number of restaurants within a 30-minute drive, Celeste and John will prepare an excellent dinner for you (by prior arrangement). Together they prepare homemade soups, a garden salad, vegetable, a choice of pork tenderloin, baked breast of chicken or fish, and tantalizing desserts. For breakfast they brought out fresh fruit and homemade breads. The morning entrée changes daily but house specialties include oven-baked pancakes, rum-raisin French toast or Celeste's variation on eggs Benedict.

We spent most of our afternoon wandering the grounds, the perennial garden and watching the animals and ducks at the pond. There's an archeological dig at the site where the blacksmith forge was located. The forge had been used to shod horses for the Confederacy during the Civil War.

While you're this close to Raphine, I suggest a drive to the Rockbridge Vineyard and then on to the Buffalo Springs Herb Farm and Wade's Mill. The Mill was constructed in 1750 and is one of the oldest mills still standing in Virginia. A number of mill products including all purpose flour, yellow and white cornmeal and biscuit mixes are available as well as the opportunity to see a historic mill in operation. Even though I am not a wine drinker, I found the best dessert wine I have ever had (V d'Or) at Rockbridge Vineyard. This wine won the Governor's award in 1995.

Oak Spring Farm Bed & Breakfast
Hwy. 11 & VA State 706; 5895 Borden Grant Trail; Raphine, VA 24472
(800) 841-8813; (540) 377-2398
Innkeepers: Celeste & John Wood
E-mail: oakspring@symweb.com
Rooms: 2; **Suites**: 1; **All Private Baths**; **Rates**: $$
Affiliations: BBAV

Payment: Amenities:

Steeles Tavern Manor Bed and Breakfast
Lexington/Staunton Area (Steeles Tavern)

You want to get away with your significant other to a place where the innkeepers have created a comfortable haven for romantic days and intimate nights. Your goal is good food, possibly a few places of interest nearby to visit and, most importantly, a place where privacy is assured. Steeles Tavern Manor would be an excellent choice. Eileen and Bill Hoernlein's goal was to create an intimate getaway and they have succeeded.

The little village of Steeles Tavern has been a haven for travelers since 1781 when David Steele, at the age of 22, settled with his wife beside the Lexington-to-Staunton turnpike. They first provided lodgings to the few passing travelers. Later, when the stage coaches began running, Steeles Tavern became a regular stopover for food and drink. Soon a country store, post office and other buildings were added to the land owned by the Steeles. It was the oat field in front of the tavern where the first public exhibition of the McCormick reaper took place in 1831. Through the years, others have followed in David's footsteps, first his son John then, later, his great-granddaughter, Irene.

Irene Steele Searson and her husband, Walter, built the present Steeles Tavern Manor in 1916 at a cost of $100,000. In the tradition of her ancestors, Irene opened her home to travelers. For years the house continued to operate at a tourist home. When Bill and Eileen purchased the 55 acres of land, Steeles Tavern Manor had become a private residence. Extensive restoration followed to convert it into this perfect getaway destination.

The 5,000-square-foot house has been meticulously decorated. Guest rooms include the best in amenities including a wine and fruit basket awaiting your arrival. The Dahila Room offers views of the Blue

Ridge Mountains and a two-person whirlpool tub. The Buttercup Room is decorated with oak furnishings, a queen-sized bed and an antique quilt. The Hyacinth Room includes a king-sized bed and two-person whirlpool. The Wisteria Suite includes its own sitting room with a view of the well-stocked bass pond, mountains and countryside. A new two-person whirlpool has been recently added to the Rose Garden Suite. All rooms include TVs and VCRs with a selection of videos available.

The innkeepers are here to pamper you, to make your getaway as memorable as possible. Afternoon tea, early morning coffee delivered to your door, breakfast in bed or served on fine china with candlelight and classical music.

Your getaway might also include a romantic candlelight five-course dinner and a complimentary bottle of wine that is available on weekends. Eileen always offers guests a choice of three entrées such as filet mignon, and chicken or fish of the day. It is accompanied by homemade soup and bread, and fresh vegetables all served at your own private table.

Steeles Tavern Manor is a lovers' getaway with places for quiet walks and private talks. Even so, within a short drive are the historic communities of Staunton to the north and Lexington to the south. At either, you will find antique shops, quaint romantic restaurants and historic sites to explore.

Steeles Tavern Manor Bed & Breakfast
Route 11; P.O. Box 39; Steeles Tavern, VA 24476
(800) 743-8666; (540) 377-6444; Fax: (540) 377-5937
Innkeepers: Eileen & Bill Hoernlein
Rooms: 3; **Suites**: 2; **All Private Baths**; **Rates**: $$$
Affiliations: BBAV, Lexington Chamber, Roanoke Chamber, RATHA
Payment: SSS CHECKS MC VISA AMEX DISCOVER
Amenities: A/C ▭ VCR ♨ ⛰ 🍴 ✎

Sugar Tree Inn
Lexington/Staunton Area (Steeles Tavern)

We were at a 2,800-foot elevation, only a mile from the Blue Ridge Parkway driving down a twisting gravel drive on the way to Sugar Tree Inn. I remember Angel asking if we had turned on the wrong road when a buck jumped from the thicket on my right. Like a forest ghost, he was gone before I could even react. I had a premonition that the treats we had been promised were just beginning.

Sugar Tree sits on 28 wooded acres with spectacular 40-mile views. The sunsets are some of the most incredible that I have ever seen and the stars in the night sky never seemed to be so bright. If it sounds like love at first sight, it was. Sugar Tree is my idea of the perfect mountain inn.

In the 1970s, a Florida minister and educational consultant fell in love with the area. He bought a large tract of land on the side of the mountain and sited Sugar Tree in the center. He then began collecting several historic log homes from the Shenandoah Valley. Each building was dismantled, numbered and stored. It took five years to accumulate the raw materials to build Sugar Tree.

After a site was bulldozed on the side of the mountain, the historic timbers and native stone were trucked to the site over the same winding gravel road we followed. Local craftsmen and women built Sugar Tree using handhewn chestnut, oak and poplar timbers. Logs (all more than 125 years old) were mortised and pegged together without nails. In 1983, Sugar Tree opened to the public.

Location is almost everything when it comes to a getaway and Sugar Tree has the location. Time provided it with other features to make it a special place for overnight guests and locals coming for dinner. In the early 1990s, innkeepers Sarah and Hal Davis took over the helm. Before becoming innkeepers, Hal and Sarah had owned an interior design

business. Once, right after they were married, they had written a book together on residential architecture. With backgrounds in art, advertising and hospitality, they brought a special blend of needed talents to Sugar Tree.

Several months were spent restoring and redecorating. A rustic elegance has been created using primitive pieces, antiques, reproductions and personal collections. There is a wood-burning fireplace in each room and the rooms have been named and themed for a particular historic or literary figure. To make sure that each guest room was perfect, Hal and Sarah have slept in every room. Finally, Sugar Tree was again opened for their April 1 through December 1 season to rave reviews.

The Sign of the Swine Tavern at Sugar Tree offers wine and beer by the glass or bottle, and dinners are available for guests any evening by reservation. On Fridays and Saturdays, locals and guests enjoy candlelight dinners from a menu carefully prepared by a master chef. A full mountain-style breakfast is served to inn guests each morning in the dining room.

While Sugar Tree's exterior is rustic, the guest rooms are large, comfortable and feature the best in furnishings, decorations and amenities. There are rooms with queen- and king-sized beds, suites featuring oversized whirlpool tubs, and marvelous views awaiting you. My premonition was right; all of Sugar Tree was a treat.

Sugar Tree Inn
Highway 56; Steeles Tavern, VA 24476
(800) 377-2197; (540) 377-2197; Fax: (540) 377-6776
Innkeepers: Sarah & Hal Davis
Rooms: 9; Suites: 2; All Private Baths; Rates: $$ - $$$
Affiliations: PAII, BBAV, Lexington Chamber, RATHA

Payment:

Amenities:

Woodruff House
Luray

As the door opened at Woodruff House, the aroma coming from the kitchen almost made me forget why I was there. The fragrance was intoxicating and I was already looking forward to dinner. As I started to mention dinner reservations, I was reminded that dinner is included with the room rate; not just dinner, but also afternoon tea and a full breakfast as well. Innkeepers Deborah and Lucas Woodruff work hard to pamper their guests, and it shows.

Woodruff House isn't one house, but two and soon to be three. The first is like stepping into a Victorian fairy tale. Every inch of the home has been beautifully restored and tastefully decorated with fine antiques, Oriental rugs, heirloom silver and imported china.

The house actually consists of two different time periods. The first part, a post and beam cabin, was constructed in the mid-1800s. You can still see some of the original structure in the third floor "Log Cabin Suite" named for the exposed high timber roof that forms both the ceiling and walls. However in 1882, the owner made major structural changes in the house to create a Victorian.

When Deborah and Lucas purchased the property in 1990, a new roof, siding and chimney caps had been installed by a former owner. However, the inside needed a great deal of work. The plumbing didn't work and there was only one working electrical outlet. With tender loving care they worked on the restoration while still holding full time jobs. It didn't take long after opening the inn to realize they needed to expand to more than two rooms and a suite. In the fall of 1993, they purchased a second house next door to the first and began the restoration work necessary to create the Rose Cottage. Recently, they purchased a third house with the goal of adding it to the property in 1997.

Woodruff House includes two guest parlors, a formal dining room, two guest rooms on the second floor and the Log Cabin Suite on the third. Similarly, the Rose Cottage has three accommodations; a suite on the main floor and two guest rooms on the second. Each room includes private bath and working fireplace. Deborah and Lucas have decorated all rooms to provide for your comfort.

Comfortable rooms and amenities, like the gazebo-covered spa in the garden, bring guests back time and again. However, it is the food at Woodruff House that seems to linger in my memory. While Deborah manages the inn, Lucas does all the cooking. Naturally, the menu changes from day to day but a sampling includes carved roast beef with oven roasted potatoes, green beans and Yorkshire pudding. Another example is Tortellini; saffron rice with black beans and marinated chicken.

Afternoon tea is offered every day with a variety of desserts such as cookies, pastries and cakes served with gourmet coffees and teas. They have their own coffee and tea label as well as their own wine label.

Luray is a perfect setting for a Victorian inn. It's like a town that time forgot. Thousands of people come each year to visit the Skyline Drive, tour the world famous Luray Caverns and wander the antique shops. However, there is still a small town atmosphere to the community.

The Woodruff House
330 Mechanic Street; Luray, VA 22835
(540) 743-1494; Fax: (540)
Innkeepers: Lucas & Deborah Woodruff
Rooms: 4; **Suites**: 2; All Private Baths; Rates: $$ - $$$$
Affiliations: NBBA, PAII, BBAV, Luray Chamber, Shenandoah Valley Travel Assoc.
Payment:
Amenities:

Cross Roads Inn
New Market

While New Market is known best for the battle which took place there during the Civil War, there are other attractions in and around the area that have brought visitors from around the world. Shenandoah, Luray, Grand and Endless Caverns are all within a short drive. Three major Virginia vineyards: Guilford Ridge, Shenandoah Vineyard and North Mountain Vineyard are also nearby.

Bryce Resort offers golf and both winter and summer skiing. You can ski Virginia's highest vertical drop, 1,110 feet, at the four-season Massanutten Resort, or play golf at Shenvalee Golf Resort. For something a bit different take a tour of eleven bedrooms dating from the 1650s to the 1930s at the Bedrooms of America Museum.

Regardless of your interest, the location and amenities at the Cross Roads Inn make it a good selection when you visit the area. It is comfortable Southern charm with a bit of European flavor. As a Virginian by birth and a graduate of the University of Virginia, innkeeper Mary-Lloyd knows the area well and supplies the Southern hospitality. The international flavor is added by her husband, Roland, who is from Salzburg, Austria. Salzburg, the birthplace of Mozart, is recognized by most Americans as the area where *The Sound of Music* was filmed.

Mary-Lloyd and Roland, together with their children, have created a very pleasant bed and breakfast in a restored 1920s late-Victorian manor house. It has been tastefully decorated with old family furnishings from both Europe and America. The bedrooms are all wallpapered in English florals and come complete with four-poster canopy beds and down comforters. The two gas-log fireplaces on the main floor and one in the master bedroom add to the ambiance of Cross Roads Inn. The hot tub on the terrace is a wonderful place to relax. For the golfer, there is a professionally maintained putting green in the back yard.

Depending on your arrival time, you may be lucky enough to enjoy the aroma of strudel as it comes fresh from the oven. Mary-Lloyd was trained as a chef in Austria and her talents shine in the gourmet breakfast she serves in the sunny breakfast room or on the terrace. The three-course meal includes homemade European bread called *Bowernbrot*, fresh fruit, and entrées of Belgian waffles, eggs Benedict or German puff pancakes. A special blend of coffee is imported from Austria and a house custom is to bring your first cup of coffee or tea to your room.

New Market's entry into the history books occurred on May 15, 1864, when 6,000 Union troops clashed with 4,500 Confederates. What first appeared to be an overwhelming victory by Union forces changed when 257 cadets from the Virginia Military Institute moved into a breach of the Confederate lines. This was the only time in American history when an entire student body was called upon to fight a war.

For the Civil War historian, Cross Roads Inn is located on part of that historic battlefield and within walking distance of downtown New Market. There you will find one of the most unique book stores in the state. Paper Treasures has an extraordinary collection of old books, maps and magazines. For the collector, they have the largest selection of the old pulp magazines I have ever seen. Both Mary-Lloyd and Roland can suggest other interesting places in the area to visit or dine.

Cross Roads Inn
9222 John Sevier Road; New Market, VA 22844
(540) 740-4157; Fax: (540) 740-4255
Innkeepers: Roland & Mary-Lloyd Freisitzer
E-mail: freisitz@shentel.net
Rooms: 5; All Private Baths; Rates: $$
Affiliations: AAA◆◆◆, BBAV, New Market Chamber, Inns of the Historic Shenandoah Valley
Payment: Amenities:

Widow Kip's Country Inn
New Market Area (Mount Jackson)

There are many reasons to visit the area around Mount Jackson. Two of the best are a covered bridge and Widow Kip's Country Inn. Other reasons, of course, would include the Shenandoah River and Caverns. Skyline Drive is less than 25 minutes away. There are also three Civil War museums in the area and a number of battlefields. Civil War re-enactments take place at several locations in the area. Still, it was the 191-foot long Meems Bottoms Covered Bridge and the reputation of Widow Kip's that drew us to the area. The rest was like icing on the cake.

The country farm house at Widow Kip's was built in the 1830s. At that time, it was the manor house for one of the largest dairy farms in the area (180 acres). The Interstate came through in the 1960s and reduced the property to its present size of seven acres. Five of those are fenced and used as pasture. Because of that, Widow Kip's is one of the few bed and breakfasts where pets are allowed (by prior arrangement). With five fenced-in acres in which to run, pets can enjoy the getaway as much as their owners.

The bed and breakfast was started in 1986 by widow Rosemary Kip. When the new owners took over, they decided to leave the name. The Widow Kip lived and worked in Washington, DC and left day to day operations to a local minister. She would come on weekends. However, as new rooms were completed and her reputation grew, the job just became too big for one person to handle. That's when Bob and Betty Luse stepped in and became the new innkeepers.

As you wander the two acres occupied by the bed and breakfast or look at the immaculately clean and well-decorated rooms, you can understand why it became a two-person job. It takes time to mow the two acres, take care of the guest swimming pool and tend to the

gardens around the house. Then, of course, there are five guest rooms in the main house plus two guest cottages to care for and a full country-style breakfast to prepare. Yet Bob and Betty keep it all looking just perfect and the guests never know all the work that goes on behind the scenes.

Throughout the house you will find quality antiques and a decorating scheme that suits the nature of a flourishing Victorian farm in the early 1900s. The common room on the main floor with its wood-burning fireplace is a favorite place for guests to relax and play a game of backgammon. The Sweet William Room is located on the first floor and, like the four rooms on the second floor, has its own private bath and working fireplace. Upstairs are the Wildflower, Marigold, Morning Glory and Hollyhock Rooms.

A small courtyard is formed by the manor house and the two guest cottages. The first, appropriately named the "Silk Purse," is a restored wash house with a single bedroom, full kitchen and sitting room. The second cottage, the "Sow's Ear," once served as a hen house before being completely restored. It now offers guests a cozy hideaway with private bath and cable TV.

Widow Kip's Country Inn
355 Orchard Drive; Mount Jackson, VA 22842
(800) 478-8714; (540) 477-2400
Innkeepers: Betty & Bob Luse
E-mail: widokips@shentel.net
Rooms: 5; Cottages: 2; All Private Baths; Rates: $$
Affiliations: Mobil★★★, BBAV, Inns of the Historic Shenandoah Valley
Payment: Amenities:

CrossTrails Bed and Breakfast
Roanoke Area (Catawba)

Two major trails, one for bikers and one for hikers, cross Virginia. The oldest of the two is the Appalachian Trail that begins in Maine and follows the mountains 2,100 miles to Georgia. The Trans-American Bike Trail, created for the bicentennial, begins at Williamsburg and stretches all the way to the west coast. You will find CrossTrails Bed & Breakfast where these two major trails cross in Roanoke County.

CrossTrails is situated on 15 acres with the Appalachian Trail describing a horseshoe around the property. With federal acquisitions in the area around them, the property has hundreds of acres of vistas that are preserved forever. It's an area that's just too pretty not to share. That's why innkeepers Bill and Katherine Cochran, who are both avid outdoor enthusiasts, purchased the property in 1987.

Katherine's early career had been working with scouting and Bill is still the outdoor editor for the *Roanoke Times*. Over the last 30 years he has covered the entire area on foot and on paper. In fact, along with his newspaper articles, Bill has more than 300 magazine articles on the outdoors.

The house is modern-contemporary with two levels. Two of the three guest rooms are located on the second level and they share a common sitting area complete with TV. While the house is well decorated throughout with antiques and family heirlooms, I think my favorite room is the great room on the main floor. I know it's the bookcase that sets this room apart. With a lot of imagination, and the help of a very good woodworker, they turned shelves from a turn-of-the-century store near Snowshoe, West Virginia into a major focal point. Because of Bill's interest in books, the house was literally built around the bookcase and its ladder. There are books on where to go and what to do but there are also classics novels. Many sections include books on the Appalachian

Trail, biking and guide books on hiking and backpacking as well as fishing and outdoor sports.

The carriage house down the hill, where the third room is located, is more modern in design. Its location offers a great opportunity to view some of the wildlife that wanders the farm. It's not unusual to see deer, grouse, quail doves, wild turkeys, a variety of song birds, as well as rabbits, woodcocks, geese and ducks. And there has been the occasional sighting of a black bear just past Catawba Creek that crosses the property. CrossTrails is located near Virginia Tech at Blacksburg and the metropolitan area of Roanoke, yet the mountain and trails make it seem a world away.

There's so much to do in the area that you may want to plan to spend a couple of days. For example, just a few miles up the road is a glider field that is one of the finest in the northern U.S. You can mountain bike, hike or perhaps just borrow a ten-speed bike and ride one of the back roads.

If you crave more sophisticated pastimes, there is always Roanoke with its museums, shopping, live theater and fine dining. Of course, for dinner you might want to try the Home Place restaurant just two miles away from CrossTrails. They serve a family style dinner and their specialty is fried chicken with mashed potatoes, gravy and green beans. It's like going to Grandma's for dinner.

CrossTrails Bed & Breakfast
5880 Blacksburg Road; Catawba, VA 24070
(540) 384-8078
Innkeepers: Bill & Katherine Cochran
E-mail: xtrails@worldnet.att.net
Rooms: 2; **Cottages**: 1; **All Private Baths**; **Rates**: $$
Affiliations: PAII, BBAV, Blacksburg Chamber, Roanoke Valley Conv. & Vis. Bureau, Appalachian Trail Conference
Payment: $$$ CHECKS **Amenities**:

Ashton Country House
Staunton

Sitting on one of the three porches at Ashton Country House, you would think that you're way out in the country. Part of what gives this illusion is the peace and quiet. It's also created by cattle grazing in the pasture beside the house. However, it *is* just an illusion because you're only minutes from downtown Staunton.

The 25 acres of rolling hills on which Ashton Country House is located helps add to the illusion of being out in the country. You can walk through the pasture to the top of hill and get a magnificent view of the Blue Ridge Mountains. From here you can also see the city of Staunton and the buildings at Mary Baldwin College.

Ashton was constructed in 1872. It's obvious that the craftsmen prided themselves on the quality of their work when building this Greek Revival mansion. Exterior and interior walls were constructed of brick and in some places those walls are nearly 18 inches thick. The soundproofing adds a real sense of privacy to the rooms.

The centerpiece of the mansion is the main hall that is nearly 40-feet long. Lofty ceilings, crown moldings, excellent quality carpets and wallpaper are set off by quality antiques and reproductions. Four guest rooms and a large suite are available for guests.

The Master Suite, largest of the guest rooms, features a queen-sized bed with a rice motif. A private sitting room adjoins the bedroom and private bath. Like the Master Suite, all the rooms include private baths, quality linens and fine antiques. The Garden Room contains a queen-sized sleigh bed and an antique armoire, both made of cherry. Other rooms include the Audubon Room, with a queen-sized four-poster cherry bed, the Country Cottage Room and the Jefferson Room. Four of the accommodations include ceramic log fireplaces.

There are always afternoon refreshments, sherry and chocolate in the rooms. Breakfast consists of various types of entrées including quiche, waffles, eggs Benedict, eggs Florentine and a variety of breakfast meats.

Innkeeper Vince DiStefano first fell in love with the valley when he came from Binghamton, New York at the age of 15 to attend Staunton Military Academy. College, family and a business kept him from returning for a number of years. Even when he and his wife, Dorie, were ready to move to the area, it took four years to find the right location.

There's so much to see and do, it's easy to see why Vince fell in love with the area. My personal favorites include the Museum of American Frontier Culture and the old railway depot. The first is a working museum containing seventeenth- and eighteenth-century farms brought from England, Germany and Northern Ireland. A nineteenth-century American farm shows the blending of those European cultures into our own unique American culture. The railway depot contains an original early twentieth-century ice cream stand. It's one of the best I have ever seen.

The entire downtown district is like stepping back in time. There are interesting shops, places to dine, and even an original movie theater. Just a few blocks from downtown is the birthplace and museum of Staunton's most famous son, Woodrow Wilson.

Ashton Country House
1205 Middlebrook Avenue; Staunton, VA 24401
(800) 296-7819; (540) 885-7819
Innkeepers: Dorie & Vince DiStefano
Rooms: 4; Suites: 1; All Private Baths; Rates: $$ - $$$
Affiliations: PAII, BBAV

Payment:

Amenities:

Frederick House
Staunton

We've stayed at Frederick House several times on trips to Staunton and we've always enjoyed ourselves. The Frederick is more like a small bed and breakfast hotel than a typical bed and breakfast inn. It is marketed as a small hotel in the European tradition.

I admire Joe and Evy Harman who have worked wonders with what was once four separate buildings. During the extensive renovations, they hauled away more than 300 tons of debris. Today, the four townhouses almost appear to be one building.

The buildings, constructed between 1810 and 1910, were all on a list of properties to be demolished. Not wanting to see these historic structures destroyed, Joe and Evy purchased the properties over several years. They have completely replaced plumbing, wiring and installed modern heating and air conditioning systems, a task that has taken more than ten years to complete. Joe and Evy are still working on the property and recently two detached houses have been purchased and are being restored.

Because each building has a different architectural design, the layout of all the accommodations is different. There are nine guest rooms and seven suites. The accommodations vary from an English basement room to a large second-floor suite. Throughout the inn you will find the works of Virginia artists, and American antiques and reproductions. All the rooms include remote controlled cable TV, radios, telephones, well-placed lights, and terry cloth bathrobes. The rooms have been sound-proofed and include private baths. Five of the rooms have working fireplaces. The rooms are scrupulously clean with quality carpets, fine wallpapers, curtains and coordinated bedspreads.

Some rooms have their own balcony or porch and many have private outside entrances. Several common areas are located throughout Frederick House. Landscaped terraces provide retreats for reading or private breakfasts. Otherwise, breakfast as well as afternoon tea are served in the

Chumley's Tearoom. A breakfast menu is printed on your coffee cup and includes apple raisin quiche, ham and cheese pie, strata with sausage, cheese with eggs and bread, granola with yogurt and fruit, hot or cold cereal, and homemade waffles with butter and syrup. A variety of drinks is also available including coffee, tea and orange, apple and grapefruit juices.

Frederick House is located near enough to downtown that it's only a short walk to a number of fine restaurants. Just a block away is McCormick's. In 1915, Cyrus McCormick, inventor of the reaper, donated funds to build a YMCA. What was once the main lobby is now a first-class restaurant.

One suggestion for something to do is the Museum of American Frontier Culture. Buildings from three farms (a German, an English and a Scotch-Irish farm) have been moved and rebuilt. A fourth farm shows the blend of these cultures in nineteenth-century America. Other things to do include visiting the Statler Brothers Complex, the Woodrow Wilson Birthplace and Museum and a walking tour of the historic areas. For a special treat you should include a stop at the soda fountain in the restored C & O train depot. It is one of the best of its type that I have seen anywhere.

Trips outside Staunton might include the Skyline Drive, the Blue Ridge Parkway and Shenandoah National Park. Wineries, vineyards and the old mill at Cyrus McCormick's Homeplace are all just a short drive from Frederick House.

Frederick House; 28 North New Street; Staunton, VA 24401
(800) 334-5575; (540) 885-4220
Innkeepers: Joe & Evy Harman
Rooms: 9; **Suites**: 7; **All Private Baths**; **Rates**: $$ - $$$
Affiliations: AAA◆◆◆, NBBA, IIA, PAII, Mobil★★, BBAV, Virginia's Inns of the Shenandoah Valley
Payment:
Amenities:

The Sampson Eagon Inn
Staunton

I had been hearing about the Sampson Eagon House for weeks before we ever arrived, not just from guests but from other innkeepers. All the conversations revolved around how elegant the property was and the quality of amenities such as the hand-ironed 320-thread count cotton sheets. What no one could have prepared us for was that with all of its elegance, the hospitality of the Sampson Eagon was just, well, homey. Of course, it's the innkeepers that create that feeling. It's done by genuinely caring about their guests.

The original structure was built by Sampson Eagon around 1800. Eagon, a blacksmith and wheelwright turned preacher, had substantial land holdings in the city. He developed such a reputation for proclaiming the gospel that the area near his home became known as Gospel Hill, a name it still bears today.

While little is known about the original structure, each new owner has made substantial changes. The second owner, Davis Kayser, a wealthy merchant and plantation owner, made several Italianate and Victorian additions. Susan Tams, the third owner, added the Colonial Revival elements. The fourth owners worked to return features that had been removed over the years such as the wrap-around porch and the Italianate portico. However, it took innkeepers Frank and Laura Mattingly three years to strip paint, replace missing fixtures, create custom millwork, upgrade utilities, modernize bathrooms and create the luxury that is Sampson Eagon today.

The three guest rooms and two suites are large enough to accommodate queen-sized beds, private telephones and remote-controlled cable TV with VCR players. A great deal of attention has been paid to making sure guests are comfortable and have everything they need. Both down pillows and non-allergic pillows are provided for the custom-made mattresses. There are movies for the VCR, a guest refrigerator, a good selection of books you can borrow and menus to all the better restaurants in town.

Breakfast is served on English china and eaten with the family sterling with beverages served in Waterford crystal in the formal dining room. Delicious

meals begin with fresh fruit and homemade breads including a bourbon-pecan roll. Grand Marnier soufflé pancakes are favorites as well as eggs Benedict and pecan Belgian waffles.

Again, I must tell that for all the elegance and pampering, Frank and Laura have created a bed and breakfast where they want their guests to feel at home. Comfortable common areas, side porches and beautifully landscaped grounds are available for guests who want to just sit back and relax. The limestone retaining wall with ornamental ironworks encircles the property and the off-street parking.

The Sampson Eagon is located a few blocks from downtown and just across the street from the Woodrow Wilson Birthplace and Museum. Staunton is also the home of the Statler Brothers, who maintain a museum and office complex within the city. The Museum of American Frontier Culture is a one-of-a-kind museum that features four homesteads, one each of German, English, Ulster Scots and Colonial American. Within a short drive is the Skyline Drive through the Shenandoah National Park and the Blue Ridge Parkway. You will find wineries, Wade's Mill, Cyrus McCormick's Homeplace and the Swannanoa Palace, which contains the works of Walter and Lao Russell.

Good food can be found at a number of local restaurants including L'Italia just a few blocks away and the Pullman Restaurant located in the old C & O Railroad Depot. The Belle Grae Inn and McCormick's Pub and Restaurant are also fine dining establishments.

The Sampson Eagon Inn
238 East Beverley Street; Staunton, VA 24401
(800) 597-9722; (540) 886-8200; Fax: (540) 886-8200
Innkeepers: Frank & Laura Mattingly
Rooms: 3; Suites: 2; All Private Baths; Rates: $$
Affiliations: AAA, Mobil, BBAV, Bed & Breakfasts of the Historic Shenandoah Valley
Payment:
Amenities:

Thornrose House at Gypsy Hill
Staunton

Located across the street from the 214-acre Gypsy Hill Park, Thornrose House is one of the oldest operating bed and breakfasts in the area. The original owners opened the doors in 1985 and in 1992 passed the baton to Suzanne and Otis Huston. The Hustons expanded the original bed & breakfast by increasing the number of rooms to five, adding private baths where needed and landscaping the grounds.

The beautifully landscaped yard is almost reason enough to stay at Thornrose. But I don't want to discount the Georgian Revival home and the work Suzanne and Otis have done inside. While there is a formal look to Thornrose with its Greek columns and the baby grand in the family room, the innkeepers have worked to create an informal atmosphere. This is a bed and breakfast where guests feel comfortable relaxing in the living room or playing the piano. A great conversation piece in the living room is the 1930s radio cabinet Suzanne and Otis found in the Niagara Falls area. Otis stripped off the paint and repaired the case. Hidden inside the cabinet is a television. It rarely is turned on, because guests would rather sit around the fireplace and tell about their adventures in Staunton.

The five guest rooms range from small but comfortable to a master bedroom with king-sized bed and windows on three sides. Furnishings throughout the house are family antiques that were purchased for comfort, not for show. Brightly lit rooms, lace curtains, quality linens, thick bath towels and private baths add to the comfort of each guest room.

Thornrose sits on an acre of beautifully-landscaped grounds that includes two sets of pergolas with Greek Revival colonnades. The one that comes directly off the veranda is covered in a hydrangea vine that is 80 years old. The other one sits out in the garden and has wisteria climbing over it.

Each afternoon there are refreshments of homemade cookies and fresh fruit. A formal tea is done regularly during the summer with scones and

small sandwiches. On the sideboard there are always ice, soft drinks and a never-empty cookie jar.

An assortment of juices, fruits and cereals is available at breakfast as well as entrées like banana pecan pancakes, waffles, egg dishes and stuffed French toast. You could stay for a week and never have the same breakfast twice.

Staunton is one of our favorite cities in Virginia and Thornrose is close to most of the major points of interest. For example, directly behind the Thornrose is the Statler Brothers Complex, a combination office and museum. The Gypsy Hill Park across the street is Staunton's oldest park and includes a swimming pool, public golf course and tennis courts. During the summer months, outdoor concerts are held regularly.

Another reason to visit Staunton is the Museum of American Frontier Culture. This unique open-air museum has four working farms with staff dressed in period costumes. The farms represent German, English and Scotch-Irish areas from where many of the Shenandoah settlers came. The fourth farm is nineteenth-century American and shows how all three cultures blended in the valley during the early years of the Commonwealth.

Restaurants in the area range from fine dining at the Pullman or McCormick's to Wright's, one of the last true drive-in restaurants in Virginia. Otis and Suzanne can help with recommendations and reservations. They also know the area well enough to recommend things to do and places to look for that special antique.

Thornrose House at Gypsy Hill
531 Thornrose Avenue; Staunton, VA 24401
(800) 861-4338; (540) 885-7026; Fax: (540) 885-6458
Innkeepers: Otis & Suzanne Huston
Rooms: 5; All Private Baths; Rates: $$
Affiliations: Mobil★★, BBAV, Staunton Chamber, Staunton Tourist Advisory Board

Payment: $$$ CHECKS

Amenities:

Anderson Cottage Bed & Breakfast
Warm Springs

One of the oldest buildings in Bath County, the Anderson Cottage Bed & Breakfast has been in owner Jean Randolph Bruns' family since the 1870s. No one knows when it was actually built, but we do know that it existed when the county was formed in 1791. Originally a log structure built to serve as a tavern or ordinary, today it is a rambling house of log and clapboard without a single right angle or straight line in the place. Its history is fascinating and within its walls you can still sense the comings and goings of the young country.

As the local tavern, news of the newly formed United States and the rest of the world would have been discussed here. You might have heard tales of the French Revolution and of King Louis XVI trying to flee France in 1791. You might even have discussed the exploits of Lewis and Clark and their journeys in 1804 to find a Northwest passage. I know that there was a feeling of being a part of it all as I sat before the fireplace and watched the flames dance in the night.

The tavern, with many additions, became a school. After the Civil War, Jean's widower great-grandfather came to the area with his three small daughters, married one of the school mistresses and with his new wife began operating an inn. The house has not been empty since the 1850s and most of the furnishings and pictures are family possessions. I think this is part of what makes history come to life and provides an example of the continuity of the place. Even the dining room table, where Jean serves breakfast, has been a part of its history since the 1850s or 60s.

The stream that flows across the property adds to the history and continuity of the place. These waters begin at the Warm Springs baths half a mile from the Cottage. They flow to the Jackson River

which combines with the Cowpasture to form the James River, flowing east past Williamsburg and Jamestown to Chesapeake Bay.

Staying at Anderson Cottage, you easily think of the rich history of the area. Jean is well acquainted with the area and has prepared a written guide for a walking tour of Warm Springs. Long before we used the baths, thousands of others, including Thomas Jefferson, came to take the cure.

Jean is a very versatile lady. She has been a newspaper reporter and the director of public relations for the University of Virginia's Medical Center. She travels each year to winter with her son and his family in Thailand where he works as a rural development specialist. Because of this, conversations at Anderson Cottage can vary from history to the here and now.

Anderson Cottage is one of Bath county's unique and welcoming places. One thing that is constant is the sense of history and hospitality. From the spring waters used to make coffee to the family-style breakfast where conversation is as important as the food Jean serves, Anderson Cottage will always be a favorite of travelers to the area.

Anderson Cottage Bed & Breakfast
Old Germantown Road; P.O. Box 176; Warm Springs, VA 24484
(540) 839-2975
Innkeeper: Jean Randolph Bruns
Rooms: 2; Suites: 2; Cottage: 1; With Private Baths: 4; With Shared Baths: 1
Rates: $$ - $$$
Affiliations: BBAV, Bath County Chamber, National Trust for Historic Preservation
Payment: CHECKS   Amenities:

Belle Hearth Bed & Breakfast
Waynesboro

Waynesboro is probably best known as the place where the Skyline Drive and the Blue Ridge Parkway meet. The Skyline Drive runs north for 105 miles through Shenandoah National Park and ends at Front Royal, Virginia. The Blue Ridge Parkway extends southwest through Virginia and North Carolina for 469 miles to the Great Smoky Mountains National Park.

Recreational opportunities abound in the area. In addition to the National Park, Sherando Lake State Park is just outside Waynesboro. Visitors to the area also come for reasons other than outdoor recreation. For example the P. Buckley Moss Museum is located in Waynesboro. Since the early 1960s, the world-renowned artist has found much of her inspiration in the area. Waynesboro is also one of the few places left in the country where you can watch the techniques of brass molding as they have been handed down through the ages at Virginia Metalcrafters, which has a showroom near downtown.

Waynesboro's location makes it a great place to stay when you're visiting the area. It sits like the hub of a wheel with Charlottesville to the east, Staunton to the west, the Skyline Drive running north and the Blue Ridge Parkway running south. In the heart of the city is the Belle Hearth Bed and Breakfast.

Named for its seven "beautiful" fireplaces, Belle Hearth was built for a Dr. Mosby in 1910. Like many doctors at the turn of the century, Mosby's offices were on the lower floor. The house's design was very typical for its day except for the number of fireplaces in the house. Guests also enjoy the wraparound porch and find it a pleasant place to relax. A more modern addition, the 16- by 32-foot swimming pool in the back yard has also become a favorite with guests.

During his 23 years in the Air Force, innkeeper Jim Rodenberg and his wife, Carolyn, had the opportunity to visit much of Europe as well as the Orient. Therefore the house is filled with antiques from around the world. There are brass lamps from Burma, a record player from Europe and other pieces from Japan, Austria and England. Their goal was not to create a museum but rather a place where guests can come and really enjoy the house as if they were living there. Victorian homes often had both European and Oriental accents, so Jim and Carolyn's collections seem to fit right in. They work to create a light, pleasant atmosphere where you can feel at home.

Three large guest rooms and a suite are available at Belle Hearth. All the accommodations have private baths and three of the guest rooms have gas log fireplaces. Cable TV and VCRs can be set up in any room or you can utilize the upstairs sun room where there are snacks, beverages and a cable TV. A dedicated line for fax and computer use for those who can't completely get away from the office is also available.

Breakfast brings many Virginia recipes to the table as well as Virginia products such as jams, jellies, bacon, ham and sausage. They serve a good old-fashioned country breakfast with Jim the cook and Carolyn making sure that everything is just right. There's always fresh fruit in season, homemade biscuits or hot breads along with eggs and breakfast meats.

Belle Hearth Bed & Breakfast
320 South Wayne Avenue; Waynesboro, VA 22980
(800) 949-6993; (540) 943-1910; Fax: (540) 942-2443
Innkeepers: Jim & Carolyn Rodenberg
Rooms: 3; Suites: 1; **All Private Baths**; Rates: $$ - $$$
Affiliations: PAII, BBAV
Payment: SSS CHECKS MC VISA
Amenities: A/C ▢ VCR ✿ ◉

The Iris Inn Bed & Breakfast
Waynesboro

There is no such thing as a typical bed and breakfast. They come in all shapes and sizes, in all types of locations. The Iris Inn is a magnificent, totally modern structure on a wooded tract in the Blue Ridge Mountains.

Innkeepers Wayne and Iris Karl looked at a lot of properties before deciding to build. Wayne, a former engineer with the Federal Aviation Administration, always looked at the properties with a very critical eye. The more he considered all the things that could go wrong with a historic property, the more he considered building a new structure. After the final decision to build was made, the next task was to find the right location.

For any business, location generally is the most important thing. With that in mind, Wayne and Iris found a secluded hilltop just southeast of Waynesboro on 21 acres of forested land overlooking the Blue Ridge Mountains. Interstate 64 is close enough to reach in minutes yet far enough away to eliminate traffic noise.

The architect and the innkeepers created a design for the building that fits perfectly in the wooded setting. The nearly 200 feet of porches which encompass the inn are favorite places for guests to relax and watch the wildlife that lives among the oaks, dogwoods, and shrubs. The massive brick and wood building, with its lookout tower and 28-foot high Great Room, just seems to belong there among the trees.

The Great Room has its own distinctive personality, much of it created by wildlife scenes painted by artist Joan Henley. Look closely for the hornets' nest high in the corner with its painted hornets and the possum hanging from the tree above the deer. This room not only serves as the reading and TV room but it's also where breakfast is served each morning. In addition to waffles and pancakes, Iris cooks eggs any style,

local bacon or sausage, and a variety of other treats that made it one of the best and most memorable breakfasts we have had in a long time.

Working with a new structure has its advantages. Wayne and Iris were able to design large rooms with modern conveniences that you would not normally expect to find in a bed and breakfast. As you head up the stairs to the second floor guest rooms, be sure to look at the painting on the walls. My favorite is the squirrels pushing the suitcase up the stairs. They looked so real, I wanted them to carry my luggage.

Each of the bright and airy rooms has been carefully decorated with functional traditional furnishings and king- or queen-sized beds. Windows provide excellent views of the surrounding woods. Bathrooms are large with plenty of room for two people to move around.

Six guest rooms are located in the main building. A seventh, located above the detached garage, is really an efficiency unit complete with kitchenette and sitting area. A new building was completed late in 1996 that houses two very large suites. These suites feature gas fireplaces, whirlpool tubs, kitchenettes and private decks.

Iris Inn is new, but the hospitality is as warm as you'll find anywhere. The amenities of Iris Inn make it one of our favorites in the Shenandoah Valley. With all there is do to in the area, we look forward to our next trip up the iris-lined curved drive.

The Iris Inn Bed & Breakfast
191 Chinquapin Drive; Waynesboro, VA 22980
(540) 943-1991
Innkeepers: Wayne & Iris Karl
Rooms: 7; All Private Baths; Rates: $$
Affiliations: Mobil, BBAV, Waynesboro Chamber
Payment:
Amenities:

Berryville Bed & Breakfast
Winchester Area (Berryville)

Not everyone who comes to Berryville Bed and Breakfast is interested in the Civil War. However, its location lends itself well to exploring this important aspect of America's history. Winchester, which is only ten miles away, changed hands 72 times during the War. Harpers Ferry, where John Brown's raid contributed so much to the beginning of the War, is only 20 miles to the north. Other major Civil War sites include Cedar Creek, Cool Spring and Kernstown.

There are other reasons to come to the Berryville Bed and Breakfast. These include steeplechases, horseback riding, antiques at the villages of Berryville, Boyce and Millwood, award-winning golf courses, a number of Virginia wineries, not to mention the beauty of the Blue Ridge Mountains and the Shenandoah Valley. Of course, the comfort and hospitality of Berryville Bed and Breakfast are reason enough. Innkeepers Don and Jan Riviere have taken an English Country style home and turned it into a very comfortable haven for travelers.

The house, located in the small community of Berryville, sits on just over an acre of well-manicured land, just blocks from downtown. Boxwoods, dogwoods and towering trees decorate the yard. The main house, built in 1915 by Amie Moore, has had two additions over the years bringing it to more than 3,200 square feet. Within, Don and Jan have created four large and beautifully decorated guest rooms.

The first is the Victorian Room with its ornately carved antique bed, English wallpaper and Persian rug. The English Garden Room's main feature is the queen-sized iron bed (pictured above). The Shenandoah Room can be rented by itself or as part of a two-room suite with the Scotland Room. It features a high-backed antique oak bed and has a theme in keeping with its location in Civil War country. The Scotland Room, appropriately, features antique oak furniture from Scotland.

The house has been decorated throughout with fine antiques, family heirlooms and quality reproductions. Three fireplaces, one in the living room, another in the TV room, and a third in the Victorian Room, add warmth to the house on cool nights.

Breakfast at Berryville is a reminder of times gone by when simple food, freshly prepared and carefully served was the rule, and not the exception. Fresh juice and fruit, country-style bacon or sausage, waffles or pancakes and eggs to order reminded me of days at grandma's house.

A number of good restaurants are close by, such as the Battletown Inn in Berryville and others in Winchester that Don and Jan can recommend. Because we were in the area for nearly a week, we made several trips to Winchester and always found something to do. I fell in love with the area and would call it one of the most hospitable cities in Virginia.

Museums, such as George Washington's Office, Stonewall Jackson's Headquarters and Abram's Delight, offer visitors to the area a bit of history. Abram's Delight, built in 1754, is the oldest home in Winchester. It has been carefully restored and decorated with period pieces. The Kurtz Cultural Center houses displays on both the Civil War and Winchester-born Patsy Cline. Whether we were shopping for antiques, looking for a good place to eat or wanting to see the local little theater, we found them all within a short drive of Berryville Bed and Breakfast.

Berryville Bed & Breakfast
100 Taylor Street; Berryville, VA 22611
(800) 826-7520; (540) 955-2200
Innkeepers: Don & Jan Riviere
Rooms: 2; **Suites**: 1; **With Private Baths**: 2; **With Shared Baths**: 1; **Rates**: $$ - $$$
Affiliations: BBAV, Berryville/Clarke County Chamber
Payment: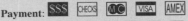

Amenities:

River House
Winchester Area (Boyce)

There's not enough room in this entire book to describe the wonder and magic of River House. Some will see it as a hideaway on the Shenandoah River filled with antiques from around the world. They will scan the bookshelves lined with a variety of reading material to find just the right book and retire to the nearest shade tree to find peace and solitude. Others will see it as a 200-year-old stage where they can act out a part in one of the innkeepers' famous murder mysteries. Some come for the food while others come for the company and the conversation.

George Washington first surveyed the area along the Shenandoah River where River House is located while still in his teens. By 1780, the tract of land became known as Ferry Farm and was part of "King" Carter's estate. A flourishing ferry business operated here at this point on the Shenandoah and the only structures were two one-story slave quarters. By 1820 the ferry had become prosperous enough that one of the slave quarters was expanded to three stories and became the ferry operator's home. The crossing became a focal point during the Civil War when General Stonewall Jackson chose the farm for a major encampment. River House functioned as a field hospital for both Yankee and Rebel troops.

In 1969, a young actress and her schoolmaster husband converted the property, which had been a restaurant and a toll house, to be the family home. Cornelia had met Donald, a young student at Princeton, when they starred in a play together. The play was a flop but the relationship a success. They came to River House to raise their children when Don became headmaster of the local school and they quickly became an important part of the community. When the last of their children were gone, they opened River House to guests. The year was 1985 and they were one of the first bed and breakfasts in the

area and one of the founding members of the state's bed and breakfast association.

River House was perfectly suited for a bed and breakfast; great location, historic property and filled with antiques. With five air-conditioned guest rooms, each with its own working fireplace, it has become a favorite stop for travelers to the Shenandoah Valley.

Good food and comfortable lodging were a matter of course but cold weather in the area always created a slow down during the winter. It was then that Cornelia and Donald added new ideas to River House that have made them famous across the country. "Enter Laughing - A weekend in the country" was created and then Murder Mysteries were added. Guests would come to stay for one of the special weekends of fine food, good wine and readings from favorite plays and comedies.

River House is now a year-round hideaway in the heart of the Shenandoah Valley. Summers bring guests to visit the historic places throughout the area. They come to search for antiques, visit wineries, and eat at some of the finest restaurants in the state. Visitors come for the Blue Ridge Mountains and all the Valley has to offer. Winters bring mystery and comedy shared with new friends over fine food in front of roaring fireplaces.

River House
Route 1, Box 135; Boyce, VA 22620
(800) 838-1476; (540) 837-1476; Fax: (540) 837-2399
Innkeepers: Cornelia & Donald Niemann
E-mail: rvrhouse@visuallink.com
Rooms: 5; All Private Baths; Rates: $$ - $$$
Affiliations: PAII, Mobil, BBAV, Winchester/Frederick County Chamber
Payment: 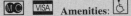 Amenities:

Inn at Vaucluse Spring
Winchester Area (Stephens City)

Not even having seen a brochure about the inn, it was the name that first captured my attention. I have always been captivated by natural springs and I had intended to go to the spring the moment I arrived. As we drove up the drive, I knew that would have to wait. There were just too many other things to see.

The Inn isn't just one building but a collection of them. The first is the Chumley Homeplace. John Chumley, a realist painter, and his wife, Bettye, purchased the property in 1963. They moved a 100+ year old two-story log cabin to the property to become their home. This is where the innkeepers have created two suites, the Chumley and the Hite. The first features a queen-sized bed, an oversized soaking tub, and a sitting area. It was from the Chumley Suite that I had my first view of the spring pond. The second suite, like the first, features a queen-sized bed, its own sitting room and includes a Jacuzzi. The Homeplace also features the log common room with a fireplace—pictured above.

In 1991, a south wing was added to the log cabin and two large modern rooms have been created here. The first, the Stephens Room, has a queen-sized bed, Jacuzzi tub and its own private deck overlooking the spring pond. A second room, the Zane, is decorated much the same as the first and has a private deck as well.

Needing an art galley, the Chumley's moved a one-and-a-half-story structure to the property in 1967. The Gallery overlooks the guest swimming pool and its guest room includes a king-sized bed, Jacuzzi tub and easy access to the pool deck.

I finally made it to the spring with its Mill House Studio. This two-story, two-room structure was moved to the property in 1972 and

served as Chumley's studio until his death in 1985. Here, looking out over the spring pond, the innkeepers have created a favorite hideaway for couples. I envied the guests who had booked the Mill House for they could hear the sounds of the spring as it ran over the sluice gate and into Meadowbrook trace.

The last building on the property sits high on the hill above the spring. This is the original manor house built in 1780 by Strother Jones. A two-story brick structure, it had been vacant for decades and was in ruins when innkeepers Mike and Karen Caplanis and their partners, Neil and Barry Myers, first looked at the property. By the time that you read this, the painstaking restoration work will have been completed and six additional rooms will have been added to the inn.

As I said, there are just so many things to see and do on the 103 acres that make up the Inn at Vaucluse Spring. So many that I haven't mentioned all the things there are to see and do in the area. These include places like Strasburg that calls itself the antique capital of Virginia. It also includes Belle Grove Plantation, one of only nine National Trust Historic Home Museums in the United States. There are the Skyline Drive and the Shenandoah National Park to the east. A short drive to the north is Winchester, which changed hands 72 times during the Civil War. Yes, there is much to do at Vaucluse. But then, the entire area offers reasons to visit.

Inn at Vaucluse Spring
140 Vaucluse Spring Lane; Stephens City, VA 22655
(800) 869-0525; (540) 869-0200; Fax: (540) 869-9546
Innkeepers: Neil & Barry Myers/Karen & Mike Caplanis
Rooms: 2; Suites: 2; Cottages: 2; All Private Baths; Rates: $$$ - $$$$
Affiliations: PAII, BBAV

Payment:

Amenities:

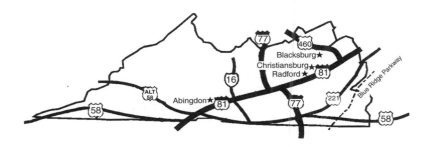

Southwestern Region

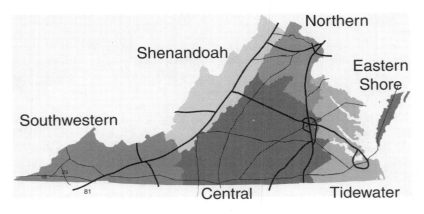

Maxwell Manor
Abingdon

The area just west of the Blue Ridge Mountains was revered by the Indians. To the north along the Ohio valley were the Shawnee and to the south the Cherokee nation. Legend has it that the Great Spirit forbade either tribe to come into this area because living would be too easy and they would become corrupt. The white man, however, jealously sought after the area.

The first settlement was a fort built in 1774. Two years later, Washington County was established by the General Assembly of Virginia. A few years later the first town west of the Blue Ridge Mountains was founded at Abingdon.

Abingdon has managed to maintain its cultural heritage, with more than 20 blocks of 200-year-old examples of National and Federal styles of architecture. The community has a lived-in feeling instead of one designed to attract the tourist trade.

Like others before her, Nancy Steele fell in love with this rich area just west of the mountains. Her quest for a suitable site to open a bed and breakfast led her to the property built by the town physician, Dr. Maxwell.

The Georgian Colonial manor house was built in 1819. Within its three acres are a duck pond, a 18- by 42-foot indoor pool and a two-person hot tub. Since there are only two guest rooms and a two-bedroom suite, you won't feel as if you're having to share it.

You'll be able to see Nancy's love of antiques in almost every room. She has decorated the Magnolia Room in nineteenth-century furniture while the Rose Room is early-twentieth century in style. The Ivy Suite is done in white wicker with green trim. The suite's wraparound windows overlook the pond and pastures. The parlor and dining room are all antique with 1800s to early-1900s Victorian furniture, silverware, china and crystal.

Abingdon is rich in culture and heritage and I think it would be impossible to not find enough things to keep you busy in the area for several days. Two stops that should be on anyone's list of things to do are the Barter Theatre and White's Mill.

The Mill, a grist and flour mill built in 1797, is the oldest water-powered mill in Southwest Virginia. While not yet fully operational, it is well worth the three-and-a-half-mile trip. The new owners are working hard to restore it to its full capability.

The Barter is Virginia's State Theater and was founded during the Depression. It takes its name from the former practice of accepting "35 cents or the equivalent in produce" as the price of admission. Ernest Borgnine, Ned Beatty, Gregory Peck and Gary Collins are counted among Barter veteran performers.

We found a number of restaurants in the area to be very good. For the history buff I would recommend a stop at either The Tavern (built in 1779 and fully restored) or the Hardware Company on Main Street. As its name implies, the latter operates in an old historic hardware store.

A new place in town is Alison's. Their rack of ribs is not to be missed! However, I have to admit that our favorite was Thomas B's. If you have a love, as I do, of a good filet mignon, then you will appreciate Thomas B's. On my trip across Virginia, I must have tried more than 40 filets. Thomas B's tied for first place.

Maxwell Manor
19215 Old Jonesboro Road; P.O. Box 13; Abingdon, VA 24211
(888) 851-1100; (540) 628-3912; Fax: (540) 628-3912
Innkeeper: Nancy C. Steele
Rooms: 2; Suites: 1; All Private Baths; Rates: $$
Affiliations: BBAV

Payment:

Amenities:

Summerfield Inn
Abingdon

Just a short walk from the Barter Theater, Virginia's State Theater, is the Summerfield Inn. Built in the early 1920s as the residence of a very prosperous lumber dealer, Summerfield is one of southwestern Virginia's premiere bed and breakfasts.

When innkeepers Don and Champe Hyatt purchased the property in 1986, there wasn't another bed and breakfast in southwestern Virginia. Since that time, they have transformed it into a small luxurious resort. Though the building was structurally sound, the work to restore it took considerable time and effort. It took new wiring, additional bathrooms, painting, and, most recently, a new cottage where three of the seven guest rooms are located.

One of the things I like about the Summerfield is that while there are many antiques, the house is not a museum The Hyatts have worked to create a place that is light, airy, cheerful and, most of all, comfortable. You feel as if you can sit back, relax and put up your feet. The role of innkeeper came easily to Champe. Her father was the manager of the highly regarded Martha Washington Inn for 25 years.

Don's rose garden includes about 35 plants with 15 different varieties. The roses were just one of the things that I liked about Summerfield Inn. I also really appreciated the guest pantries in the manor house and the guest cottage. There's something special about a homemade cookie and a cold drink after a day of exploring. And there's a lot in the area to see while staying at Summerfield. Of course, if you're just looking to relax, I can personally recommend the comfortable rockers on the wraparound porch. Abingdon is located at just over 2,000 feet above sea level and the weather is generally just right for an evening of sitting on the porch.

If you want to see the area, you will find that Don and Champe are very familiar with all there is to see and do. I know that some of their

recommendations would include the Virginia Creeper Trail, White's Mill and of course the Barter Theatre.

The Virginia Creeper Trail is a 34-mile multiple-use trail that connects Abingdon with the Virginia/North Carolina border. It began as an Indian footpath and later was used by pioneers such as Daniel Boone. In the early 1900s, the railroad ran along it. The railroad stopped running many years ago, but the trail remains as one of the best hikes west of the Blue Ridge Mountains.

An evening at the Barter Theatre is, I think, a must for anyone visiting the area. Started during the Depression, the theater got its name from its policy of accepting produce in exchange for admission. The Barter is professional theater at its best. Over the years the cast has included Ernest Borgnine, Ned Beatty, Gregory Peck and Gary Collins, to name a few.

Dining is also a pleasure in the area because there are a number of very good restaurants to visit. I can recommend the Hardware Company in the historic downtown area and The Tavern, located in Abingdon's oldest building. My personal favorite is Thomas B's. If you like steak, ask for the filet mignon. Be sure to inquire about the special steak sauce which has been added since our visit to the restaurant. If you mention this book, they might even tell you the story behind the sauce.

Summerfield Inn
101 West Valley Street; Abingdon, VA 24210
(800) 668-5905; (540) 628-5905
Innkeepers: Champe & Don Hyatt
E-mail: suminn@naxs.com
Rooms: 7; **All Private Baths; Rates: $$ - $$$**
Affiliations: BBAV, Abingdon Chamber
Payment: 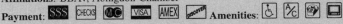 Amenities:

Brush Mountain Inn Bed & Breakfast
Blacksburg

Brush Mountain Inn, operated by Mode Johnson, is a beautiful cottage deep in the woods at the base of Brush (or Brushy) Mountain, located on 20 acres adjacent to the Jefferson National Forest.

Much larger that the typical cottage, the house is built of laminated cedar with knotty pine floors and walls. The timber-frame great room is complemented by a 20-foot stone fireplace of native mountain stone. The decor throughout is Scandinavian-style furniture and rustic family antiques. There's an eclectic country look about the place with its cedar post beds and night tables. The bed and breakfast is located well away from the road, giving it a great feeling of privacy.

The Sunset Room on the second floor has its own small balcony, a double bed and a large private bath complete with whirlpool, a glass surround shower and twin pedestal sinks. The other guest room, appropriately named the Forest View Room, is located in back and is much larger with a queen-sized bed, TV, refrigerator and its own private entrance.

From the deck or balcony outside your room you can see a variety of wildlife including deer, fox, many species of birds and even the occasional black bear. For the hiker, there is a deer trail leading to the National Forest and a mountain bike trail as well. There are also a number of well-marked trails just a 10- to 15-minute drive away in the National Forest.

During the week, Mode works as Assistant to the Vice-president in charge of special projects at Virginia Tech. One of his major accomplishments was that of project manager for the historic Hotel Roanoke. This project took four years to complete and cost more than 28 million dollars. Over the years Mode has traveled to all 50 states and it was during his travels that he first became interested in bed and breakfasts. His experiences have helped to create a very comfortable retreat.

Through the week he serves a continental breakfast and on weekends he proves his culinary expertise with a full country breakfast.

While Blacksburg is a small college town best known as the home of Virginia Tech, it is also close to a number of major attractions in Western Virginia. The 690,000-acre Jefferson National Forest offers many activities including hiking on more than 950 miles of marked trails, fishing and bird watching. The Cascades Recreation Area is a favorite stop that features a 66-foot cascade waterfall and is located nearby in Pembroke. The world's second oldest river, the New River, is one of Blacksburg's most popular tubing areas.

Smithfield Plantation House, built in 1745, is an official Virginia landmark and was home of two Virginia Governors. The Fine Arts Center for the New River Valley, the Virginia Tech Museum of Geological Sciences and the Museum of Natural History are all within an easy drive of Brush Mountain Inn.

Many visitors to the area find that the short drive to Roanoke is worthwhile. You could spend several days in the Roanoke area visiting Virginia's Museum of Transportation, Explore Park and the Mill Mountain Zoo. Mill Mountain Theater is another Roanoke attraction. As in any good-sized college town, you will find that there is almost any type of restaurant in Blacksburg that you might want. As a long time resident of the area, Mode can help with sample menus and reservations.

Brush Mountain Inn Bed & Breakfast
3030 Mt. Tabor Road; Blacksburg, VA 24060
(540) 951-7530
Innkeeper: Mode Johnson
E-mail: brushmtn@vt.edu
Rooms: 2; **All Private Baths; Rates**: $$
Affiliations: BBAV
Payment: Amenities: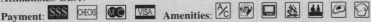

Evergreen—The Bell-Capozzi House
Blacksburg Area (Christiansburg)

Bears! Dozens and dozens of bears. That will always be my memory of Evergreen. Of course, I will also remember the pool and sitting on the front porch watching the rain, but most of all I will remember the bears.

These are VIP Bears (Very Important Bears) and they're very sophisticated, not cutsey stuffed toys. For example, in the library there is William Shakesbear and Rembearant. At the grand piano there is Libearace. It all started with innkeeper Barbara Bell-Capozzi never having a teddy bear as she grew up, so her children began giving her bears about 20 years ago. Today there are more than a hundred of them. The amazing thing is they fit perfectly in the Victorian home. I think my personal favorites were Rhett Beartler, Scarlett O'Beara, Humphrey Beargart and Lauren Bearcall. Barbara's favorite is Cyrano Debearzerack. He has a long detachable nose.

Part of what helps the bears fit in so well is that the house is so large. There are 17 rooms within four floors covering more than 6,300 square feet. The house has eight bedrooms and nine bathrooms. However, since it is located in a residential district, Evergreen has only five large guest rooms available.

The exact date the house was constructed isn't clear, but is believed to have been between 1892 and 1894. The land was a vacant lot when it was sold in 1887. The house was on the lot at the next recorded tax history in 1903. It is believed to be one of the oldest houses in Christiansburg. It was constructed for Betty Junkin, sister of Stonewall Jackson's first wife.

Barbara's husband, Rocco, a graduate of the University of Cincinnati, is an engineer by profession. Even though he and Barbara have lived at the Evergreen for the last 19 years, the house required some changes before it could open as a bed and breakfast. Of course they improved

the wiring, put in new plumbing, ceilings and additional insulation. Rocco added two bathrooms on the second floor, and added five rooms and three baths to the third floor. This 100+ year old house still has its original slate roof. Other changes over the years have included a ten-foot windowed porch with fireplace as well as a pool and bath house available for guest use.

There are many antiques and family heirlooms throughout the house, such as the piano in the library that was built in 1887 in Berlin and shipped to the United States. There are nearly 140 feet of wraparound porches with plenty of rockers for guests to just sit and relax. If you're looking for a good book, the library has about 2,000 volumes from which to choose.

Each guest room is different from the others. I think my personal favorite is the Toy Room. Here you will find old trains and a variety of collectibles. Do you remember the mechanical horse you rode while your mom shopped? Well, there is one in the room and I'm told it still works. Other rooms are more Victorian in design but I still like this room the best. It brings out the kid in me.

Breakfast is typical of what you would expect in southwestern Virginia, and I really appreciated that. There are homemade biscuits, real country ham or pork tenderloin, scrambled eggs and buckwheat pancakes. You may even find a bowl of cheese grits sitting among the breakfast dishes on the polished antique dining room table.

Evergreen—The Bell-Capozzi House
201 East Main Street; Christiansburg, VA 24073
(888) 382-7372; (540) 382-7372; Fax: (540) 382-4376
Innkeepers: Rocco & Barbara Bell-Capozzi
E-mail: evrgreninn@aol.com
Rooms: 5; All Private Baths; Rates: $$ - $$$
Affiliations: PAII, BBAV, Radford Chamber, Christiansburg Chamber, Blacksburg Chamber
Payment: MC VISA AMEX DISCOVER Amenities: A/C VCR

Alleghany Inn
Blacksburg Area (Radford)

The Blue Ridge Mountains limited the western expansion of Colonial America until the early 1740s when the first settlers moved into present day southwestern Virginia. The hardships of living in this new territory were almost unbelievable. There were no roads across the mountains, only trails created first by buffalo and deer and later used by the Indians and the settlers. Supplies took weeks to arrive and the only protection was the valley militia formed by Colonel James Patton. It looked as if there would be war in the east between the French and English. Yet the land around the New River Valley was rich, and so settlers came to begin a new life along the second-oldest river in the world.

In 1745, Colonel Patton was granted 120,000 acres. In the early 1750s he sold a small homestead near what is now Radford to the Ingles family. As the French and Indian War heated up, Shawnee Indians began to attack the settlers west of the mountains. Then on July 30, 1755, a band of Shawnees abducted 23-year-old Mary Draper Ingles and her two young sons.

Since 1971, the story of Mary's escape and her 850-mile trek to warn settlers of a second attack has been re-created each summer in *The Long Way Home*. This outdoor dramatization of the novel, Follow the River by James Alexander Thom was recently the basis of a made-for-television movie. The amphitheater is located beside the Ingles Homestead in Radford.

The Alleghany Inn is located just a short drive from the amphitheater and only a block and a half from Radford University. It was built in 1905 on property that had been owned by Governor Tyler through the 1800s. Tyler sold the property to J.H. Barnette, treasurer of the

City of Radford. The house built by Barnette still contains all of its original oak and Virginia heart pine in pristine condition.

Recently remodeled to include central air-conditioning and heat, the Alleghany has five guest rooms and a suite/apartment available for family weekends or long-term corporate use. All guest rooms have queen-sized beds, color cable TV and private phones. The suite, with its own kitchenette, provides a master bedroom with queen-sized bed and separate sitting room. It even has its own washer and dryer and a private entrance.

I would say our breakfast was one of the best we had in Virginia. In addition to country ham cured on the premises, there was brown sugar walnut bacon, eggs to order, fresh baked biscuits with homemade jelly and several types of fresh fruit. Operated as an inn, the Alleghany serves excellent dinners five nights a week. Their chef uses local ingredients from nearby gardens and farms. With 18 years of experience, he turns out some really great meals including rack of lamb, chicken primavera and, of course, a very good filet mignon. Radford's location makes it a convenient stop for visiting in the area. A variety of activities are available including fishing, hunting, canoeing, and touring along the Blue Ridge Parkway. You might also want to visit Smithfield Plantation.

Alleghany Inn
1123 Grove Avenue; P.O. Box 747; Radford, VA 24141
(540) 731-4466; Fax: (540) 731-1533
Innkeepers: Jeff & Lori Jarvis
E-mail: ALGHNYIN@aol.com
Rooms: 3; **Suites**: 4; **All Private Baths; Rates**: $$ - $$$$
Affiliations: Mobil, BBAV, Blacksburg Chamber, Radford Chamber
Payment: $$$ CHECKS M/C VISA AMEX DISCOVER Diner's Club CARTE BLANCHE
Amenities: ♿ A/C ✏ 🔥 🖥 VCR 👥 🏨 🍴 🛏 📧

Bed & Breakfast and Inn Directory

Working on as tight a schedule as we did to stay at 112 bed and breakfasts and inns in just five and a half months, we missed many excellent inns across the state. The following directory covers an additional 88 properies that we were unable to visit, for a total of 200.

We hope you enjoy your travels across Virginia as much as we did.

The following abbreviations are used in this guide:

RATES

$	50 and under
$$	51-100
$$$	101-150
$$$$	151-250
$$$$$	251 and over

AFFILIATIONS

AAA	American Automobile Association
ABBA	American Bed & Breakfast Association
BBAV	Bed & Breakfast Association of Virginia
IIA	Independent Innkeepers Association
NBBA	National Bed & Breakfast Association
PAII	Professional Association of Innkeepers International
RATHA	Rockbridge Area Travel and Hospitality Association
USB&B	United States Bed & Breakfast Association

Abingdon

Crooked Cabin
301 East Main Street
Abingdon, VA 24210
(540) 628-9583
Fax: (540) 623-1414
Rooms: 3; Rates: $$$$
Rent the entire cabin for your own private getaway, reunions or business meetings. Walk to Barter Theatre, VA Creeper Trail, downtown historic district, shopping & restaurants.

Inn on Town Creek
P.O. Box 1745
Abingdon, VA 24212
(540) 628-4560
Fax: (540) 628-9611
Innkeepers: Dr. Roger and Linda Neal
Rooms: 5; Suites: 2; Rates: $$$
Affiliations: BBAV
Experience a touch of elegance and a wealth of hospitality. Close to hiking trails, theatre and fine restaurants.

Maxwell Manor
19215 Old Jonesboro Road
P.O. Box 13
Abingdon, VA 24211
(888) 851-1100; (540) 628-3912
Fax: (540) 628-3912
Innkeepers: Nancy C. Steele
Rooms: 2; Suites: 1: Rates: $$
Affiliations: BBAV
Featured on Page: 242

River Garden Bed & Breakfast
19080 North Fork River Road
Abingdon, VA 24210
(800) 952-4296; (540) 676-0335
Innkeepers: Carol & Bill Crump
Rooms: 4; Rates: $$

Summerfield Inn
101 West Valley Street
Abingdon, VA 24210
(800) 668-5905; (540) 628-5905

Innkeepers: Champe & Don Hyatt
Rooms: 7; Rates: $$ - $$$
Affiliations: BBAV
Featured on Page: 244

White Birches B&B
268 Whites Mill Road
Abingdon, VA 24210
(800) 247-2437; (540) 676-2140
Fax: (540) 676-2146
Innkeepers: Paulette & Michael Wartella
Rooms: 3; Rates: $$
Affiliations: BBAV
email whitebirches@maxs.com

Amherst

Dulwich Manor
550 Richmond Highway
Amherst, VA 24521
(804) 946-7207
Innkeepers: Bob & Judy Reilly
Rooms: 6; Rates: $$
Affiliations: Mobil★★★, BBAV
Featured on Page: 158

Fair View Bed & Breakfast
2416 Lowesville Road
(Route 778)
Amherst, VA 24521
(804) 277-8500
Fax: (804) 277-8311
Innkeepers: Judy & Jim Noon
Rooms: 3; Rates: $$
Affiliations: BBAV
Featured on Page: 160

Appomattox

The Babcock House
Route 2, Box 822A
Appomattox, VA 24522
(804) 352-7532
Innkeepers: Barbara Carr, Lue Coleman, Deb Powell
Rooms: 4; Suites: 1; Rates: $$
Affiliations: PAII, BBAV

Arrington

Harmony Hill Bed & Breakfast
Wilson Hill Road; Route 2, Box 4A3
Arrington, VA 22922
(804) 263-7750
Innkeepers: Joanne & Bob Cuoghi
Rooms: 5; Rates: $$
Affiliations: PAII

Ashland

Henry Clay Inn
114 North Railroad Avenue
Ashland, VA 23005
(800) 343-4565; (804) 798-3100
Innkeepers: Carol, Martin &
AnnCarol Houston
Rooms: 14; Suites: 1; Rates: $$ - $$$
Affiliations: PAII, Mobil★★★, BBAV
*Georgian revival-style inn located on
train tracks in one of the prettiest small
towns left on the east coast. Come
enjoy our rocking chairs and porches.*

Belle Haven

**Bay View Waterfront Bed &
Breakfast**
35350 Copes Drive
Belle Haven, VA 23306
(800) 442-6966; (757) 442-6963
Innkeepers: Wayne &
Mary Will Browning
Rooms: 3; Suites: 1; Rates: $$ - $$$
Affiliations: BBAV
Featured on Page: 18

Berryville

Berryville Bed & Breakfast
100 Taylor Street
Berryville, VA 22611
(800) 826-7520; (540) 955-2200
Innkeepers: Don & Jan Riviere
Rooms: 2; Rates: $$ - $$$
Affiliations: BBAV
Featured on Page: 234

The Battletown Inn
102 West Main Street
P.O. Box 205
Berryville, VA 22611
(800) 282-4106; (540) 955-4100
Innkeepers: Susan Bailey & Jeff
Lindstrom
Rooms: 12 Rates: $$ - $$$

Blacksburg

Brush Mountain Inn
3030 Mt. Tabor Road
Blacksburg, VA 24060
(540) 951-7530
Innkeepers: Mode Johnson
Rooms: 2; Rates: $$
Affiliations: BBAV
Featured on Page: 246

Blackstone

Epes House Bed & Breakfast
210 College Avenue
Blackstone, VA 23824
(804) 292-7941
Innkeepers: James & Connie Barfell
Rooms: 3; Rates: $$
Affiliations: BBAV
Featured on Page: 126

Boston

Thistle Hill Bed & Breakfast Inn
5541 Sperryville Pike
Boston, VA 22713
(540) 987-9142; Fax: (540) 987-9122
Innkeepers: Charles & Marianne
Wilson
Rooms: 2; Rates: $$ - $$$
Affiliations: BBAV
Featured on Page: 106

Bowling Green

Mansion View Bed & Breakfast
16041 Richmond Turnpike
P.O. Box 787

Bowling Green, VA 22427
(800) 251-9335; (804) 633-4377
Fax: (540) 251-9335
Innkeepers: Dennis & Jane Donachy
Rooms: 5; Rates: $$
Affiliations: BBAV
Featured on Page: 88

Boyce

River House
Route 1, Box 135
Boyce, VA 22620
(800) 838-1476; (540) 837-1476
Fax: (540) 837-2399
Innkeepers: Cornelia & Donald
Niemann
Rooms: 5; Rates: $$ - $$$
Affiliations: PAII, Mobil, BBAV
Featured on Page: 236

Brookneal

Staunton Hill
RR 2, Box 244B
Brookneal, VA 24528
(804) 326-4048
Fax: (804) 376-5929
Innkeepers: David & Janet Bruce
Rooms: 20 Rates: $$ - $$$
Affiliations: ABBA, BBAV
Featured on Page: 128

Cape Charles

Bay Avenue's Sunset B&B
108 Bay Avenue
Cape Charles, VA 23310
(888) 422-9283; (757) 331-2424
Fax: (757) 331-4877
Innkeepers: Al Longo & Joyce Tribble
Rooms: 4; Rates: $$
Affiliations: ABBA, NBBA, PAII,
AAA◆◆◆, Mobil★★, BBAV
Featured on Page:

Cape Charles House
645 Tazewell Avenue

Cape Charles, VA 23310
(757) 331-4920
Fax: (757) 331-4960
Innkeepers: Bruce & Carol Evans
Rooms: 4; Rates: $$ - $$$
Affiliations: BBAV
Featured on Page: 20

Chesapeake Charm B&B
202 Madison Avenue
Cape Charles, VA 23310
(800) 546-9215; (757) 331-2676
Innkeepers: Phyllis & Barry Tyndall
Rooms: 3; Rates: $$
Affiliations: BBAV
Featured on Page: 22

Nottingham Ridge Bed & Breakfast
28184 Nottingham Ridge Lane
Cape Charles, VA 23310
(757) 331-1010
Innkeepers: Bonnie Nottingham Scott
Rooms: 3; Suites: 1; Rates: $$ - $$$
Affiliations: ABBA, IIA
*Acres of private beach on bay. The tip
of VAs Eastern Shore. Swimming,
biking, birding and golfing.*

Wilson-Lee House Bed & Breakfast
403 Tazewell Avenue
Cape Charles, VA 23310
(757) 331-1954
Fax: (757) 331-8133
Innkeepers: David Phillips &
Leon Parham
Rooms: 6; Rates: $$ - $$$
Affiliations: BBAV
*Six luxurious rooms with AM/FM
stereo clock/radio/CD players,
hairdryers, guest robes, all private
baths. Whirlpool, bicycle built for two.*
wlhbnb@aol.com

Catawba

CrossTrails Bed & Breakfast
5880 Blacksburg Road
Catawba, VA 24070

(540) 384-8078
Innkeepers: Bill & Katherine Cochran
Rooms: 2; Rates: $$
Affiliations: PAII, BBAV
Featured on Page: 218

Champlain

Linden House Bed & Breakfast
P.O. Box 23
Champlain, VA 22438
(800) 622-1202; (804) 443-1170
Fax: (804) 443-0107
Innkeepers: Ken & Sandra Pounsberry
Rooms: 4; Suites: 2; Rates: $$ - $$$
Affiliations: ABBA, AAA, BBAV
Featured on Page: 44

Charles City

Edgewood Plantation Inn
4800 John Tyler Memorial Highway
Charles City, VA 23030
(804) 829-2962
Innkeepers: Julian & Dot Boulward
Rooms: 5; Suites: 2; Rates: $$$ - $$$$
Affiliations: ABBA, IIA, BBAV

North Bend Plantation
12200 Weyanoke Road
Charles City, VA 23030
(800) 841-1479; (804) 829-5176
Fax: (804) 829-6828
Innkeepers: George &
  Ridgely Copland
Rooms: 4; Suites: 1; Rates: $$$
Affiliations: ABBA, USB&B, BBAV
Featured on Page: 70

Orange Hill Bed & Breakfast
18401 Glebe Lane
Charles City, VA 23030
(804) 829-6453
Fax: (804) 829-6453
Innkeepers: Dorothy & Skip Bergoine
Rooms: 3; Rates: $$ - $$$
Affiliations: BBAV
Experience country quiet. Relaxation

*at its best. Only minutes to Colonial
Williamsburg, historic plantations,
shopping and golf.*

Charlottesville

1817 Historic Bed & Breakfast, The
1211 West Main Street
Charlottesville, VA 22903
(800) 730-7443; (804) 979-7353
Fax: (804) 979-7209
Innkeepers: Candace DeLoach
Rooms: 3; Suites: 2; Rates: $$ - $$$$
Affiliations: BBAV
Featured on Page: 130

Inn at Monticello, The
1188 Scottsville Road
Highway 20 South
Charlottesville, VA 22902
(804) 979-3593
Fax: (804) 296-1344
Innkeepers: Rebecca & Norm
  Lindway
Rooms: 5; Rates: $$$
Affiliations: PAII, Mobil, BBAV
Featured on Page: 132

Inn at Sugar Hollow Farm, The
P.O. Box 5705
Charlottesville, VA 22905
(804) 823-7086
Fax: (804) 823-2002
Innkeepers: Richard & Hayden Cabell
Rooms: 3; Suites: 2; Rates: $$ - $$$
Affiliations: PAII, BBAV
Featured on Page: 134

Quarters, The
611 Preston Place
P.O. Box 5737
Charlottesville, VA 22903
(804) 979-7264; Fax: (804) 293-7791
Innkeepers: Mary Hill Caperton
Suites: 1; Rates: $$$
Affiliations: BBAV
Featured on Page: 136

Chatham

Eldon—The Inn at Chatham
1037 Chalk Level Road
State Road 685
Chatham, VA 24531
(804) 432-0935
Innkeepers: Joy & Bob Lemm
Rooms: 3; Suites: 1; Rates: $$ - $$$
Affiliations: BBAV
Featured on Page: 146

Chesterfield

Bellmont Manor Bed & Breakfast
6600 Belmont Road
Chesterfield, VA 23832
(800) 809-9041; (804) 745-0106
Fax: (804) 745-0740
Innkeepers: Uly Gooch &
  Worth Kenyon
Rooms: 4; Rates: $$
Affiliations: BBAV
Featured on Page: 166

Chincoteague

Cedar Gables Seaside Inn
P.O. Box 1006
Chincoteague, VA 23336
(888) 491-2944; (757) 336-1096
Fax: (757) 336-6860
Innkeepers: Fred & Claudia Greenway
Rooms: 3; Suites: 2; Rates: $$$ - $$$$
*This brand new waterfront inn features
rooms that include fireplace, whirlpool
bath, telephone, cable, TV, private
exterior entrance, balcony or deck
overlooking the water, in-room
refrigerators and luxurious furnish-
ings. Other amenities include a heated
swimming pool, hot tub, sun decks,
screened porch, waterside dock and
secluded shade garden.*

Channel Bass Inn
6228 Church Street
Chincoteague, VA 23336
(800) 221-5620; (757) 336-6686
Fax: (757) 336-6599
Innkeepers: David &
  Barbara Wiedenheft
Rooms: 5; Suites: 1; Rates: $$ - $$$$
See Article on Page: 26

Garden and the Sea Inn
4188 Nelson Road
P.O. Box 275
New Church, VA 23415
(800) 824-0672; (757) 824-0672
Fax: (757) 824-5605
Innkeepers: Tom & Sara Baker
Rooms: 6; Rates: $$ - $$$$
Affiliations: PAII, Mobil★★★, BBAV
Featured on Page: 30

Inn at Poplar Corner
4248 Main Street
P.O. Box 905
Chincoteague, VA 23336
(800) 336-6787; (757) 336-6115
Fax: (757) 336-5776
Innkeepers: David & JoAnne Snead
  and Tom & Jacque Derrickson
Rooms: 4; Rates: $$ - $$$
Affiliations: BBAV
See Article on Page: 28

Island Manor House; (1848)
4160 Main Street
Chincoteague, VA 23336
(800) 852-1505; (757) 336-5436
Innkeepers: Carol &
  Charles Kalmykow
Rooms: 8; Rates: $$ - $$$
Affiliations: BBAV
Featured on Page: 24

Main Street House Bed & Breakfast
4356 Main Street
P.O. Box 126
Chincoteague, VA 23336
(800) 491-2027; (757) 336-6030
Innkeepers: Kathryn & Dennis Holland
Rooms: 2; Rates: $$
Affiliations: BBAV

Miss Molly's Inn
4141 Main Street
Chincoteague, VA 23336
(800) 221-5620; (757) 336-6686
Fax: (757) 336-1342
Innkeepers: David & Barbara Wiedenheft
Rooms: 7; Rates: $$ - $$$
Affiliations: Mobil, BBAV
Featured on Page: 26

Watson House, The
4240 Main Street; P.O. Box 905
Chincoteague, VA 23336
(800) 336-6787; (757) 336-1564
Fax: (757) 336-5776
Innkeepers: David & JoAnne Snead &
Tom & Jacque Derrickson
Rooms: 6; Rates: $$ - $$$
Affiliations: AAA◆◆◆, BBAV
Featured on Page: 28

Year of the Horse Inn
3583 Main Street
Chincoteague, VA 23336
(800) 680-0090; (757) 336-3221
Innkeepers: Carlton Bond
Rooms: 3; Suites: 1; Rates: $$
Affiliations: ABBA, BBAV
*Water view from balcony-100 ft. pier
for guests. Great sunsets.*

Christiansburg

Evergreen—The Bell-Capozzi House
201 East Main Street
Christiansburg, VA 24073
(888) 382-7372; (540) 382-7372
Fax: (540) 382-4376
Innkeepers: Rocco &
Barbara Bell-Capozzi
Rooms: 5; Rates: $$ - $$$
Affiliations: PAII, BBAV
Featured on Page: 248

Clifton Forge

Longdale Inn
6209 Longdale Furnace Road

Clifton Forge, VA 24422
(800) 862-0386; (540) 862-0892
Fax: (540) 862-3554
Innkeepers: Bob Cormier
Rooms: 8; Suites: 2; Rates: $$ - $$$
Affiliations: PAII, BBAV
Featured on Page: 178

Cluster Springs

**Oak Grove Plantation Bed &
Breakfast**
1245 Cluster Springs Road
P.O. Box 45
Cluster Springs, VA 24535
(804) 575-7137
Innkeepers: Pickett Craddock
Rooms: 3; Rates: $$
Affiliations: BBAV
Featured on Page: 148

Columbia

Upper Byrd Bed & Breakfast
6452 River Road West
Columbia, VA 23038
(804) 842-2240
Innkeepers: Ivona D. Kaz-Jepsen
Rooms: 2; Rates: $$
Affiliations: ABBA

Covington

Milton Hall Bed & Breakfast Inn
207 Thorny Lane
Covington, VA 24426
(540) 965-0196
Innkeepers: John & Veronica Eckert
Rooms: 5; Suites: 1; Rates: $$ - $$$
Affiliations: BBAV
Featured on Page: 180

Culpeper

Fountain Hall
609 South East Street
Culpeper, VA 22701
(800) 298-4748; (540) 825-8200

Fax: (540) 825-7716
Innkeepers: Steve & Kathi Walker
Rooms: 4; Suites: 2; Rates: $$ - $$$
Affiliations: AAA◆◆◆, Mobil★★★,
  BBAV
Featured on Page: 84

Eastville

Eastville Manor
6058 Willow Oak Road
P.O. Box 1005
Eastville, VA 23347
(757) 678-7378
Innkeepers: Melody & Bill Scalley
Rooms: 2; Suites: 1; Rates: $$ - $$$$
Affiliations: PAII
*Romantic Victorian centrally located to
all the Eastern Shore has to offer.
Public fine dining for lunch or dinner!*

Elkton

JoAnne's Bed & Breakfast
Route 2, Box 276
Elkton, VA 22827
(540) 298-9723
Innkeepers: JoAnne Frederick
Rooms: 3; Rates: $ - $$
Affiliations: ABBA
*Quiet farm, breathtaking view, craft
shops on premises.*

Spotswood Inn Bed & Breakfast
403 East Rockingham Street
Elkton, VA 22827
(540) 298-0246
Innkeepers: Neil W. & Elsie M. Cox
Rooms: 4; Rates: $$
*Elegant lodging in Virginia's
Shenandoah Valley.*

Exmore

Gladstone House, The
12108 Lincoln Avenue
P.O. Box 296
Exmore, VA 23350

(800) 262-4837; (757) 442-4614
Fax: (757) 442-4678
Innkeepers: Pat & Al Egan
Rooms: 3; Rates: $$
Affiliations: NBBA, AAA◆◆◆, BBAV
Featured on Page: 34

Fairfax

Bailiwick Inn, The
4023 Chain Bridge Road
Fairfax, VA 22030
(800) 366-7666; (703) 691-2266
Fax: (703) 934-2112
Innkeepers: Bob & Annette Bradley
Rooms: 14; Suites: 1; Rates: $$$
Affiliations: ABBA, IIA, PAII, Mobil,
  BBAV
Featured on Page: 120

Fancy Gap

Cascade Mountain Inn
P.O. Box 264
Fancy Gap, VA 24328
(540) 728-2300
Innkeepers: Jerry & Sherrie Weyant
Rooms: 19; Suites: 2; Rates: $$ - $$$$
*On Blue Ridge Pkwy milepost 199.
Tennis courts, heated pool*

Farmville

"Linden" Bed & Breakfast
Route 5, Box 2810
Farmville, VA 23901
(804) 223-8443
Innkeepers: Gretchen & Bob Rogers
Rooms: 2; Rates: $$ - $$$
Affiliations: BBAV
Featured on Page: 150

Floyd

Stonewall Bed & Breakfast
Wendi Pate Trail
Floyd, VA 24091
(540) 745-2861

Innkeepers: Ray & Joy Batiato
Rooms: 4; Suites: 1; Rates: $$

Fredericksburg

La Vista Plantation
4420 Guinea Station Road
Fredericksburg, VA 22408
(800) 529-2823; (540) 898-8444
Fax: (540) 898-9414
Innkeepers: Michele &
   Edward Schiesser
Rooms: 1; Suites: 1; Rates: $$
Affiliations: NBBA, BBAV
Featured on Page: 86

Front Royal

Chester House
43 Chester Street
Front Royal, VA 22630
(800) 621-0441; (540) 635-3937
Fax: (540) 636-8695
Innkeepers: Bill & Ann Wilson
Rooms: 5; Suites: 1; Rates: $$ - $$$
Affiliations: Mobil★★★, BBAV
Featured on Page: 182

Killahevlin
1401 North Royal Avenue
Front Royal, VA 22630
(800) 847-6132; (540) 636-7335
Fax: (540) 636-8694
Innkeepers: Susan & John Lang
Rooms: 4; Suites: 2; Rates: $$$
Affiliations: ABBA, PAII, BBAV
Featured on Page: 184

Woodward House on Manor Grade
413 South Royal Avenue
Front Royal, VA 22630
(800) 635-7011; (540) 635-7010
Fax: (540) 635-8217
Innkeepers: Joan & Bob Kaye
Rooms: 3; Suites: 5; Rates: $$$
Affiliations: ABBA, NBBA, BBAV
Featured on Page: 186

Glade Spring

Dunburn Farms B&B
33175 Mast Road
Glade Spring, VA 24340
(540) 475-5667
Innkeepers: John Lentz
Rooms: 5; Rates: $$

Gloucester

Airville Plantation
6423 T.C. Walker Road
Gloucester, VA 23061
(804) 694-0287; Fax: (804) 694-0287
Innkeepers: Lawrence &
   Kathleen Cohen
Rooms: 3; Rates: $$$ - $$$$
Affiliations: BBAV
Featured on Page: 74

Goodview

Stone Manor Bed & Breakfast
1135 Stone Manor Place
Goodview, VA 24095
(540) 297-1414
Innkeepers: Don & Mary Davis
Rooms: 3; Rates: $$
Affiliations: BBAV
Located on beautiful Smith Mtn. Lake.
690' waterfront docks, pool, fishing
and full breakfast.

Gordonsville

Rabbit Run Bed & Breakfast
305 North High Street
P.O. Box 535
Gordonsville, VA 22942
(800) 791-9205; (540) 832-2892
Fax: (540) 832-0801
Innkeepers: Virginia Hulvey &
   Elizabeth Hupp
Rooms: 4; Rates: $ - $$
Affiliations: BBAV

Sleepy Hollow Farm Bed & Breakfast
16280 Blue Ridge Turnpike
Gordonsville, VA 22942
(800) 215-4804; (540) 832-5555
Fax: (540) 832-2515
Innkeepers: Beverley Allison &
Dorsey Allison Comer
Rooms: 6; Suites: 3; Rates: $$ - $$$
Affiliations: NBBA, BBAV
Featured on Page: 98

Tivoli
9171 Tivoli Drive
Gordonsville, VA 22942
(800) 840-2225; (540) 832-2225
Fax: (540) 832-3691
Innkeepers: Phil & Susie Audibert
Rooms: 4; Rates: $$$
Affiliations: PAII, BBAV
Featured on Page: 100

Goshen

Hummingbird Inn, The
Wood Lane; P.O. Box 147
Goshen, VA 24439
(800) 397-3214; (540) 997-9065
Fax: (540) 997-0289
Innkeepers: Diana & Jeremy Robinson
Rooms: 5; Rates: $$ - $$$
Affiliations: PAII, AAA◆◆◆, BBAV
Featured on Page: 204

Hampton

Victoria House
4501 Victoria Blvd.
Hampton, VA 23669
(757) 722-2658
Innkeepers: Martha & C.H. Rowe
Rooms: 2; Rates: $$ - $$$
Affiliations: BBAV

Harrisonburg

Kingsway Bed & Breakfast
3581 Singers Glen Road
Harrisonburg, VA 22801
(540) 867-9696

Innkeepers: Chester G. &
Verna E. Leaman
Rooms: 3; Rates: $$

Boxwood Bed & Breakfast
Route 1, Box 130
Hinton, VA 22831
(540) 867-5772
Fax: (540) 867-5701
Innkeepers: Nancy Bondurant Jones
Rooms: 3; Rates: $$
Near trout streams, historic sites,
antique shops and James Madison
University.

Hot Springs

Kings Victorian Inn
Route 1, Box 622
Hot Springs, VA 24445
(540) 839-3134
Innkeepers: Richard & Liz King
Rooms: 6; Rates: $$ - $$$
Affiliations: BBAV
Featured on Page: 192

Leesburg

Norris House Inn, The
108 Loudoun Street SW
Leesburg, VA 20175
(800) 644-1806; (703) 777-1806
Fax: (703) 771-8051
Innkeepers: Pam & Don McMurray
Rooms: 6; Rates: $$ - $$$
Affiliations: BBAV
Featured on Page: 90

Lexington

Applewood Inn
Buffalo Bend Road; P.O. Box 1348
Lexington, VA 24450
(800) 463-1902; (540) 463-1962
Fax: (540) 463-6996
Innkeepers: Linda & Christian Best
Rooms: 3; Suites: 1; Rates: $$ - $$$
Affiliations: PAII, BBAV
Featured on Page: 194

A B&B at Llewellyn Lodge
603 South Main Street
Lexington, VA 24450
(800) 882-1145; (540) 463-3233
Fax: (540) 464-3122
Innkeepers: John & Ellen Roberts
Rooms: 6; Rates: $$
Affiliations: NBBA, PAII, BBAV
Featured on Page: 196

Brierley Hill Country Inn
Route 2, Box 21A Borden Road
Lexington, VA 24450
(800) 422-4925; (540) 464-8421
Fax: (540) 464-8925
Innkeepers: Carole Speton
Rooms: 5; Suites: 1; Rates: $$ - $$$
Affiliations: NBBA, PAII, BBAV
Featured on Page: 198

D&Ds Bed & Breakfast
#2 Wild Turkey Road
Lexington, VA 24450
(800) 496-4133; (540) 463-6298
Fax: (540) 463-6299
Innkeepers: Mr. & Mrs. David E. Hall
Suites: 1; Rates: $$$
Affiliations: ABBA
Located in the heart of the
Shenandoah Valley only minutes from
the Natural Bridge, VA Horse Center
and near W&L University and VMI.

Historic Country Inns of Lexington
11 North Main Street
Lexington, VA 24450
(540) 463-2044
Fax: (540) 463-7262
Innkeepers: Don Fredenburg Meredith
Rooms: 31; Suites: 12; Rates: $$$ - $$$$
Affiliations: IIA, PAII, Mobil★★★
Lovely town - History, VMI and W&L,
theater. Three gracious inns, intimate
dining, amenities. All welcome.

Inn at Union Run, The
Route 3, Box 68
Lexington, VA 24450

(800) 528-6466; (540) 463-9715
Fax: (540) 463-3526
Innkeepers: Roger & Jeanette Serens
Rooms: 4; Suites: 4; Rates: $$ - $$$
Affiliations: ABBA, PAII, BBAV
Featured on Page: 200

Seven Hills Inn
408 South Main Street
Lexington, VA 24450
(888) 845-3801; (540) 463-4715
Fax: (540) 463-6526
Innkeepers: Shirley Ducommun
Rooms: 7; Rates: $$ - $$$
Affiliations: BBAV
Featured on Page: 202

Stoneridge Bed & Breakfast
Stoneridge Lane; P.O. Box 38
Lexington, VA 24450
(800) 491-2930; (540) 463-4090
Fax: (540) 463-6078
Innkeepers: Norm &
  Barbara Rollenhagen
Rooms: 4; Suites: 1; Rates: $$ - $$$
Affiliations: PAII, BBAV
A fine, old home with the welcomes of
Southern hospitality, of secluded
getaway, of antebellum history.

Lincoln

Springdale Country Inn

Lincoln, VA 20160
(800) 388-1832; (540) 338-1832
Fax: (540) 338-1839
Innkeepers: Nancy & Roger Fones
Rooms: 9; Suites: 2; Rates: $$$
Affiliations: PAII, BBAV
Featured on Page: 92

Locust Dale

Inn at Meander Plantation
HCR 5, Box 460A
Locust Dale, VA 22948
(800) 385-4936; (540) 672-4912

Fax: (540) 672-4912
Innkeepers: Suzanne Thomas,
Suzie & Bob Blanchard
Rooms: 3; Suites: 4; Rates: $$$ - $$$$
Affiliations: NBBA, PAII, BBAV
Featured on Page: 102

Louisa

Ginger Hill Bed & Breakfast
47 Holly Springs Drive
Louisa, VA 23093
(540) 967-3260
Fax: (540) 967-2555
Innkeepers: Ronald A. &
Virginia F. Ellis
Rooms: 2; Rates: $$ - $$$
Affiliations: BBAV
Featured on Page: 138

Lovettesville

Victorian Charm
13073 Lutheran Church Road
Lovettesville, VA 20180
(540) 822-9120
Innkeepers: Charline Whitman
Rooms: 2; Rates: $$
Affiliations: IIA
*Turn-of-the-century Victorian home,
"Romance & Relaxation"*

Luray

Locust Grove Inn
1456 North Egypt Bend Drive
Luray, VA 22835
(540) 743-1804
Innkeepers: Rod & Isabel Graves
Rooms: 5; Rates: $$
Affiliations: BBAV
*A 1765 log home on the Shenandoah
River. Unforgettable scenery, one-of-a-
kind interiors.*

Mayneview Bed & Breakfast
439 Mechanic Street
Luray, VA 22835

(540) 743-7921
Innkeepers: Shar Mayne
Rooms: 5; Rates: $$ - $$$
Affiliations: Mobil★★★
*Victorian home with spectacular
mountain views, spa, private baths,
fireplaces, featherbeds, gourmet meals &
afternoon tea awaits you! Come join us.*

Shadow Ridge Cabin
774 Lakewood Road
Luray, VA 22835
(540) 743-7529
Innkeepers: Gwynne & Emalice Jewell
Rooms: 1; Rates: $$
*Secluded cabin with 20-mile views of
Shenandoah Valley. Modern and fully
equipped. Deck, fireplace - very romantic.*

Shenandoah River Inn
201 Stagecoach Road
Luray, VA 22835
(540) 743-1144
Innkeepers: Paul E. Bramell
Rooms: 3; Rates: $$ - $$$
Affiliations: BBAV
*Historic 1812 stagecoach inn &
ferryboat stop. All rooms have pvt.
baths, frplcs, king/queen beds.
Secluded romantic 4-acre site. Mtntop
cabin avail. 30-mile views.*

Spring Farm Bed & Breakfast
13 Wallace Avenue
Luray, VA 22835
(800) 203-2814; (540) 743-4701
Fax: (540) 743-7851
Innkeepers: Susan Murphy &
Thelma Mayes
Rooms: 4; Suites: 1; Rates: $$ - $$$
*Coziest retreat in the Shenandoah
Valley. Warm hospitality, spectacular
views, luscious breakfast. Near Luray
Caverns & Skyline Drive. Weddings &
reunions welcome.*

Woodruff House, The
330 Mechanic Street

Luray, VA 22835
(540) 743-1494
Innkeepers: Lucas &
   Deborah Woodruff
Rooms: 4; Suites: 2; Rates: $$ - $$$$
Affiliations: NBBA, PAII, AAA,
   BBAV
Featured on Page: 212

Wisteria Bed & Breakfast
1126 Marksville Road
Stanley, VA 22851
(540) 778-3347
Innkeepers: Eric & Nicola Portch
Rooms: 4; Rates: $$$
Affiliations: BBAV
Elegant century-old Victorian on 15-acre estate. Spacious antique-furnished rooms with mountain views, private baths and king- or queen-sized beds. All inclusive packages & gift certificates available.

Lynchburg

Federal Crest Inn
1101 Federal Street
Lynchburg, VA 24504
(800) 818-6155; (804) 845-6155
Fax: (804) 845-1445
Innkeepers: Phil & Ann Ripley
Rooms: 2; Suites: 3; Rates: $$ - $$$
Affiliations: PAII, BBAV
Featured on Page: 152

Lynchburg Mansion Inn Bed & Breakfast
405 Madison Street
Lynchburg, VA 24504
(800) 352-1199; (804) 528-5400
Innkeepers: Bob & Mauranna Sherman
Rooms: 3; Suites: 2; Rates: $$ - $$$
Affiliations: PAII, Mobil★★★, BBAV
Featured on Page: 154

Madison House Bed & Breakfast, The
413 Madison Street
Lynchburg, VA 24504

(800) 828-6422; (804) 528-1503
Fax: (804) 528-4412
Innkeepers: Irene & Dale Smith
Rooms: 3; Suites: 1; Rates: $$ - $$$
Affiliations: NBBA, Mobil, BBAV
Featured on Page: 156

The Cricket Guest House
1511 Langhorne Road
Lynchburg, VA 24503
(804) 384-1511
Innkeepers: Virginia & Mel O'Klock
Rooms: 1; Suites: 1; Rates: $$ - $$$
Affiliations: IIA
Gourmet breakfast in formal setting. Elegant 1919 home designed by noted architect & set in beautiful gardens by master gardener, interior designer.

Lyndhurst

Cabin Creekwood
Route 1, Box 444J
Lyndhurst, VA 22952
(540) 943-8552
Innkeepers: Stan & Deb Horst
Rooms: 0; Rates: $$
Fully furnished resort mountain cabins near the Blue Ridge Parkway milepost 13.

Madison

Shenandoah Springs Country Inn Bed & Breakfast
P.O. Box 770
Madison, VA 22727
(540) 923-4300
Innkeepers: Anne & Doug Farmer
Rooms: 4; Rates: $$ - $$$
Affiliations: BBAV
Featured on Page: 104

Madison Heights

Winridge Bed & Breakfast
Winridge Drive
Route 1, Box 362
Madison Heights, VA 24572

(804) 384-7220
Fax: (804) 384-1399
Innkeepers: LoisAnn & Ed Pfister &
Pfamily
Rooms: 3; Rates: $$
Affiliations: BBAV
Featured on Page: 162

Manassas

Benneth House Bed & Breakfast
9252 Bennett Drive
Manassas, VA 20110
(703) 368-6121
Innkeepers: Jean & Curtis Harrover
Rooms: 1; Rates: $$
Affiliations: BBAV

Meadows of Dan

Spangler B&B
RR 2, Box 108
Meadows of Dan, VA 24120
(540) 952-2454
Innkeepers: Harold & Martha Spangler
Rooms: 3; Suites: 1; Rates: $$
Affiliations: ABBA
*Victorian 1903 farmhouse, antiques. 3
1/2-acre lake w/fishing, boating. Blue
Ridge Parkway milepost 180. Near
Mabry Mill. Good hiking.*

Middleburg

Middleburg Country Inn
209 East Washington Street
Middleburg, VA 22117
(800) 262-6082; (540) 687-6082
Fax: (540) 687-5603
Innkeepers: Susan & John Pettibone
Rooms: 6; Suites: 2
  Rates: $$$ - $$$$$
Affiliations: ABBA, PAII, Mobil
Featured on Page: 94

The Longbarn
P.O. Box 208
Middleburg, VA 20118

(540) 687-4137
Fax: (540) 687-4044
Innkeepers: Chiara Langley
Rooms: 3; Rates: $$ - $$$
Affiliations: ABBA, BBAV

Welbourne
22314 Welbourne Farm Lane
Middleburg, VA 20117
(540) 687-3201
Innkeepers: Nat & Sherry Morison
Rooms: 6; Rates: $$
*1775 ,7th-generation family home on
600-acre farm in Virginia's hunt
country. Civil War history, Virginia
Historic Landmark, Nat'l Register of
Historic Places.*

Midlothian

Uli Manor
14042 Southshore Road
Midlothian, VA 23112
(804) 739-9817
Fax: (804) 639-1909
Innkeepers: Bill & Jennifer Chvala
Rooms: 2; Rates: $$ - $$$
Affiliations: BBAV
Featured on Page: 168

Montebello

Dutch House Geselligkeit
655 Fork Mount Lane
Montebello, VA 24464
(540) 377-2119
Innkeepers: Elme & Barbara Blommer
Rooms: 3; Rates: $
In Blue Ridge Mtns. 3 mi. off P'way.

Monterey

Bobbie's Bed & Breakfast
HC 02, Box 5
Monterey, VA 24465
(540) 468-2308
Innkeepers: Bobbie & Ross Hefner
Rooms: 3; Rates: $

Mount Jackson

Widow Kip's Country Inn
355 Orchard Drive
Mount Jackson, VA 22842
(800) 478-8714; (540) 477-2400
Innkeepers: Betty & Bob Luse
Rooms: 5; Rates: $$
Affiliations: Mobil★★★, BBAV
Featured on Page: 216

Nellysford

Mark Addy, The
56 Rodes Farm Drive
Nellysford, VA 22958
(800) 278-2154; (804) 361-1101
Innkeepers: John S. Maddox &
   Saverio Anselmo
Rooms: 9; Suites: 1; Rates: $$ - $$$
Affiliations: NBBA, PAII, BBAV
Featured on Page: 172

Trillium House @ Wintergreen
Wintergreen Drive
P.O. Box 280
Nellysford, VA 22958
(800) 325-9126; (804) 325-9126
Fax: (804) 325-1099
Innkeepers: Betty & Ed Dinwiddie
Rooms: 10; Suites: 2; Rates: $$$
Affiliations: IIA, PAII, AAA, Mobil,
   BBAV
Featured on Page: 174

New Market

A Touch of Country
9329 Congress Street
New Market, VA 22844
(540) 740-8030
Innkeepers: Dawn Kasow/Jean
Schoellig
Rooms: 6; Rates: $$
Affiliations: BBAV

Cross Roads Inn
9222 John Sevier Road

New Market, VA 22844
(540) 740-4157
Fax: (540) 740-4255
Innkeepers: Roland &
   Mary-Lloyd Freisitzer
Rooms: 5; Rates: $$
Affiliations: AAA◆◆◆, BBAV
Featured on Page: 214

Red Shutter Farmhouse B&B
Route 1, Box 376
New Market, VA 22844
(540) 740-4281
Fax: (540) 740-4661
Innkeepers: Geo & Juanita Miller
Rooms: 4; Suites: 1; Rates: $$
Affiliations: BBAV

Newport

Riverbend Farm Bed & Breakfast
Route 2, Box 561B
Newport, VA 24128
(540) 544-7849
Fax: (540) 544-7849
Innkeepers: Ray & Betty Collins
Rooms: 2; Suites: 1; Rates: $$
Affiliations: BBAV
*Located on 35 acres. Our log and
stone home offers guests the peace &
quiet of rural Virginia. We offer our
guests fly-fishing for large trout on our
stream.*

Norfolk

Page House Inn
323 Fairfax Avenue
Norfolk, VA 23507
(800) 599-7659; (757) 625-5033
Fax: (757) 623-9451
Innkeepers: Stephanie &
   Ezio DiBelardino
Rooms: 4; Suites: 2; Rates: $$ - $$$
Affiliations: PAII, AAA◆◆◆◆,
   Mobil★★★, BBAV
Featured on Page: 40

North Garden

Inn at the Crossroads
5010 Plank Road; Routes 29 & 692
North Garden, VA 22959
(804) 979-6452
Innkeepers: John & Maureen Deis
Rooms: 4; Suites: 1; Rates: $$ - $$$
Affiliations: BBAV
Featured on Page: 140

Onancock

76 Market Street Bed & Breakfast
P.O. Box 316
Onancock, VA 23417
(757) 787-7600
Innkeepers: Nancy Watts Sprague
Rooms: 3; Rates: $$
Affiliations: IIA
Restored Victorian. Walk to harbor or restaurants. Come by boat or car and rock on the front porch.

Orange

Holladay House
155 West Main Street
Orange, VA 22960
(800) 358-4422; (540) 672-4893
Fax: (540) 672-3028
Innkeepers: Phebe & Pete Holladay
Rooms: 4; Suites: 2; Rates: $$$-$$$$
Affiliations: PAII, Mobil, BBAV
Featured on Page: 96

Mayhurst Mansion Inn
12460 Mayhurst Lane
Orange, VA 22960
(540) 672-2243
Innkeepers: Bob & Peg Harmon
Rooms: 5; Suites: 1; Rates: $$$$
Affiliations: BBAV
Romantic 1859 Italianate Victorian plantation home on 37 historic acres. Charming setting under old trees with pond. Newly renovated with fireplaces in beautiful romantic rooms, some with

double whirlpools. Enjoy a scrumptious breakfast in bed. A Virginia Landmark & Natl. Historic Registry. Located on Route 15 South, Orange, nearby Monticello, wineries, Civil War sites, Montpelier, 25 mi. to Charlottesville, 80 mi. to DC.

Paeonian Springs

Cornerstone Bed & Breakfast
19882 Clarks Gap Road
Paeonian Springs, VA 20129
(540) 882-3722
Innkeepers: Molly &
  Dick Cunningham
Rooms: 2; Rates: $$
Affiliations: IIA, PAII

Palmyra

Palmer Country Manor
Route 2, Box 1390
Palmyra, VA 22963
(800) 253-4306; (804) 589-1300
Fax: (804) 589-1300
Innkeepers: Gregory &
  Kathleen Palmer
Rooms: 2; Rates: $$$
Affiliations: AAA♦♦♦, BBAV
Featured on Page: 142

Pamplin

Sleepy Lamb Bed & Breakfast
HCR 1, Box 34
Pamplin, VA 23958
(804) 248-6289
Innkeepers: Ron & Judy Bernaldo
Rooms: 3; Rates: $$
Affiliations: BBAV
Featured on Page: 124

Penn Laird

Hearth N' Holly Inn
Route 2, Box 325
Penn Laird, VA 22846

(800) 209-1379; (540) 434-6766
Innkeepers: Dennis & Doris Brown
Rooms: 3; Rates: $$
Affiliations: BBAV
Featured on Page: 188

Petersburg

Mayfield Inn
3348 West Washington Street
P.O. Box 2265
Petersburg, VA 23804
(800) 538-2381; (804) 861-6775
Fax: (804) 863-1971
Innkeepers: Cherry Turner
Rooms: 2; Suites: 2; Rates: $$
Affiliations: BBAV
Featured on Page: 164

Port Haywood

Inn at Tabb's Creek Landing
Route 14, Mathews County
P.O. Box 219
Port Haywood, VA 23138
(804) 725-5136
Innkeepers: Cabell &
Catherine Venable
Rooms: 2; Suites: 2; Rates: $$$
Affiliations: ABBA, BBAV
Featured on Page: 38

Portsmouth

Olde Towne Inn
420 Middle Street
Portsmouth, VA 23704
(800) 353-0278; (757) 397-5462
Innkeepers: Dede & John Braley
Rooms: 3; Suites: 1; Rates: $$ - $$$
Affiliations: BBAV
Featured on Page: 42

Providence Forge

Jasmine Plantation Bed &
  Breakfast Inn
4500 North Courthouse Road

Providence Forge, VA 23140
(800) 639-5368; (804) 966-9836
Fax: (804) 966-5679
Innkeepers: Joyce & Howard Vogt
Rooms: 6; Suites: 1; Rates: $$ - $$$
Affiliations: PAII, BBAV
Featured on Page: 76

Radford

Alleghany Inn
1123 Grove Avenue; P.O. Box 747
Radford, VA 24141
(540) 731-4466; Fax: (540) 731-1533
Innkeepers: Jeff & Lori Jarvis
Rooms: 3; Suites: 4; Rates: $$ - $$$$
Affiliations: Mobil, BBAV
Featured on Page: 250

Hideaway Bed and Breakfast
3474 Lone Oak Road
Radford, VA 24141
(540) 731-3126
Innkeepers: Bev & Joe Lineweaver
Rooms: 2; Suites: 1; Rates: $ - $$
Relax and enjoy nature from contem-
porary lakeside farmhouse. A/C and
whirlpool. I-85 Exit 105

Raphine

Oak Spring Farm Bed & Breakfast
5895 Borden Grant Trail
Hwy. 11 & VA State 706
Raphine, VA 24472
(800) 841-8813; (540) 377-2398
Innkeepers: Celeste & John Wood
Rooms: 2; Suites: 1; Rates: $$
Affiliations: BBAV
Featured on Page: 206

Willow Pond Farm Bed & Breakfast
137 Pisgah Road
Raphine, VA 24472
(800) 945-6763; (540) 348-1310
Fax: (540) 348-1359
Innkeepers: Carol Ann &
  Walter Schendel

Rooms: 4; Rates: $$$
Affiliations: IIA
*Secluded elegance in the country. 174-
acre farmstead, romantic getaways. Sit
on our screened-in porch and dream of
a quieter time. Stroll around the pond.*

Reedville

Cedar Grove Bed & Breakfast Inn
2535 Fleeton Road
Reedville, VA 22539
(800) 497-8215; (804) 453-3915
Fax: (804) 453-2650
Innkeepers: Susan & Bob Tipton
Rooms: 3; Rates: $$ - $$$
Affiliations: BBAV
*Victorian sea captain's home on
Chesapeake Bay. Sandy beach.*

Morris House, The
Lower Main Street; P.O. Box 163
Reedville, VA 22539
(804) 453-7016; Fax: (804) 453-9032
Innkeepers: Heath & Erin Dill
Rooms: 2; Suites: 2; Rates: $$ - $$$
Affiliations: PAII, BBAV
Featured on Page: 46

Remington

Highland Farm Inn B&B
10981 Lee's Mill Road
Remington, VA 22734
(540) 439-0088
Innkeepers: Ralph & Linda Robinson
Rooms: 3; Rates: $$ - $$$
*A secluded thoroughbred farm
overlooking the Rappahannock River
in the hunt & wine country of VA. In-
ground pool & ponds. Golf nearby. 50
min. from Wash. DC.*

Richmond

The Emmanuel Hutzler House
2036 Monument Avenue
Richmond, VA 23220

(804) 353-6900
Fax: (804) 355-5053
Innkeepers: Lyn M. Benson &
John E. Richardson
Rooms: 2; Suites: 2; Rates: $$ - $$$
Affiliations: Mobil★★★
*Totally renovated 1914, 8,000-sq.-ft.
Italianate renaissance on stunning
historic avenue. Lovely fabrics,
wallpapers, architectural detail,
antiques & warm but soothing colors.*

The William Catlin House
2304 East Broad Street
Richmond, VA 23223
(804) 780-3746
Innkeepers: Josephine & Robert Martin
Rooms: 5; Rates: $$
Affiliations: Mobil★★

Salem

Inn at Burwell Place
601 West Main Street
Salem, VA 24153
(800) 891-0250; (540) 387-0250
Fax: (540) 387-3279
Innkeepers: Rebecca Martin
Rooms: 2; Suites: 2; Rates: $$ - $$$
*Unsurpassed elegance. 1907 mansion
with full vintage bathrooms. 77'
veranda with view of Blue Ridge Mtns.
Fireplace, whirlpool tubs, robes, TV, A/
C, 4-poster beds, antiques, polo towels
& sheets, custom European bedspreads. Walk to antique shops. Full
country breakfast.*

Scottsville

Deerfield Bed & Breakfast
RR 3, Box 573
Scottsville, VA 24590
(800) 545-1744; (804) 286-6306
Innkeepers: John & Callie Bowers
Rooms: 2; Rates: $$$
Affiliations: BBAV
Overlooking the James River.

**High Meadows Inn &
  Mountain Sunset Inn**
High Meadows Lane
Scottsville, VA 24590
(800) 232-1832; (804) 286-2218
Fax: (804) 289-2124
Innkeepers: Peter Sushka &
  Mary Jae Abbitt
Rooms: 7; Suites: 4; Rates: $$$
Affiliations: IIA, PAII, BBAV
Featured on Page: 144

Sweetwater Guest House
Route 3, Box 535
Scottsville, VA 24590
(757) 286-3279
Innkeepers: Jan & Ric Pederson
Rooms: 3; Suites: 1; Rates: $$

Smith Mountain Lake

Manor at Taylor's Store, The
Route 1, Box 533
Smith Mountain Lake, VA 24184
(800) 248-6267; (540) 721-3951
Fax: (540) 721-5243
Innkeepers: Lee & Mary Lynn Tucker
Rooms: 3; Suites: 6; Rates: $$ - $$$$
Affiliations: NBBA, PAII, Mobil,
  BBAV
Featured on Page: 170

Smithfield

Isle of Wight Inn
345 South Church Street
Smithfield, VA 23430
(800) 357-3245; (757) 357-3176
Innkeepers: Bob Hart
Rooms: 6; Suites: 4; Rates: $$ - $$$

Smithfield Station
415 South Church Street
Smithfield, VA 23430
(757) 357-7700
Fax: (757) 357-7700
Innkeepers: Ron & Tina Pack
Rooms: 15; Suites: 2; Rates: $$ - $$$$

Affiliations: ABBA, BBAV
*Enjoy our waterfront inn. Treat
yourself to fine or casual dining
outside or in. The marina offers
floating docks, bath-house and
swimming pool.*

Sperryville

Apple Hill Farm Bed & Breakfast
117 Old Hollow Road
Sperryville, VA 22740
(800) 326-4583; (540) 987-9454
Fax: (540) 987-3139
Innkeepers: Wayne & Dot Waller
Rooms: 4; Rates: $$ - $$$
Affiliations: IIA, PAII
Featured on Page: 118

Stanardsville

Edgewood Farm Bed & Breakfast
1186 Middle River Road
Stanardsville, VA 22973
(800) 985-3782; (804) 985-3782
Fax: (804) 985-6904
Innkeepers: Eleanor & Norman C.
  Schwartz, Jr.
Rooms: 4; Rates: $$
Affiliations: BBAV
*Be pampered at our romantic B&B -
Fireplaces, sumptuous breakfasts, off
the beaten path.*

Stanley

Milton House Bed & Breakfast Inn
P.O. Box 366
Stanley, VA 22851
(800) 816-3731; (540) 778-2495
Fax: (540) 778-3451
Innkeepers: John & Karin Tipton
Rooms: 3; Suites: 3; Rates: $$ - $$$
*Private log cabin suites with fireplaces
and hot tubs. Candlelight dinners. Near
Luray Caverns, Skyline Drive, canoeing,
horseback riding and great fishing.*

Staunton

Ashton Country House
1205 Middlebrook Avenue
Staunton, VA 24401
(800) 296-7819; (540) 885-7819
Innkeepers: Dorie & Vince DiStefano
Rooms: 4; Suites: 1; Rates: $$ - $$$
Affiliations: PAII, BBAV
Featured on Page: 220

Belle Grae Inn
515 West Frederick Street
Staunton, VA 24401
(888) 541-5151; (540) 886-5151
Fax: (540) 886-6641
Innkeepers: Michael Organ
Rooms: 7; Suites: 7; Rates: $$ - $$$$
Affiliations: ABBA, IIA, Mobil★★★
Historic Victorian inn located in
downtown Staunton. Romantic
ambiance rooms with fireplaces.
Southern hospitality and excellent
cuisine. Dinner nightly.

Frederick House
28 North New Street
Staunton, VA 24401
(800) 334-5575; (540) 885-4220
Innkeepers: Joe & Evy Harman
Rooms: 9; Suites: 7; Rates: $$ - $$$
Affiliations: IIA, NBBA, PAII,
AAA◆◆◆, Mobil★★, BBAV
Featured on Page: 222

Montclair Bed & Breakfast
320 North New Street
Staunton, VA 24401
(540) 885-5761
Innkeepers: Mark & Sheri Bang
Rooms: 4; Rates: $$
Affiliations: BBAV
Italianate townhouse in the downtown
historic district.

Sampson Eagon Inn, The
238 East Beverley Street
Staunton, VA 24401
(800) 597-9722; (540) 886-8200
Fax: (540) 886-8200
Innkeepers: Frank & Laura Mattingly
Rooms: 3; Suites: 2; Rates: $$
Affiliations: AAA◆◆◆, Mobil, BBAV
Featured on Page: 224

Thornrose House at Gypsy Hill
531 Thornrose Avenue
Staunton, VA 24401
(800) 861-4338; (540) 885-7026
Fax: (540) 885-6458
Innkeepers: Otis & Suzanne Huston
Rooms: 5; Rates: $$
Affiliations: Mobil★★, BBAV
Featured on Page: 226

Steeles Tavern

Steeles Tavern Manor Bed & Breakfast
Route 11; P.O. Box 39
Steeles Tavern, VA 24476
(800) 743-8666; (540) 377-6444
Fax: (540) 377-5937
Innkeepers: Eileen & Bill Hoernlein
Rooms: 3; Suites: 2; Rates: $$$
Affiliations: BBAV
Featured on Page: 208

Sugar Tree Inn
Highway 56
Steeles Tavern, VA 24476
(800) 377-2197; (540) 377-2197
Fax: (540) 377-6776
Innkeepers: Sarah & Hal Davis
Rooms: 9; Suites: 2; Rates: $$ - $$$
Affiliations: PAII, BBAV
Featured on Page: 210

Stephens City

Inn at Vaucluse Spring
140 Vaucluse Spring Lane
Stephens City, VA 22655
(800) 869-0525; (540) 869-0200
Fax: (540) 869-9546
Innkeepers: Neil & Barry Myers

Karen & Mike Caplanis
Rooms: 2; Suites: 2; Rates: $$$ - $$$$
Affiliations: PAII, BBAV
Featured on Page: 238

Strasburg

Hotel Strasburg
213 Holliday Street
Strasburg, VA 22657
(800) 348-8327; (540) 465-9191
Fax: (540) 465-4788
Innkeepers: Gary & Carol Rutherford
Rooms: 20; Suites: 9; Rates: $$$$

Sonner House B&B
208 West Queen Street
Strasburg, VA 22657
(800) 829-4809; (540) 564-4712
Innkeepers: Mary & Sam Hutchings
Rooms: 3; Rates: $$
Affiliations: IIA, BBAV
The 1757 weatherboard over log featured in "Country Home Magazine" is part of the historic walking tour of Strasburg.

Surry

Seward House Bed & Breakfast
193 Colonial Trail East
P.O. Box 352
Surry, VA 23883
(757) 294-3810
Innkeepers: Jacqueline Bayer &
   Cynthia Erskine
Rooms: 3; Suites: 1; Rates: $$
Affiliations: BBAV
Featured on Page: 78

Trevilians

Prospect Hill Plantation Inn
2887 Poindexter Road
Trevilians, VA 23093
(800) 277-0844; (540) 967-2574
Fax: (540) 967-0102
Innkeepers: Michael & Laura Sheehan

Rooms: 10; Suites: 3; Rates: $$$$$
Affiliations: IIA, PAII
Prospect Hill is a 1732 plantation with 13 accommodations, 5 in the Manor House and 8 in dependencies, featuring Jacuzzi tubs and breakfast-in-bed. Our guests enjoy sipping iced tea by the pool. Fifteen miles east of Charlottesville, Prospect Hill is a short drive to Monticello, The University of Virginia, The Skyline Drive and many Virginia wineries. Romantic candlelight dinners are served by reservation. AAA, Four Diamond Award.

Urbanna

Hewick Plantation
VSH 602/615
P.O. Box 82
Urbanna, VA 23175
(800) 484-7514; (804) 758-4214
Fax: (804) 758-4080
Innkeepers: Helen & Ed Battleson
Rooms: 2; Rates: $$ - $$$
Affiliations: BBAV
Featured on Page: 80

Virginia Beach

Angie's Guest Cottage
302 24th Street
Virginia Beach, VA 23451
(757) 428-4690
Innkeepers: Barbara Yates and Parents
Rooms: 6; Rates: $ - $$
Affiliations: BBAV
Featured on Page: 48

Barclay Cottage
400 16th Street
Virginia Beach, VA 23451
(757) 422-1956
Innkeepers: Peter & Claire Catanese
Rooms: 5; Rates: $$
Affiliations: AAA◆◆◆, BBAV
Featured on Page: 50

Church Point Manor
4001 Church Point Road
Virginia Beach, VA 23455
(757) 460-2657
Fax: (757) 460-2845
Innkeepers: Angela Craig &
Peter Gagnon
Rooms: 9; Suites: 1; Rates: $$$ - $$$$
Affiliations: PAII, BBAV
Featured on Page: 52

Wachapreague

Burton House Bed & Breakfast
P.O. Box 182
Wachapreague, VA 23480
(757) 787-4560
Innkeepers: Pat & Tom Hart
Rooms: 7; Rates: $$

**Hart's Harbor House Bed &
Breakfast**
P.O. Box 182
Wachapreague, VA 23480
(757) 787-4848
Innkeepers: Patricia Hart
Rooms: 3; Rates: $$
Affiliations: BBAV
Waterfront cottages and marina.

Warm Springs

Anderson Cottage Bed & Breakfast
Old Germantown Road; P.O. Box 176
Warm Springs, VA 24484
(540) 839-2975
Innkeepers: Jean Randolph Bruns
Rooms: 2; Suites: 2; Rates: $$ - $$$
Affiliations: BBAV
Featured on Page: 228

Hidden Valley Bed & Breakfast
P.O. Box 53
Warm Springs, VA 24484
(540) 839-3178
Innkeepers: Ron & Pam Stidham
Rooms: 3; Rates: $$
Affiliations: BBAV

*Award-winning restoration in Greek
revival mansion. Located in GW
National Forest. Great fly-fishing,
hiking & mountain biking. Pets
welcome. Working farm.*

Warrenton

Black Horse Inn
8393 Meetze Road
Warrenton, VA 20187
(540) 349-4020
Fax: (540) 349-4242
Innkeepers: Lynn Pirozzoli
Rooms: 6; Suites: 1
Rates: $$$ - $$$$$
Affiliations: BBAV
*Only 45 minutes from Wash. DC. In the
heart of Virginia horse and wine
country. Elegant & romantic. Wed-
dings, reunions, corporate retreats.*

Warsaw

Greenwood B&B
99 Maple Street
Warsaw, VA 22572
(804) 333-4353
Innkeepers: Bob & Donie Wilson
Rooms: 4; Rates: $

Washington

Caledonia Farm—1812
47 Dearing Road
Flint Hill, VA 22627
(800) 262-1812; (540) 675-3693
Fax: (540) 675-3693
Innkeepers: Phil Irwin
Rooms: 1; Suites: 1; Rates: $$ - $$$
Affiliations: NBBA, BBAV
Featured on Page: 116

Fairlea Farm Bed & Breakfast
636 Mount Salem Avenue
P.O. Box 124
Washington, VA 22747
(540) 675-3679

Fax: (540) 675-1064
Innkeepers: Susan & Walt Longyear
Rooms: 3; Suites: 1; Rates: $$ - $$$
Affiliations: NBBA, USB&B, BBAV
Featured on Page: 108

Foster-Harris House
189 Main Street; P.O. Box 333
Washington, VA 22747
(800) 666-0153; (540) 675-3757
Innkeepers: Phyllis Marriott
Rooms: 3; Suites: 1; Rates: $$$
Affiliations: PAII, BBAV
Featured on Page: 110

Gay Street Inn
P.O. Box 237
Washington, VA 22747
(540) 675-3288
Innkeepers: Robin & Donna Kevis
Rooms: 3; Suites: 1; Rates: $$ - $$$
Affiliations: PAII, BBAV
*Come and enjoy our 4-room renovated
1850 farmhouse located in the historic
town of Washington, VA in the foothills
of VA on the morningside of Blue
Ridge Mtns.*

Middleton Inn
176 Main Street; P.O. Box 254
Washington, VA 22747
(800) 816-8157; (540) 675-2020
Fax: (540) 675-1050
Innkeepers: Mary Ann Kuhn
Rooms: 4; Rates: $$$$ - $$$$$
Affiliations: PAII, Mobil★★★, BBAV
Featured on Page: 112

Sunset Hills Farm Bed & Breakfast
105 Christmas Tree Lane
Washington, VA 22747
(880) 980-2580; (540) 987-8804
Fax: (540) 987-9742
Innkeepers: Betty & Leon Hutcheson
Rooms: 2; Suites: 1; Rates: $$$$
Affiliations: BBAV
Featured on Page: 114

Waynesboro

Belle Hearth Bed & Breakfast
320 South Wayne Avenue
Waynesboro, VA 22980
(800) 949-6993; (540) 943-1910
Fax: (540) 942-2443
Innkeepers: Jim & Carolyn Rodenberg
Rooms: 3; Suites: 1; Rates: $$ - $$$
Affiliations: PAII, BBAV
Featured on Page: 230

Iris Inn Bed & Breakfast, The
191 Chinquapin Drive
Waynesboro, VA 22980
(540) 943-1991
Innkeepers: Wayne & Iris Karl
Rooms: 7; Rates: $$
Affiliations: Mobil, BBAV
Featured on Page: 232

Weyers Cave

Inn at Keezletown Road
Route 1, Box 14
Weyers Cave, VA 24486
(800) 465-0100; (540) 234-0644
Innkeepers: Alan & Sandy Inabinet
Rooms: 4; Rates: $$
Affiliations: AAA♦♦♦, BBAV
Featured on Page: 190

White Post

L'Auberge Provencale
P.O. Box 119
White Post, VA 22663
(800) 638-1702; (540) 837-1375
Fax: (540) 837-2004
Innkeepers: Celeste & Alain Borel
Rooms: 9; Suites: 2; Rates: $$$ - $$$$
Affiliations: IIA, PAII, Mobil★★★
*Premiere French country inn in
Virginia's hunt country. Romantic inn
with world-renowned cuisine.
Fireplaces, candlelight, excellent
service.*

Williamsburg

Applewood Colonial Bed & Breakfast
605 Richmond Road
Williamsburg, VA 23185
(800) 899-2753; (757) 229-0205
Fax: (757) 229-9405
Innkeepers: Marty Jones/Jan Brown
Rooms: 3; Suites: 1; Rates: $$ - $$$
Affiliations: ABBA, NBBA, PAII, AAA, BBAV
Featured on Page: 54

Candlewick Bed & Breakfast
800 Jamestown Road
Williamsburg, VA 23185
(800) 418-4949; (757) 253-8693
Innkeepers: Mary Peters
Rooms: 3; Suites: 1; Rates: $$$
Affiliations: ABBA, BBAV

Cedars Bed & Breakfast
616 Jamestown Road
Williamsburg, VA 23185
(800) 296-3591; (757) 229-3591
Fax: (757) 229-0756
Innkeepers: Carol, James & Bróna Malecha
Rooms: 6; Suites: 2; Rates: $$ - $$$
Affiliations: PAII, AAA, BBAV
Featured on Page: 56

Colonial Capital Bed & Breakfast
501 Richmond Road
Williamsburg, VA 23185
(800) 776-0570; (757) 229-0233
Fax: (757) 253-7667
Innkeepers: Barbara & Phil Craig
Rooms: 4; Suites: 1; Rates: $$ - $$$
Affiliations: PAII, Mobil, BBAV
Featured on Page: 58

Colonial Gardens Bed & Breakfast
1109 Jamestown Road
Williamsburg, VA 23185
(800) 886-9715; (757) 220-8087
Fax: (757) 253-1495

Innkeepers: Scottie & Wilmot Phillips
Rooms: 2; Suites: 2; Rates: $$$
Affiliations: BBAV
Featured on Page: 60

Fox Grape Bed & Breakfast
701 Monumental Avenue
Williamsburg, VA 23185
(800) 292-3699; (757) 229-6914
Innkeepers: Bob & Pat Orendorff
Rooms: 4; Rates: $$
Warm hospitality awaits you just 5 blocks north of Colonial area. Furnished with antiques, cross stitch, quilts & folk art. Pat enjoys reading and doing cross stitch. Bob carves walking sticks & makes folk art-style Noah's Arks & nursery rhyme collectables.

Indian Springs Bed & Breakfast
330 Indian Springs Road
Williamsburg, VA 23185
(800) 262-9165; (757) 220-0726
Innkeepers: Paul & Kelly Supplee
Rooms: 1; Suites: 2; Rates: $$ - $$$
Affiliations: Mobil, BBAV

Liberty Rose Bed & Breakfast
1055 Jamestown Road
Williamsburg, VA 23185
(800) 545-1825; (757) 253-1260
Innkeepers: Brad & Sandra Hirz
Rooms: 2; Suites: 2; Rates: $$$ - $$$$
Affiliations: NBBA, USB&B, AAA◆◆◆◆, Mobil, BBAV
Featured on Page: 62

Magnolia Manor
700 Richmond Road
Williamsburg, VA 23185
(800) 462-6667; (757) 220-9600
Fax: (757) 253-0088
Innkeepers: Bill & Robyn Eshleman
Rooms: 2; Suites: 2; Rates: $$$ - $$$$
Affiliations: BBAV
Featured on Page: 64

Newport House B&B
710 South Henry Street
Williamsburg, VA 23185
(757) 229-1775; Fax: (757) 229-6408
Innkeepers: John & Cathy Millar
Rooms: 2; Rates: $$$
Affiliations: ABBA, BBAV
*Williamsburg's most authentic B&B;
designed 1756, furnished in period;
500 yds. to historic area; Colonial
dancing Tuesdays.*

Piney Grove at Southall's Plantation
P.O. Box 1359
Williamsburg, VA 23187
(804) 829-2480
Innkeepers: The Gordineer Family
Rooms: 4; Rates: $$$ - $$$$
Affiliations: PAII, AAA◆◆◆, BBAV
Featured on Page: 72

Primrose Cottage Bed & Breakfast
706 Richmond Road
Williamsburg, VA 23185
(888) 800-1705; (757) 229-6421
Fax: (757) 259-0717
Innkeepers: Inge Curtis
Rooms: 4; Rates: $$ - $$$
Affiliations: BBAV
Featured on Page: 66

War Hill Inn
4560 Long Hill Road
Williamsburg, VA 23188
(800) 743-0248; (757) 565-0248
Innkeepers: Shirley, Bill & Will Lee
Rooms: 3; Suites: 1; Rates: $$ - $$$
Affiliations: AAA◆◆◆, Mobil, BBAV
Featured on Page: 68

Williamsburg Manor
600 Richmond Road
Williamsburg, VA 23185
(800) 422-8011; (757) 220-8011
Fax: (757) 220-0245
Innkeepers: Laura Reeves
Rooms: 5; Rates: $$ - $$$
Affiliations: BBAV

*Walking distance, gourmet breakfast,
romantically charming.*

**Williamsburg Sampler Bed &
Breakfast**
922 Jamestown Road
Williamsburg, VA 23185
(800) 722-1169; (757) 253-0398
Fax: (757) 253-2669
Innkeepers: Helen & Ike Sisane
Rooms: 2; Suites: 2; Rates: $$$
Affiliations: Mobil★ ★ ★
*Governor declared 18th-c plantation
style home built in the year of the
bicentennial "Inn Of The Year." Come
for atmosphere. Stay for "Skip Lunch"
breakfast.*

Willis Wharf

Ballard House Bed 'N Breakfast
12527 Ballard Drive
Willis Wharf, VA 23486
(757) 442-2206
Innkeepers: Jo & Kim Penland
Rooms: 3; Suites: 1; Rates: $ - $$
Affiliations: IIA, BBAV
Children and pets welcome.

Woodstock

Azalea House Bed & Breakfast
551 South Main Street
Woodstock, VA 22664
(540) 459-3500
Innkeepers: Margaret &
  Price McDonald
Rooms: 4; Rates: $$
Affiliations: BBAV

Inn at Narrow Passage
US 11 South; P.O. Box 608
Woodstock, VA 22664
(800) 459-8002; (540) 459-8000
Fax: (540) 459-8001
Innkeepers: Ellen & Ed Markel
Rooms: 12 Rates: $$ - $$$
Affiliations: IIA, PAII, Mobil

*Historic 1740 log inn on Shenandoah
River. Guests enjoy hiking, fishing,
riding, historic sites, vineyards & fine
restaurants.*

River'd Inn
1972 Artz Road
Woodstock, VA 22664
(800) 637-4561; (540) 459-5369
Fax: (540) 459-8241
Innkeepers: Diana Edwards
Rooms: 8; Rates: $$$ - $$$$$
Affiliations: PAII, BBAV
*Luxury accommodations, elegant
dining; fireplaces/Jacuzzis, mountain/
river quiet setting. Open year round.*

Yorktown

Marl Inn Bed & Breakfast
P.O. Box 572
Yorktown, VA 23690
(800) 799-6207; (757) 898-9268
Fax: (757) 898-3587
Innkeepers: Eugene C. Marlin
Rooms: 2; Suites: 2; Rates: $$ - $$$
Affiliations: ABBA, BBAV
*Located in restored Colonial area.
Bikes available for touring American
Revolution battlegrounds/Historic
reception centers. Pkwy to Wmsbg/
Jamestown & Busch Gardens.*

Index

We'd love to hear from you...

about your experiences at not only the bed and breakfasts and inns featured in this guide, but also at the restaurants we have suggested.

We would also like to hear of bed and breakfasts or inns we may have missed and that you feel should be included in future editions. Your comments about area restaurants or places of interest that our readers might like to know about would also be appreciated.

Don Vandeventer

You can write to me care of:

Down Home Publications
P.O. Box 1899
Candler, NC 28715